HOUSE OF THE HOLY GHOST

The Story of the Holy Ghost
444 Devotions

Do You Really Know the Holy Spirit?

Mary King

authorHOUSE®

AuthorHouse™
1663 Liberty Drive
Bloomington, IN 47403
www.authorhouse.com
Phone: 833-262-8899

Published by AuthorHouse 11/11/2021

ISBN: 978-1-6655-4425-2 (sc)
ISBN: 978-1-6655-4424-5 (hc)
ISBN: 978-1-6655-4439-9 (e)

Library of Congress Control Number: 2021923223

Print information available on the last page.

Any people depicted in stock imagery provided by Getty Images are models, and such images are being used for illustrative purposes only. Certain stock imagery © Getty Images.

This book is printed on acid-free paper.

NOTE TO PUBLISHERS AND WRITERS:
The author of these books allows any author to copy and paste up to one full page of the text without written request to the author or publisher. In lieu of the writing of permission, the author only asks the authors and publishers to mention the title of the book and the author's name at the place where the page (or less) is copied and pasted into *each* of their text and into their article or book or books.

When the copied text contains Scripture, the references must be satisfied by each of the Scripture publishers; as is deemed customary by all publishers of the Holy Bible.

444 devotions in a Bible Study
followed by
10 commentary outlines

EXPLANATION POINT
When an entire sentence was anointed as this book was being prepared, there will be an explanation point at the end of that sentence. When a word or phrase was anointed, only that double anointed word or phrase was highlighted.

COMMENTARY WRITTEN BY YOU
You want to know more about the Holy Spirit, the Spirit of Christ. In the back of this book are lists where you can write 10 commentaries about the Spirit of God for your own fun with the Spirit.

HOUSE OF THE HOLY GHOST
How well do you know the Holy Ghost?

Do you know?

Who was the first Spirit-filled person?
How did God describe the transfer of the Spirit?
How can we know we are in the Spirit?
How many in the upper room received the Holy Ghost?
So how can Jesus be God?
Who baptizes us with the Holy Ghost?
What do we have by one Spirit?
Daddy always gives favor to His children because of who He is!
Does God want His Spirit to flow from you?
Did Jesus say the Spirit would speak in you when you speak in faith in Him?
Who asked, "Have ye received the Holy Ghost?"
Do you want Jesus to take up for you?
On the Day of Pentecost, who interpreted and how were the words understood?
How could she be filled with the Holy Ghost before Pentecost?
Who said, "The Holy Ghost fell on them, as on us?" And who was he talking about?
Can a person be filled and baptized with the Holy Ghost at the same time?
How can we know the perfect will of God?
There are many but what is one promise God has made to all?
Who was first to talk about the Spirit?

As Mary was studying to publish the HOLY GHOST BIBLE (400 sets of Scriptures of and about the Holy Spirit) someone said it would make an interesting devotion. She agreed and that is HOUSE OF THE HOLY GHOST. For 7 years she studied to compile and write these books to tell the story of the HOLY GHOST in a compact way to draw nearer to Jesus and get to know the Spirit of God better at the same time.

date_____
AND THE SPIRIT OF GOD

Genesis 1:1 – 3 (KJV)
[1] In the beginning God created the heaven and the earth.
[2] And the earth was without form, and void; and darkness *was* upon the face of the deep. And the Spirit of God moved upon the face of the waters.
[3] And God said, Let there be light: and there was light.

God was first to talk about His Spirit! God told us what the Spirit was doing **before time.** "For those who live according to the flesh set their minds on the things of the flesh, but those *who live* according to the Spirit, the things of the Spirit" **Romans 8:5 (NKJV).**
In the beginning, Christ Jesus was called and equipped.
Since God is Spirit, how can Jesus be God? Since the Spirit made Gideon strong in spirit and gave strength to Samson and carried Ezekiel, how does He relate to us today?

_____
_____
_____
_____
_____
_____
_____

date_____
BREATHED…BREATH OF LIFE

Genesis 2:4 – 7 (KJV)
[4] These *are* the generations of the heavens and of the earth when they were created, in the day that the LORD God made the earth and the heavens,
[5] And every plant of the field before it was in the earth, and every herb of the field before it grew: for the LORD God had not caused it to rain upon the earth, and *there was* not a man to till the ground.
[6] But there went up a mist from the earth, and watered the whole face of the ground.
[7] And the LORD God formed man *of* the dust of the ground, and breathed into his nostrils the breath of life; and man became a living soul.

When the breath of life **came upon** the first Adam, first-blood began to **flow** (Leviticus 17:11). God walked the bride down the aisle and the creation of marriage on earth was **made by God** while they stood **in the light** (1:3 – 2:25). (see 2:7, Isaiah 42:5, John 20:23; Matthew 16:18; Ephesians 5:32) Why did God want His Spirit in us?

_____
_____
_____

HEARD THY (GOD) VOICE IN THE GARDEN

Genesis 3:8 – 11, 20 – 21 (KJV)

8 And they heard the voice of the LORD God walking in the garden in the cool of the day: and Adam and his wife hid themselves from the presence of the LORD God amongst the trees of the garden.

9 And the LORD God called unto Adam, and said unto him, Where *art* thou?

10 And he said, I heard thy voice in the garden, and I was afraid, because I *was* naked; and I hid myself.

11 And he said, Who told thee that thou *wast* naked? Hast thou eaten of the tree, whereof I commanded thee that thou shouldest not eat?

20 And Adam called his wife's name Eve; because she was the mother of all living.

21 Unto Adam also and to his wife did the LORD God make coats of skins, and clothed them.

God Himself made the first love sacrifice to endue Adam and Eve in the clothes of grace.

_____

_____

_____

_____

THE LORD HAD RESPECT

Genesis 4:1 – 4 (KJV)

1 And Adam knew Eve his wife; and she conceived, and bare Cain, and said, I have gotten a man from the LORD.

2 And she again bare his brother Abel. And Abel was a keeper of sheep, but Cain was a tiller of the ground.

3 And in process of time it came to pass, that Cain brought of the fruit of the ground an offering unto the LORD.

4 And Abel, he also brought of the firstlings of his flock and of the fat thereof. And the LORD had respect unto Abel and to his offering:

Cain and Abel had a choice and freedom and the same parents and environment and doctrine and teachings (Genesis 1 – 3). Cain yielded to a temptation to disobey. God wanted them to do what He said and the way He said. Were they both obedient to God?

_____

_____

_____

_____

_____

_____

date_____

LAMECH...NOAH...SHEM

Genesis 5:28 – 32 (KJV)
28 And Lamech lived an hundred eighty and two years, and begat a son:
29 And he called his name Noah, saying, This *same* shall comfort us concerning our work and toil of our hands, because of the ground which the LORD hath cursed.
30 And Lamech lived after he begat Noah five hundred ninety and five years, and begat sons and daughters:
31 And all the days of Lamech were seven hundred seventy and seven years: and he died.
32 And Noah was five hundred years old: and Noah begat Shem, Ham, and Japheth.

Wisdom is the pattern so God shows us things to come by showing us legacies of others. We learn wisdom by studying the wisdom from the Bible. Solomon wrote:
"Let us hear the conclusion of the whole matter: Fear God and keep His commandments, For this is man's all" **Ecclesiastes 12:13 (NKJV).**

_____
_____
_____
_____
_____

date_____

MY (THE LORD'S) SPIRIT

Genesis 6:1, 2, 3, 17 (KJV)
1 And it came to pass, when men began to multiply on the face of the earth, and daughters were born unto them,
2 That the sons of God saw the daughters of men that they *were* fair; and they took them wives of all which they chose.
3 And the LORD said, My spirit shall not always strive with man, for that he also *is* flesh: yet his days shall be an hundred and twenty years.
17 And, behold, I, even I, do bring a flood of waters upon the earth, to destroy all flesh, wherein *is* the breath of life, from under heaven; *and* every thing that *is* in the earth shall die.

God saw that someone needed to be saved or would be rescued, so **He caused a change** and waited for the time for **Noah's ark of grace. Predestination is God knew.**

_____
_____
_____
_____
_____
_____
_____

date_____
LORD SAID UNTO NOAH

Genesis 7:1, 2, 5, 23 (KJV)
[1] And the LORD said unto Noah, Come thou and all thy house into the ark; for thee have I seen righteous before me in this generation.
[2] Of every clean beast thou shalt take to thee by sevens, the male and his female: and of beasts that *are* not clean by two, the male and his female.
[5] And Noah did according unto all that the LORD commanded him.
[23] And every living substance was destroyed which was upon the face of the ground, both man, and cattle, and the creeping things, and the fowl of the heaven; and they were destroyed from the earth: and Noah only remained *alive*, and they that *were* with him in the ark.

Noah's animals piled into the ark in order and were **in hibernation** from the time God shut the door; until Noah chose a raven and a dove to send out **God's window, God's opportunity given to or set before a person.**

_____
_____
_____
_____
_____
_____

date_____
NOAH BUILDED AN ALTAR

Genesis 8:4, 18, 20 – 22 (KJV)
[4] And the ark rested in the seventh month, on the seventeenth day of the month, upon the mountains of Ararat.
[18] And Noah went forth, and his sons, and his wife, and his sons' wives with him:
[20] And Noah builded an altar unto the LORD; and took of every clean beast, and of every clean fowl, and offered burnt offerings on the altar.
[21] And the LORD smelled a sweet savour; and the LORD said in his heart, I will not again curse the ground any more for man's sake; for the imagination of man's heart *is* evil from his youth; neither will I again smite any more every thing living, as I have done.
[22] While the earth remaineth, seedtime and harvest, and cold and heat, and summer and winter, and day and night shall not cease.

We see Jesus on the cross when God saw the offering on the altar and God permanently removed a curse, replacing it with the principle of seedtime and harvest.

_____
_____
_____
_____
_____

A TOKEN OF THE COVENANT

Genesis 9:12, 13, 15, 17, 18 (KJV)
¹² And God said, This *is* the token of the covenant which I make between me and you and every living creature that *is* with you, for perpetual generations:
¹³ I do set my bow in the cloud, and it shall be for a token of a covenant between me and the earth.
¹⁵ And I will remember my covenant, which *is* between me and you and every living creature of all flesh; and the waters shall no more become a flood to destroy all flesh.
¹⁷ And God said unto Noah, This *is* the token of the covenant, which I have established between me and all flesh that *is* upon the earth.
¹⁸ And the sons of Noah, that went forth of the ark, were Shem, and Ham, and Japheth: and Ham *is* the father of Canaan.

God's bow, a sign, **a weapon of covenant was God's signature of grace in the sky. His grace was given before we needed it and because we could not deserve it (9:20 – 25).**

_____
_____
_____
_____
_____

THESE ARE THE FAMILIES

Genesis 10:1, 32 (KJV)
¹ Now these *are* the generations of the sons of Noah, Shem, Ham, and Japheth: and unto them were sons born after the flood.
³² These *are* the families of the sons of Noah, after their generations, in their nations: and by these were the nations divided in the earth after the flood.

Noah's congregation would be only 8 people, but God waited 120 years for the 8ᵗʰ person to believe in the LORD, as Noah prepared the ark. (see 15:6; Matthew 1)
God loved us so much He gave His only sinless perfect Son in our place so we could believe in the Lord Jesus Christ and **receive Him as Lord for all eternity.**
God has a plan: He set an assignment, calling, opportunity, gift, talent, skill and purposes on a road map for every life. All this was a **concept** in the mind of God before time began. He knew then who would accept the mission and He turns the earth in the midst of it all to accomplish His faith, His promise, His mission, His gift and His grace.

_____
_____
_____
_____

date_____

NOTHING WILL BE RESTRAINED

Genesis 11:5 – 7, 9 (KJV)

5 And the LORD came down to see the city and the tower, which the children of men builded.

6 And the LORD said, Behold, the people *is* one, and they have all one language; and this they begin to do: and now nothing will be restrained from them, which they have imagined to do.

7 Go to, let us go down, and there confound their language, that they may not understand one another's speech.

9 Therefore is the name of it called Babel; because the LORD did there confound the language of all the earth: and from thence did the LORD scatter them abroad upon the face of all the earth.

Oh the power of corporate prayer! What would happen if we (God and us) were in one accord?

_____
_____
_____
_____
_____
_____
_____
_____

date_____

BUILDED AN ALTAR UNTO THE LORD

Genesis 12:1, 2, 4, 8 (KJV)

1 Now the LORD had said unto Abram, Get thee out of thy country, and from thy kindred, and from thy father's house, unto a land that I will shew thee:

2 And I will make of thee a great nation, and I will bless thee, and make thy name great; and thou shalt be a blessing:

4 So Abram departed, as the LORD had spoken unto him; and Lot went with him: and Abram *was* seventy and five years old when he departed out of Haran.

8 And he removed from thence unto a mountain on the east of Bethel, and pitched his tent, *having* Bethel on the west, and Hai on the east: and there he builded an altar unto the LORD, and called upon the name of the LORD.

Abram obeyed the God of glory who appeared to him asking him to move **nearer to God** (Acts 7:1 – 4). How? He took his wife and left the family who wouldn't worship God.

_____
_____
_____
_____
_____

THERE AT THE FIRST

Genesis 13:3, 4, 14, 15(KJV)
3 And he went on his journeys from the south even to Bethel, unto the place where his tent had been at the beginning, between Bethel and Hai;
4 Unto the place of the altar, which he had made there at the first: and there Abram called on the name of the LORD.
14 And the LORD said unto Abram, after that Lot was separated from him, Lift up now thine eyes, and look from the place where thou art northward, and southward, and eastward, and westward:
15 For all the land which thou seest, to thee will I give it, and to thy seed for ever.

We also can return to the place where we first met with the LORD. We can listen again (13:1 – 15). What word lets us know God focuses on the future generations? (see 2 Peter 1:15)

_____
_____
_____
_____
_____
_____
_____
_____

WHEN ABRAM HEARD

Genesis 14:13 – 15 (KJV)
13 And there came one that had escaped, and told Abram the Hebrew; for he dwelt in the plain of Mamre the Amorite, brother of Eshcol, and brother of Aner: and these *were* confederate with Abram.
14 And when Abram heard that his brother was taken captive, he armed his trained *servants*, born in his own house, three hundred and eighteen, and pursued *them* unto Dan.
15 And he divided himself against them, he and his servants, by night, and smote them, and pursued them unto Hobah, which *is* on the left hand of Damascus.

Abram had his own military when he needed them and **they wanted to fight for him.** Abram had given them everything. They were his soldiers and they won.

_____
_____
_____
_____
_____
_____
_____

date_____

LOOK NOW TOWARD HEAVEN

Genesis 15:1, 5 – 7 (KJV)

¹ After these things the word of the LORD came unto Abram in a vision, saying, Fear not, Abram: I *am* thy shield, *and* thy exceeding great reward.

⁵ And he brought him forth abroad, and said, Look now toward heaven, and tell the stars, if thou be able to number them: and he said unto him, So shall thy seed be.

⁶ And he believed in the LORD; and he counted it to him for righteousness.

⁷ And he said unto him, I *am* the LORD that brought thee out of Ur of the Chaldees, to give thee this land to inherit it.

God put His righteousness into the account of Abram. He does that for us through Jesus (2 Corinthians 5:21). God had delivered Abram. "…brought him forth…Look… stars…" Now where do you think the LORD took Abram when He brought him out to see the stars?

_____
_____
_____
_____
_____
_____
_____

date_____

ANGEL OF THE LORD FOUND HER

Genesis 16:7 – 8, 10 – 11 (KJV)

⁷ And the angel of the LORD found her by a fountain of water in the wilderness, by the fountain in the way to Shur.

⁸ And he said, Hagar, Sarai's maid, whence camest thou? and whither wilt thou go? And she said, I flee from the face of my mistress Sarai.

¹⁰ And the angel of the LORD said unto her, I will multiply thy seed exceedingly, that it shall not be numbered for multitude.

¹³ And she called the name of the LORD that spake unto her, Thou God seest me: for she said, Have I also here looked after him that seeth me?

God has found you too, whether you are by the fountain or in the wilderness, to say to you, **"Try again."**

_____
_____
_____
_____
_____
_____
_____
_____
_____

I (GOD) WILL BLESS HER

Genesis 17:3, 5, 15 – 17 (KJV)
[3] And Abram fell on his face: and God talked with him, saying,
[5] Neither shall thy name any more be called Abram, but thy name shall be Abraham; for a father of many nations have I made thee.
[15] And God said unto Abraham, As for Sarai thy wife, thou shalt not call her name Sarai, but Sarah *shall* her name *be*.
[16] And I will bless her, and give thee a son also of her: yea, I will bless her, and she shall be *a mother* of nations; kings of people shall be of her.
[17] Then Abraham fell upon his face, and laughed, and said in his heart, Shall *a child* be born unto him that is an hundred years old? and shall Sarah, that is ninety years old, bear?

When God breathed on Abraham and Sarah, the Spirit of God came upon them and they had been **baptized with the breath of God**. (see Matthew 1:1)

_____
_____
_____
_____
_____
_____

IS ANY THING TOO HARD FOR THE LORD?

Genesis 18:13 – 14, 17 – 19 (KJV)
[13] And the LORD said unto Abraham, Wherefore did Sarah laugh, saying, Shall I of a surety bear a child, which am old?
[14] Is any thing too hard for the LORD? At the time appointed I will return unto thee, according to the time of life, and Sarah shall have a son.
[17] And the LORD said, Shall I hide from Abraham that thing which I do;
[18] Seeing that Abraham shall surely become a great and mighty nation, and all the nations of the earth shall be blessed in him?
[19] For I know him, that he will command his children and his household after him, and they shall keep the way of the LORD, to do justice and judgment; that the LORD may bring upon Abraham that which he hath spoken of him.

Nothing is out of the reach of God! Nothing is too hard for the LORD. (see Jeremiah 32:16, 17; Psalm 2:8) Why did God tell Abraham what He was going to do?

_____
_____
_____
_____

THERE CAME TWO ANGELS

GOD CAME TO ABIMELECH

Genesis 19:1 – 3 (KJV)

¹ And there came two angels to Sodom at even; and Lot sat in the gate of Sodom: and Lot seeing *them* rose up to meet them; and he bowed himself with his face toward the ground;

² And he said, Behold now, my lords, turn in, I pray you, into your servant's house, and tarry all night, and wash your feet, and ye shall rise up early, and go on your ways. And they said, Nay; but we will abide in the street all night.

³ And he pressed upon them greatly; and they turned in unto him, and entered into his house; and he made them a feast, and did bake unleavened bread, and they did eat.

Lot was rescued after he brought in and fed strangers in his home (19:10 – 11). How much could the power of kindness do for you?

_____
_____
_____
_____
_____
_____
_____
_____

Genesis 20:3, 6, 7 (KJV)

³ But God came to Abimelech in a dream by night, and said to him, Behold, thou *art but* a dead man, for the woman which thou hast taken; for she *is* a man's wife.

⁶ And God said unto him in a dream, Yea, I know that thou didst this in the integrity of thy heart; for I also withheld thee from sinning against me: therefore suffered I thee not to touch her.

⁷ Now therefore restore the man *his* wife; for he *is* a prophet, and he shall pray for thee, and thou shalt live: and if thou restore *her* not, know thou that thou shalt surely die, thou, and all that *are* thine.

Just name it! God will take up for you. That woman was Sarai, Sarah.

Since God spoke to a man like Abimelech, He can speak to anyone. Who do you want God to speak to on your behalf as He did for Sarah, the wife of Abraham?

_____
_____
_____
_____
_____
_____
_____

date_____
AT THE SET TIME

Genesis 21:1, 2, 5, 22 (KJV)
[1] And the LORD visited Sarah as he had said, and the LORD did unto Sarah as he had spoken.
[2] For Sarah conceived, and bare Abraham a son in his old age, at the set time of which God had spoken to him.
[5] And Abraham was an hundred years old, when his son Isaac was born unto him.
[22] And it came to pass at that time, that Abimelech and Phichol the chief captain of his host spake unto Abraham, saying, God *is* with thee in all that thou doest:

God returned youth to her, just as He had promised (18:10). (see Matthew 1:2)

_____
_____
_____
_____
_____
_____
_____
_____
_____
_____

date_____
PROVIDE HIMSELF A LAMB

Genesis 22:2, 8, 11, 12 (KJV)
[2] And he said, Take now thy son, thine only *son* Isaac, whom thou lovest, and get thee into the land of Moriah; and offer him there for a burnt offering upon one of the mountains which I will tell thee of.
[8] And Abraham said, My son, God will provide himself a lamb for a burnt offering: so they went both of them together.
[11] And the angel of the LORD called unto him out of heaven, and said, Abraham, Abraham: and he said, Here *am* I.
[12] And he said, Lay not thine hand upon the lad, neither do thou any thing unto him: for now I know that thou fearest God, seeing thou hast not withheld thy son, thine only *son* from me.

Abraham obeyed God in the portrait of Jesus Christ (Hebrews 11:19). (see John 13:35)

_____
_____
_____
_____
_____
_____
_____

date_____

ABRAHAM HEARKENED
UNTO EPHRON

Genesis 23:1, 2, 16, 17 (KJV)
[1] And Sarah was an hundred and seven and twenty years old: *these were* the years of the life of Sarah.
[2] And Sarah died in Kirjatharba; the same *is* Hebron in the land of Canaan: and Abraham came to mourn for Sarah, and to weep for her.
[16] And Abraham hearkened unto Ephron; and Abraham weighed to Ephron the silver, which he had named in the audience of the sons of Heth, four hundred shekels of silver, current *money* with the merchant.
[17] And the field of Ephron, which *was* in Machpelah, which *was* before Mamre, the field, and the cave which *was* therein, and all the trees that *were* in the field, that *were* in all the borders round about, were made sure

Ephron could never boast that Abraham owed more since Abraham paid the full price. (see Matthew 4:8 – 10; 27:59 – 64; Proverbs 29:24;)

_____
_____
_____
_____
_____
_____
_____

date_____

THEY BLESSED REBEKAH

Genesis 24:58 – 61 (KJV)
[58] And they called Rebekah, and said unto her, Wilt thou go with this man? And she said, I will go.
[59] And they sent away Rebekah their sister, and her nurse, and Abraham's servant, and his men.
[60] And they blessed Rebekah, and said unto her, Thou *art* our sister, be thou *the mother* of thousands of millions, and let thy seed possess the gate of those which hate them.
[61] And Rebekah arose, and her damsels, and they rode upon the camels, and followed the man: and the servant took Rebekah, and went his way.

The blessing of Rebekah is powerful and generational (24:19).

_____
_____
_____
_____
_____
_____
_____
_____
_____
_____

SHE WENT TO ENQUIRE OF THE LORD

Genesis 25:21 – 24 (KJV)

²¹ And Isaac intreated the LORD for his wife, because she *was* barren: and the LORD was intreated of him, and Rebekah his wife conceived.

²² And the children struggled together within her; and she said, If *it be* so, why *am* I thus? And she went to enquire of the LORD.

²³ And the LORD said unto her, Two nations *are* in thy womb, and two manner of people shall be separated from thy bowels; and *the one* people shall be stronger than *the other* people; and the elder shall serve the younger.

²⁴ And when her days to be delivered were fulfilled, behold, *there were* twins in her womb.

The prophecy was the answer from the LORD (25:21 – 34).

_____
_____
_____
_____
_____
_____
_____
_____

THE LORD APPEARED TO HIM (ISAAC)

Genesis 26:2 – 5 (KJV)

² And the LORD appeared unto him, and said, Go not down into Egypt; dwell in the land which I shall tell thee of:

³ Sojourn in this land, and I will be with thee, and will bless thee; for unto thee, and unto thy seed, I will give all these countries, and I will perform the oath which I sware unto Abraham thy father;

⁴ And I will make thy seed to multiply as the stars of heaven, and will give unto thy seed all these countries; and in thy seed shall all the nations of the earth be blessed;

⁵ Because that Abraham obeyed my voice, and kept my charge, my commandments, my statutes, and my laws.

Isaac was blessed, being that he was the seed of Abraham! (see Philippians 1:3 – 7)

_____
_____
_____
_____
_____
_____

THE DEW OF HEAVEN

Genesis 27:26 – 29 (KJV)

²⁶ And his father Isaac said unto him, Come near now, and kiss me, my son. ²⁷ And he came near, and kissed him: and he smelled the smell of his raiment, and blessed him, and said, See, the smell of my son *is* as the smell of a field which the LORD hath blessed:

²⁸ Therefore God give thee of the dew of heaven, and the fatness of the earth, and plenty of corn and wine:

²⁹ Let people serve thee, and nations bow down to thee: be lord over thy brethren, and let thy mother's sons bow down to thee: cursed *be* every one that curseth thee, and blessed *be* he that blesseth thee.

The father's blessing came down as the dew from heaven couldn't be cancelled. God has affirmed us as His children and we have abundance of His Word and plenty of His Spirit.

_____
_____
_____
_____
_____
_____
_____
_____
_____

HE (JACOB) DREAMED...A LADDER

Genesis 28:12 – 15 (KJV)

¹² And he dreamed, and behold a ladder set up on the earth, and the top of it reached to heaven: and behold the angels of God ascending and descending on it.

¹³ And, behold, the LORD stood above it, and said, I *am* the LORD God of Abraham thy father, and the God of Isaac: the land whereon thou liest, to thee will I give it, and to thy seed;

¹⁴ And thy seed shall be as the dust of the earth, and thou shalt spread abroad to the west, and to the east, and to the north, and to the south: and in thee and in thy seed shall all the families of the earth be blessed.

¹⁵ And, behold, I *am* with thee, and will keep thee in all *places* whither thou goest, and will bring thee again into this land; for I will not leave thee, until I have done *that* which I have spoken to thee of.

A generational blessing was promised to Jacob! Is your faith level little or great?

_____
_____
_____
_____

WHAT SHALL THY WAGES BE?

Genesis 29:9, 10, 11, 14, 15 (KJV)
⁹ And while he yet spake with them, Rachel came with her father's sheep: for she kept them.
¹⁰ And it came to pass, when Jacob saw Rachel the daughter of Laban his mother's brother, and the sheep of Laban his mother's brother, that Jacob went near, and rolled the stone from the well's mouth, and watered the flock of Laban his mother's brother.
¹¹ And Jacob kissed Rachel, and lifted up his voice, and wept.
¹⁴ And Laban said to him, Surely thou *art* my bone and my flesh. And he abode with him the space of a month.
¹⁵ And Laban said unto Jacob, Because thou *art* my brother, shouldest thou therefore serve me for nought? tell me, what *shall* thy wages *be*?

It's time for the boss to ask you what you want to be paid. What will you answer?

_____
_____
_____
_____
_____
_____
_____

THE LORD HAS BLESSED

Genesis 30:25, 27, 28, 29, 30 (KJV)
²⁵ And it came to pass, when Rachel had born Joseph, that Jacob said unto Laban, Send me away, that I may go unto mine own place, and to my country.
²⁷ And Laban said unto him, I pray thee, if I have found favour in thine eyes, *tarry: for* I have learned by experience that the LORD hath blessed me for thy sake.
²⁸ And he said, Appoint me thy wages, and I will give *it*.
²⁹ And he said unto him, Thou knowest how I have served thee, and how thy cattle was with me.
³⁰ For *it was* little which thou hadst before I *came*, and it is *now* increased unto a multitude; and the LORD hath blessed thee since my coming: and now when shall I provide for mine own house also?

Laban saw the LORD's blessing on Jacob and offered Jacob any salary to stay. Laban didn't believe in God and yet he needed to hire the one who was blessed by God.

_____
_____
_____
_____

date_____

GOD CAME TO LABAN THE SYRIAN

Genesis 31:22 – 24 (KJV)

²² And it was told Laban on the third day that Jacob was fled.

²³ And he took his brethren with him, and pursued after him seven days' journey; and they overtook him in the mount Gilead.

²⁴ And God came to Laban the Syrian in a dream by night, and said unto him, Take heed that thou speak not to Jacob either good or bad.

Jacob had been faithful to his employer (Laban) and to God who visited Laban in a dream **on Jacob's behalf**. God watches how employers treat His faithful. Jacob was faithful to God; regardless of what Laban did and God was putting **miracles** into Jacob's account (31:1 – 12). We know it is right when the Bible has a precedent for it. What would you like for God to visit someone about on your behalf?

_____
_____
_____
_____
_____
_____
_____

date_____

MY (JACOB'S) LIFE IS PRESERVED

Genesis 32:24, 25, 28, 29, 30 (KJV)

²⁴ And Jacob was left alone; and there wrestled a man with him until the breaking of the day.

²⁵ And when he saw that he prevailed not against him, he touched the hollow of his thigh; and the hollow of Jacob's thigh was out of joint, as he wrestled with him.

²⁸ And he said, Thy name shall be called no more Jacob, but Israel: for as a prince hast thou power with God and with men, and hast prevailed.

²⁹ And Jacob asked *him*, and said, Tell *me*, I pray thee, thy name. And he said, Wherefore *is* it *that* thou dost ask after my name? And he blessed him there.

³⁰ And Jacob called the name of the place Peniel: for I have seen God face to face, and my life is preserved.

Jacob spent a whole night alone with God and he was **clothed with God's power**. What does God want you to be relentless about for His kingdom? (James 1:5)

_____
_____
_____
_____
_____

date_____

GOD HATH DEALT GRACIOUSLY

Genesis 33:8 – 11 (KJV)

⁸ And he said, What *meanest* thou by all this drove which I met? And he said, *These are* to find grace in the sight of my lord.

⁹ And Esau said, I have enough, my brother; keep that thou hast unto thyself.

¹⁰ And Jacob said, Nay, I pray thee, if now I have found grace in thy sight, then receive my present at my hand: for therefore I have seen thy face, as though I had seen the face of God, and thou wast pleased with me.

¹¹ Take, I pray thee, my blessing that is brought to thee; because God hath dealt graciously with me, and because I have enough. And he urged him, and he took *it*.

Jacob saw God's promise when he saw **his brother's forgiveness.** (see Matthew 5:16) All God's promises for them and for us are 'Yes' and 'Amen' for the glory of God who has anointed us (2 Corinthians 1:20 – 21).

_____

_____

_____

_____

_____

date_____

DINAH

Genesis 34:1 – 4 (KJV)

¹ And Dinah the daughter of Leah, which she bare unto Jacob, went out to see the daughters of the land.

² And when Shechem the son of Hamor the Hivite, prince of the country, saw her, he took her, and lay with her, and defiled her.

³ And his soul clave unto Dinah the daughter of Jacob, and he loved the damsel, and spake kindly unto the damsel.

⁴ And Shechem spake unto his father Hamor, saying, Get me this damsel to wife.

Shechem, a Hivite, didn't believe in God, so he could believe in anything and steal anything without remorse. I'm surprised at this story being in the Bible until I realized God wants us to learn wisdom on all levels from His own words. We could be wrong but the words of God's Spirit will never be wrong. What can we learn from Him?

_____

_____

_____

_____

_____

_____

_____

GOD APPEARED TO JACOB AGAIN

Genesis 35:1, 9, 10, 11, 13 (KJV)
[1] And God said unto Jacob, Arise, go up to Bethel, and dwell there: and make there an altar unto God, that appeared unto thee when thou fleddest from the face of Esau thy brother.
[9] And God appeared unto Jacob again, when he came out of Padanaram, and blessed him.
[10] And God said unto him, Thy name *is* Jacob: thy name shall not be called any more Jacob, but Israel shall be thy name: and he called his name Israel.
[11] And God said unto him, I *am* God Almighty: be fruitful and multiply; a nation and a company of nations shall be of thee, and kings shall come out of thy loins;
[13] And God went up from him in the place where he talked with him.

God came down for the meeting in His name. (see Matthew 18:20; John 10:27)
Afterward, Jacob and his brother became too wealthy to live near each other.

_____
_____
_____
_____
_____

BECAUSE OF THEIR CATTLE

Genesis 36:1, 5 – 8 (KJV)
[1] Now these *are* the generations of Esau, who *is* Edom.
[5] And Aholibamah bare Jeush, and Jaalam, and Korah: these *are* the sons of Esau, which were born unto him in the land of Canaan.
[6] And Esau took his wives, and his sons, and his daughters, and all the persons of his house, and his cattle, and all his beasts, and all his substance, which he had got in the land of Canaan; and went into the country from the face of his brother Jacob.
[7] For their riches were more than that they might dwell together; and the land wherein they were strangers could not bear them because of their cattle.
[8] Thus dwelt Esau in mount Seir: Esau *is* Edom.

The brothers, Jacob and Esau, loved and forgave each other, but when they were passed away, their descendents forgot to pass on forgiveness. Could one person remember?

_____
_____
_____
_____

date_____
STRIPT JOSEPH OUT OF HIS COAT

Genesis 37:23, 24, 31, 32 (KJV)
²³ And it came to pass, when Joseph was come unto his brethren, that they stript Joseph out of his coat, *his* coat of *many* colours that *was* on him;
²⁴ And they took him, and cast him into a pit: and the pit *was* empty, *there was* no water in it.
³¹ And they took Joseph's coat, and killed a kid of the goats, and dipped the coat in the blood;
³² And they sent the coat of *many* colours, and they brought *it* to their father; and said, This have we found: know now whether it *be* thy son's coat or no.

The beginning of a ministry looks like trouble!
While Joseph was gone, Judah his brother lied to a woman and then caught the woman in sin; but when Judah realized he was no better than her, he gave her grace. That woman is Tamar and she is in the genealogy of Jesus (Matthew 1:1 – 3). (see John 8:1 – 11)

_____
_____
_____
_____
_____

date_____
DISCERN

Genesis 38:11, 25, 26 (KJV)
¹¹ Then said Judah to Tamar his daughter in law, Remain a widow at thy father's house, till Shelah my son be grown: for he said, Lest peradventure he die also, as his brethren *did*. And Tamar went and dwelt in her father's house.
²⁵ When she *was* brought forth, she sent to her father in law, saying, By the man, whose these *are, am* I with child: and she said, Discern, I pray thee, whose *are* these, the signet, and bracelets, and staff.
²⁶ And Judah acknowledged *them*, and said, She hath been more righteous than I; because that I gave her not to Shelah my son. And he knew her again no more.

Tamar called for **total honesty**. Every child is intricately made and is precious to God (Psalm 139:13 – 14). God offers grace to all who will receive. (see Matthew 1:1 – 3) His answer is always "life and life" (John 10:10). God sees the person before creation. Can we imagine how excited He is when the child He saw before creation is conceived?

_____
_____
_____
_____

THE LORD WAS WITH JOSEPH

Genesis 39:2 – 5 (KJV)

² And the LORD was with Joseph, and he was a prosperous man; and he was in the house of his master the Egyptian.

³ And his master saw that the LORD *was* with him, and that the LORD made all that he did to prosper in his hand.

⁴ And Joseph found grace in his sight, and he served him: and he made him overseer over his house, and all *that* he had he put into his hand.

⁵ And it came to pass from the time *that* he had made him overseer in his house, and over all that he had, that the LORD blessed the Egyptian's house for Joseph's sake; and the blessing of the LORD was upon all that he had in the house, and in the field.

The Lord made the difference for Joseph no matter where he was. (see 39:20 – 23)
Joseph remained faithful to God even though life was crashing around him!

_____
_____
_____
_____
_____
_____

TELL ME THEN, I PRAY YOU

Genesis 40:5 – 8 (KJV)

⁵ And they dreamed a dream both of them, each man his dream in one night, each man according to the interpretation of his dream, the butler and the baker of the king of Egypt, which *were* bound in the prison.

⁶ And Joseph came in unto them in the morning, and looked upon them, and, behold, they *were* sad.

⁷ And he asked Pharaoh's officers that *were* with him in the ward of his lord's house, saying, Wherefore look ye *so* sadly to day?

⁸ And they said unto him, We have dreamed a dream, and *there is* no interpreter of it. And Joseph said unto them, *Do* not interpretations *belong* to God? tell me *them*, I pray you.

Joseph was concerned for the others and confident he would hear the voice of God.

_____
_____
_____
_____
_____
_____
_____
_____

date_____

IN WHOM THE SPIRIT OF GOD IS

Genesis 41:9,12, 14, 38 (KJV)

⁹ Then spake the chief butler unto Pharaoh, saying, I do remember my faults this day:

¹² And *there was* there with us a young man, an Hebrew, servant to the captain of the guard; and we told him, and he interpreted to us our dreams; to each man according to his dream he did interpret.

¹⁴ Then Pharaoh sent and called Joseph, and they brought him hastily out of the dungeon: and he shaved *himself*, and changed his raiment, and came in unto Pharaoh.

³⁸ And Pharaoh said unto his servants, Can we find *such a one* as this *is*, a man in whom the Spirit of God *is*?

As the king needed Joseph, **the powerful are about have dreams and need you,** the one who refuses to compromise when compromise is more convenient.

Joseph's Witness was the Spirit of God.

_____

_____

_____

_____

_____

date_____

I (REUBEN) WILL BRING HIM TO THEE AGAIN

Genesis 42:35 – 37 (KJV)

³⁵ And it came to pass as they emptied their sacks, that, behold, every man's bundle of money *was* in his sack: and when *both* they and their father saw the bundles of money, they were afraid.

³⁶ And Jacob their father said unto them, Me have ye bereaved *of my children*: Joseph *is* not, and Simeon *is* not, and ye will take Benjamin *away*: all these things are against me.

³⁷ And Reuben spake unto his father, saying, Slay my two sons, if I bring him not to thee: deliver him into my hand, and I will bring him to thee again.

Jacob, (Joseph's dad) has been blaming himself for Joseph's death; but God was saving lives; making everything turn out for good. What are you blaming on yourself?

_____

_____

_____

_____

_____

_____

_____

JOSEPH SAW BENJAMIN

Genesis 43:14 – 17 (KJV)
[14] And God Almighty give you mercy before the man, that he may send away your other brother, and Benjamin. If I be bereaved *of my children*, I am bereaved.
[15] And the men took that present, and they took double money in their hand, and Benjamin; and rose up, and went down to Egypt, and stood before Joseph.
[16] And when Joseph saw Benjamin with them, he said to the ruler of his house, Bring *these* men home, and slay, and make ready; for *these* men shall dine with me at noon.
[17] And the man did as Joseph bade; and the man brought the men into Joseph's house.

Throughout Joseph's trials, he had sat before the LORD and now the brethren (who had been cruel to him**) sit before him.** (see Psalm 23:5; John 4:1 – 30) Who does God want you to see differently, love more and influence for the Lord?

LET THE LAD GO

Genesis 44:32 – 33 (KJV)
[32] For thy servant became surety for the lad unto my father, saying, If I bring him not unto thee, then I shall bear the blame to my father for ever.
[33] Now therefore, I pray thee, let thy servant abide instead of the lad a bondman to my lord; and let the lad go up with his brethren.

Like Joseph, **the one who was opposing you (before) is now afraid to oppose you. Joseph's brothers didn't know who they were talking to.**
Judah said, not knowing he was talking to Joseph, "Take me instead. Let me be the guarantee instead of the boy."
When the Romans came to arrest Jesus, He said to the Romans (about His disciples), "Let them go." Jesus took up for all of us at that moment. We have all done wrong, but God has given us Goodness anyway. Not one of us could pay for our sin. Like Joseph, **our opposition doesn't know who they are talking to.**

_____
_____
_____
_____
_____
_____

date_____
WHEN HE (JACOB) SAW THE WAGONS

Genesis 45:7, 25 – 27 (KJV)
7 And God sent me before you to preserve you a posterity in the earth, and to save your lives by a great deliverance.
25 And they went up out of Egypt, and came into the land of Canaan unto Jacob their father,
26 And told him, saying, Joseph *is* yet alive, and he *is* governor over all the land of Egypt. And Jacob's heart fainted, for he believed them not.
27 And they told him all the words of Joseph, which he had said unto them: and when he saw the wagons which Joseph had sent to carry him, the spirit of Jacob their father revived:

When you are in a place where people don't want you around, then you are on a road to prestige, privilege and power from the God of heaven! That was Joseph's road and his faithfulness toward God and willingness to wait kept him going right. (Genesis 37 – 45)

_____
_____
_____
_____
_____
_____

date_____
IN THE WAGONS... PHARAOH...SENT

Genesis 46:1 – 3, 5 (KJV)
1 And Israel took his journey with all that he had, and came to Beersheba, and offered sacrifices unto the God of his father Isaac.
2 And God spake unto Israel in the visions of the night, and said, Jacob, Jacob. And he said, Here *am* I.
3 And he said, I *am* God, the God of thy father: fear not to go down into Egypt; for I will there make of thee a great nation:
5 And Jacob rose up from Beersheba: and the sons of Israel carried Jacob their father, and their little ones, and their wives, in the wagons which Pharaoh had sent to carry him.

The wagons are coming and they are yours! What **a pattern!** God had prepared beyond what any of them could have **dreamed** (Genesis 46:1 – 5). He can do it. He will do it for you (Jeremiah 33:3). The pattern is the wisdom.

_____
_____
_____
_____
_____

date_____

THOU HAST SAVED OUR LIVES

Genesis 47:15, 20, 24, 25 (KJV)

¹⁵ And when money failed in the land of Egypt, and in the land of Canaan, all the Egyptians came unto Joseph, and said, Give us bread: for why should we die in thy presence? for the money faileth..

²⁰ And Joseph bought all the land of Egypt for Pharaoh; for the Egyptians sold every man his field, because the famine prevailed over them: so the land became Pharaoh's.

²⁴ And it shall come to pass in the increase, that ye shall give the fifth *part* unto Pharaoh, and four parts shall be your own, for seed of the field, and for your food, and for them of your households, and for food for your little ones.

²⁵ And they said, Thou hast saved our lives: let us find grace in the sight of my lord, and we will be Pharaoh's servants.

Joseph exchanged their wealth for food from the seeds they had brought to Joseph before. God had always been watching over the books while Joseph lived in faith trusting God.

_____
_____
_____
_____

date_____

ONE PORTION ABOVE

Genesis 48:3, 4, 21, 22 (KJV)

³ And Jacob said unto Joseph, God Almighty appeared unto me at Luz in the land of Canaan, and blessed me,

⁴ And said unto me, Behold, I will make thee fruitful, and multiply thee, and I will make of thee a multitude of people; and will give this land to thy seed after thee *for* an everlasting possession.

²¹ And Israel said unto Joseph, Behold, I die: but God shall be with you, and bring you again unto the land of your fathers.

²² Moreover I have given to thee one portion above thy brethren, which I took out of the hand of the Amorite with my sword and with my bow.

Israel/Jacob, 147, (Joseph's father who thought Joseph had died) had saved that *one portion above* for Joseph because **dreams come true!** Israel/Jacob never gave up on Joseph's dreams, because when he heard them, **he believed.** What is your dream?

_____
_____
_____
_____
_____

GATHER YOURSELVES TOGETHER

Genesis 49:1, 2, 22, 23, 24 (KJV)
[1] And Jacob called unto his sons, and said, Gather yourselves together, that I may tell you *that* which shall befall you in the last days.
[2] Gather yourselves together, and hear, ye sons of Jacob; and hearken unto Israel your father.
[22] Joseph *is* a fruitful bough, *even* a fruitful bough by a well; *whose* branches run over the wall:
[23] The archers have sorely grieved him, and shot *at him*, and hated him:
[24] But his bow abode in strength, and the arms of his hands were made strong by the hands of the mighty *God* of Jacob; (from thence *is* the shepherd, the stone of Israel:)

When our dad isn't with us, we can pray in faith for God to give us **the blessing Jacob gave to his son Joseph** and God will, because He wants us to be blessed (49:25, 26).

GOD MEANT IT UNTO GOOD

Genesis 50:17 – 20 (KJV)
[17] So shall ye say unto Joseph, Forgive, I pray thee now, the trespass of thy brethren, and their sin; for they did unto thee evil: and now, we pray thee, forgive the trespass of the servants of the God of thy father. And Joseph wept when they spake unto him.
[18] And his brethren also went and fell down before his face; and they said, Behold, we *be* thy servants.
[19] And Joseph said unto them, Fear not: for *am* I in the place of God?
[20] But as for you, ye thought evil against me; *but* God meant it unto good, to bring to pass, as *it is* this day, to save much people alive.

After or during a time of ministering, **every minister can say those words** to someone. Ministers go through hard things, **for the sake of others**. Ministers serve for the sake of others and the beginning isn't easy; **but the ending will save lives.**

_____

_____

_____

_____

_____

_____

_____

I AM THAT I AM

Exodus 3:2, 4, 13, 14 (KJV)

[2] And the angel of the LORD appeared unto him in a flame of fire out of the midst of a bush: and he looked, and, behold, the bush burned with fire, and the bush *was* not consumed.

[4] And when the LORD saw that he turned aside to see, God called unto him out of the midst of the bush, and said, Moses, Moses. And he said, Here *am* I.

[13] And Moses said unto God, Behold, *when* I come unto the children of Israel, and shall say unto them, The God of your fathers hath sent me unto you; and they shall say to me, What *is* his name? what shall I say unto them?

[14] And God said unto Moses, I AM THAT I AM: and he said, Thus shalt thou say unto the children of Israel, I AM hath sent me unto you.

When Moses built the tabernacle by God's pattern, **the fire became the Spirit** for the **tabernacle of worship**. God can do anything (19:2). Does God want a meeting place?

_____
_____
_____
_____
_____
_____

FILLED WITH THE SPIRIT OF WISDOM

Exodus 28:1 – 4 (KJV)

[1] And take thou unto thee Aaron thy brother, and his sons with him, from among the children of Israel, that he may minister unto me in the priest's office, *even* Aaron, Nadab and Abihu, Eleazar and Ithamar, Aaron's sons.

[2] And thou shalt make holy garments for Aaron thy brother for glory and for beauty.

[3] And thou shalt speak unto all *that are* wise hearted, whom I have filled with the spirit of wisdom, that they may make Aaron's garments to consecrate him, that he may minister unto me in the priest's office.

[4] And these *are* the garments which they shall make; a breastplate, and an ephod, and a robe, and a broidered coat, a mitre, and a girdle: and they shall make holy garments for Aaron thy brother, and his sons, that he may minister unto me in the priest's office.

The Spirit of wisdom was given for seamstresses in the house of God! (see 29:7, 8, 9) Did the makers of clothing matter to God? Is the Spirit of wisdom the same as the Spirit?

_____
_____
_____
_____

date_____

SPIRIT OF GOD...IN ALL... WORKMANSHIP

Exodus 31:1 – 3 (KJV)
[1] And the LORD spake unto Moses, saying,
[2] See, I have called by name Bezaleel the son of Uri, the son of Hur, of the tribe of Judah:
[3] And I have filled him with the spirit of God, in wisdom, and in understanding, and in knowledge, and in all manner of workmanship,

The characteristics of God in man will build His house! God is the Source of His work!
Where do wisdom and gifts come from? (Colossians 1:9; 1 Corinthians 12:4) Is the Spirit of God and the Spirit of wisdom the same?

_____
_____
_____
_____
_____
_____
_____
_____
_____

date_____

STIRRED...(THEIR) SPIRIT MADE WILLING

Exodus 35:21, 22, 29 (KJV)
[21] And they came, every one whose heart stirred him up, and every one whom his spirit made willing, *and* they brought the LORD'S offering to the work of the tabernacle of the congregation, and for all his service, and for the holy garments.
[22] And they came, both men and women, as many as were willing hearted, *and* brought bracelets, and earrings, and rings, and tablets, all jewels of gold: and every man that offered *offered* an offering of gold unto the LORD.
[29] The children of Israel brought a willing offering unto the LORD, every man and woman, whose heart made them willing to bring for all manner of work, which the LORD had commanded to be made by the hand of Moses.

He is the Source of His skills for the furnishing and finishing of His house! The willing heart is a heart with the faith to give! You cannot out-give God! (see 2 Timothy 1:6; Isaiah 1:19; Hebrews 10:24) Why did God connect His Spirit to our spirit?

_____
_____
_____

date_____

FILLED HIM WITH THE SPIRIT OF GOD

Exodus 35:30 – 34 (KJV)

[30] And Moses said unto the children of Israel, See, the LORD hath called by name Bezaleel the son of Uri, the son of Hur, of the tribe of Judah;

[31] And he hath filled him with the spirit of God, in wisdom, in understanding, and in knowledge, and in all manner of workmanship;

[32] And to devise curious works, to work in gold, and in silver, and in brass,

[33] And in the cutting of stones, to set *them*, and in carving of wood, to make any manner of cunning work.

[34] And he hath put in his heart that he may teach, *both* he, and Aholiab, the son of Ahisamach, of the tribe of Dan.

Moses said, "See." They had seen the evidence of the Spirit of God (35:30 – 31)!

The Spirit gave them masteries in embroidery, carpentry, artwork and jewelry.

_____
_____
_____
_____
_____
_____

date_____

I (LORD) WILL TAKE OF THE SPIRIT

Numbers 11:11, 14, 16, 17 (KJV)

[11] And Moses said unto the LORD, Wherefore hast thou afflicted thy servant? and wherefore have I not found favour in thy sight, that thou layest the burden of all this people upon me?

[14] I am not able to bear all this people alone, because *it is* too heavy for me.

[16] And the LORD said unto Moses, Gather unto me seventy men of the elders of Israel, whom thou knowest to be the elders of the people, and officers over them; and bring them unto the tabernacle of the congregation, that they may stand there with thee.

[17] And I will come down and talk with thee there: and I will take of the spirit which *is* upon thee, and will put *it* upon them; and they shall bear the burden of the people with thee, that thou bear *it* not thyself alone.

The LORD transfers His Spirit by faith to make His burden (the burden He gave Moses) easier and his calling lighter! (Matthew 11:28 – 28) (see Luke 10:1; Nehemiah 9:20)

_____
_____
_____
_____
_____

date_____

THE SPIRIT RESTED UPON THEM...PROPHESIED

Numbers 11:22 – 25 (KJV)
²² Shall the flocks and the herds be slain for them, to suffice them? or shall all the fish of the sea be gathered together for them, to suffice them?
²³ And the LORD said unto Moses, Is the LORD'S hand waxed short? thou shalt see now whether my word shall come to pass unto thee or not.
²⁴ And Moses went out, and told the people the words of the LORD, and gathered the seventy men of the elders of the people, and set them round about the tabernacle.
²⁵ And the LORD came down in a cloud, and spake unto him, and took of the spirit that *was* upon him, and gave *it* unto the seventy elders: and it came to pass, *that*, when the spirit rested upon them, they prophesied, and did not cease.

The LORD came down and the Shekinah came to earth! Did the Spirit transfer from the LORD to the ordinary? Is anything too hard for the LORD?

_____
_____
_____
_____

date_____

TWO...THE SPIRIT RESTED UPON THEM

Numbers 11:26 – 27 (KJV)
²⁶ But there remained two *of the* men in the camp, the name of the one *was* Eldad, and the name of the other Medad: and the spirit rested upon them; and they *were* of them that were written, but went not out unto the tabernacle: and they prophesied in the camp.
²⁷ And there ran a young man, and told Moses, and said, Eldad and Medad do prophesy in the camp.

The Spirit comes by faith. There is no distance in prayer and no distance in faith. Yet God required a tabernacle to be built for Him even in the desert. (see 2 Chronicles 1 – 7) What did the Spirit do and cause to happen?

_____
_____
_____
_____
_____
_____
_____
_____
_____
_____
_____

date_____
LORD WOULD PUT HIS SPIRIT UPON THEM

Numbers 11:27 – 29 (KJV)

27 And there ran a young man, and told Moses, and said, Eldad and Medad do prophesy in the camp.

28 And Joshua the son of Nun, the servant of Moses, *one* of his young men, answered and said, My lord Moses, forbid them.

29 And Moses said unto him, Enviest thou for my sake? would God that all the LORD'S people were prophets, *and* that the LORD would put his spirit upon them!

The Word of God clarifies and confirms the Word of God (1 Corinthians 14). Moses said it and wrote it before Paul was born and wrote it. When God gave the mouthpiece to Aaron He was showing us all that we all can prophesy! (Exodus 4:13 – 15) Why didn't Joshua think the others could prophesy too? Did Moses want everyone to prophesy?

_____
_____
_____
_____
_____
_____
_____

date_____
ANOTHER SPIRIT WITH HIM

Numbers 14:22 – 24 (KJV)

22 Because all those men which have seen my glory, and my miracles, which I did in Egypt and in the wilderness, and have tempted me now these ten times, and have not hearkened to my voice;

23 Surely they shall not see the land which I sware unto their fathers, neither shall any of them that provoked me see it:

24 But my servant Caleb, because he had another spirit with him, and hath followed me fully, him will I bring into the land whereinto he went; and his seed shall possess it.

Caleb had taken a stand. Caleb and Joshua had been 2 against 2 million. Caleb received the Spirit and the Spirit was with him. When Caleb asked for certain land, God would make sure he got it because Caleb had turned to the Spirit of faith in the one living God (Hebrews 3:1 – 4:1). (see Luke 10:38 – 42; Numbers 14:19 – 24)

_____
_____
_____
_____
_____
_____

date_____

IN WHOM IS THE SPIRIT

Numbers 27:15 – 20 (KJV)
[15] And Moses spake unto the LORD, saying,
[16] Let the LORD, the God of the spirits of all flesh, set a man over the congregation,
[17] Which may go out before them, and which may go in before them, and which may lead them out, and which may bring them in; that the congregation of the LORD be not as sheep which have no shepherd.
[18] And the LORD said unto Moses, Take thee Joshua the son of Nun, a man in whom *is* the spirit, and lay thine hand upon him;
[19] And set him before Eleazar the priest, and before all the congregation; and give him a charge in their sight.
[20] And thou shalt put *some* of thine honour upon him, that all the congregation of the children of Israel may be obedient.

The spirit of honor will fight our battles for us! (see 1 Corinthians 11:23; 1 John 1:3)

_____
_____
_____
_____
_____
_____

date_____

JOSHUA...FULL OF THE SPIRIT OF WISDOM

Deuteronomy 34:5, 7, 9 (KJV)
[5] So Moses the servant of the LORD died there in the land of Moab, according to the word of the LORD.
[7] And Moses *was* an hundred and twenty years old when he died: his eye was not dim, nor his natural force abated.
[9] And Joshua the son of Nun was full of the spirit of wisdom; for Moses had laid his hands upon him: and the children of Israel hearkened unto him, and did as the LORD commanded Moses.

When the Spirit was transferred, it was **a taste of the Pentecost to come** when God would pour out His Spirit for everyone (Numbers 27:18; Acts 2:17, 18).

_____
_____
_____
_____
_____
_____
_____
_____

EVEN OTHNIEL...THE SPIRIT OF THE LORD

Judges 3:9 – 10 (KJV)
⁹ And when the children of Israel cried unto the LORD, the LORD raised up a deliverer to the children of Israel, who delivered them, *even* Othniel the son of Kenaz, Caleb's younger brother. ¹⁰ And the Spirit of the LORD came upon him, and he judged Israel, and went out to war: and the LORD delivered Chushanrishathaim king of Mesopotamia into his hand; and his hand prevailed against Chushanrishathaim.

By the Spirit of grace, Othniel became a judge and a military leader for his country in **justice and protection** (3:7 – 11). You can accomplish a higher level. You are stronger than you think. He will lift you higher. "even Othniel" He **represents the unlikely**, like Gideon, Moses and Simon and like the young John who trusted in God (Acts 10:5; John 18:25 – 27, 21:20; 1 Corinthians 15:3 – 5). What's the difference between **empowered by the Spirit and walking in the Spirit**?

_____
_____
_____
_____
_____

SPIRIT OF THE LORD CAME UPON GIDEON

Judges 6:23, 28, 29, 34 (KJV)
²³ And the LORD said unto him, Peace *be* unto thee; fear not: thou shalt not die.
²⁸ And when the men of the city arose early in the morning, behold, the altar of Baal was cast down, and the grove was cut down that *was* by it, and the second bullock was offered upon the altar *that was* built.
²⁹ And they said one to another, Who hath done this thing? And when they enquired and asked, they said, Gideon the son of Joash hath done this thing. ³⁴ But the Spirit of the LORD came upon Gideon, and he blew a trumpet; and Abiezer was gathered after him.

Gideon was afraid but **the Spirit came on him.** Gideon was afraid, but **God honored Gideon's obedience**. Through faith **from the Spirit**, the unknown Gideon became known as General Gideon. What did the Spirit give to Gideon so Gideon could obey God? (see Acts 4:13, 31)

_____
_____
_____
_____
_____

SPIRIT...BEGAN TO MOVE HIM (SAMSON)

Judges 13:3, 4, 24, 25 (KJV)
3 And the angel of the LORD appeared unto the woman, and said unto her, Behold now, thou *art* barren, and bearest not: but thou shalt conceive, and bear a son.
4 Now therefore beware, I pray thee, and drink not wine nor strong drink, and eat not any unclean *thing*:
24 And the woman bare a son, and called his name Samson: and the child grew, and the LORD blessed him.
25 And the Spirit of the LORD began to move him at times in the camp of Dan between Zorah and Eshtaol.

The Spirit of the LORD works in the physical realm. **What do you want to call on God for and conceive in faith** that you have not been able to bring forth in your strength? (see Jeremiah 33:3; 2 Peter 1:20 – 21)

_____
_____
_____
_____
_____
_____
_____
_____
_____

SPIRIT OF THE LORD CAME MIGHTILY

Judges 14:5 – 7 (KJV)
5 Then went Samson down, and his father and his mother, to Timnath, and came to the vineyards of Timnath: and, behold, a young lion roared against him.
6 And the Spirit of the LORD came mightily upon him, and he rent him as he would have rent a kid, and *he had* nothing in his hand: but he told not his father or his mother what he had done.
7 And he went down, and talked with the woman; and she pleased Samson well.

The Spirit gave strength to one. The lion wanted Samson for lunch but that lion became lunch to Samson after he tore it up as if it were a piece of paper. The Spirit of the LORD gave protection to Samson when he wanted to receive. What or who wants to harm you?

_____
_____
_____
_____
_____
_____
_____

date_____
THE SPIRIT...CAME UPON HIM (SAMSON)

Judges 14:1, 2, 4, 19 (KJV)
[1] And Samson went down to Timnath, and saw a woman in Timnath of the daughters of the Philistines.

[2] And he came up, and told his father and his mother, and said, I have seen a woman in Timnath of the daughters of the Philistines: now therefore get her for me to wife.

[4] But his father and his mother knew not that it *was* of the LORD, that he sought an occasion against the Philistines: for at that time the Philistines had dominion over Israel.

[19] And the Spirit of the LORD came upon him, and he went down to Ashkelon, and slew thirty men of them, and took their spoil, and gave change of garments unto them which expounded the riddle. And his anger was kindled, and he went up to his father's house.

One facet of this story tells us about the man Samson who left his wife (14:1 – 20). His wife was a Philistine, but God still saw them both as one, so God required even Samson to treat her as costly porcelain if he wanted God's help (1 Peter 3:7).

_____
_____
_____

date_____
THE SPIRIT OF THE LORD CAME MIGHTILY

Judges 15:12 – 14 (KJV)
[12] And they said unto him, We are come down to bind thee, that we may deliver thee into the hand of the Philistines. And Samson said unto them, Swear unto me, that ye will not fall upon me yourselves.

[13] And they spake unto him, saying, No; but we will bind thee fast, and deliver thee into their hand: but surely we will not kill thee. And they bound him with two new cords, and brought him up from the rock.

[14] *And* when he came unto Lehi, the Philistines shouted against him: and the Spirit of the LORD came mightily upon him, and the cords that *were* upon his arms became as flax that was burnt with fire, and his bands loosed from off his hands.

The Spirit of God knew what Samson would do but the **Spirit of the LORD had still given him the gift of strength** to **weaken the enemy** (13:5). **Since there are no wasted words here, why is "mightily" in verse 14?** (see Genesis 17:1 – 2; Jeremiah 32:27)

_____
_____
_____
_____

date_____

SPIRIT OF THE LORD WILL COME

1 Samuel 10:5 – 7 (KJV)

[5] After that thou shalt come to the hill of God, where *is* the garrison of the Philistines: and it shall come to pass, when thou art come thither to the city, that thou shalt meet a company of prophets coming down from the high place with a psaltery, and a tabret, and a pipe, and a harp, before them; and they shall prophesy:

[6] And the Spirit of the LORD will come upon thee, and thou shalt prophesy with them, and shalt be turned into another man.

[7] And let it be, when these signs are come unto thee, *that* thou do as occasion serve thee; for God *is* with thee.

Samuel anointed the first king with oil and the LORD anointed him with the Spirit (9:15 – 17). Samuel advised Saul to **take advantage of the moment.** When the Spirit of the LORD came on him, God was with him. (see Genesis 39:3; Luke 3:21 – 22; 11:20) **Instruments and the word of the Lord came together** with vessels of the Lord.

_____

_____

_____

_____

date_____

THE SPIRIT...CAME... PROPHESIED

1 Samuel 10:8 – 10 (KJV)

[8] And thou shalt go down before me to Gilgal; and, behold, I will come down unto thee, to offer burnt offerings, *and* to sacrifice sacrifices of peace offerings: seven days shalt thou tarry, till I come to thee, and shew thee what thou shalt do.

[9] And it was *so*, that when he had turned his back to go from Samuel, God gave him another heart: and all those signs came to pass that day.

[10] And when they came thither to the hill, behold, a company of prophets met him; and the Spirit of God came upon him, and he prophesied among them.

Samuel poured oil on Saul in the name of the Lord (10:1). Saul got a new heart. Later also, when the Spirit of God comes on Zacharias, he prophesies (Luke 1:67)! How much do you need to happen, to reconcile, to restore, to see, **in one day**? (10:9) (see Luke 10:29 – 37)

_____

_____

_____

_____

_____

date_____

SPIRIT OF GOD CAME UPON SAUL

1 Samuel 11:5 – 7 (KJV)
⁵ And, behold, Saul came after the herd out of the field; and Saul said, What *aileth* the people that they weep? And they told him the tidings of the men of Jabesh.
⁶ And the Spirit of God came upon Saul when he heard those tidings, and his anger was kindled greatly.
⁷ And he took a yoke of oxen, and hewed them in pieces, and sent *them* throughout all the coasts of Israel by the hands of messengers, saying, Whosoever cometh not forth after Saul and after Samuel, so shall it be done unto his oxen. And the fear of the LORD fell on the people, and they came out with one consent.

Saul made an illustration that no one would forget and an army of 330,000 gathered with him and Saul's career as a captain began in a day on the day the Spirit empowered him to a take a stand (1 Samuel 10:1 – 11:8). (see Luke 17:1 – 4; Matthew 5:44)

_____
_____
_____
_____
_____
_____

date_____

THE SPIRIT OF THE LORD DEPARTED

1 Samuel 16:14, 23 (KJV)
¹⁴ But the Spirit of the LORD departed from Saul, and an evil spirit from the LORD troubled him.
²³ And it came to pass, when the *evil* spirit from God was upon Saul, that David took an harp, and played with his hand: so Saul was refreshed, and was well, and the evil spirit departed from him.

Saul was being warned again and again to stay in the presence. (see 10:5; 18:10 – 12; 1 Corinthians 12:10)
When my mama was hospitalized, I saw a warning from the LORD on the medicine being given to her. It was a warning sign to stop her from taking it. I requested it be stopped but someone gave it to her and in the 3 days mama was unable to move. Then the doctor came in the morning and saw her and ordered that medicine stopped. Mama was out of bed and herself again the next morning.

_____
_____
_____
_____
_____

date_____

HE WILL MAKE THEE AN HOUSE...HOUSE

2 Samuel 7:11, 25, 27 (KJV)

[11] And as since the time that I commanded judges *to be* over my people Israel, and have caused thee to rest from all thine enemies. Also the LORD telleth thee that he will make thee an house.

[25] And now, O LORD God, the word that thou hast spoken concerning thy servant, and concerning his house, establish *it* for ever, and do as thou hast said.

[27] For thou, O LORD of hosts, God of Israel, hast revealed to thy servant, saying, I will build thee an house: therefore hath thy servant found in his heart to pray this prayer unto thee.

David spoke to God repeating **God's words** back to God who did it for His word sake (7:18, 21). We are each a temple for His Spirit, a **house of the Holy Ghost, prepared individually for the corporate and individual habitation of God**. (see 1 Corinthians 6:19; John 14:1 – 3, 17) We are called to **enter** His presence.

_____

_____

_____

_____

date_____

THE SPIRIT OF THE LORD SPAKE BY ME (DAVID)

2 Samuel 23:1 – 3 (KJV)

[1] Now these *be* the last words of David. David the son of Jesse said, and the man *who was* raised up on high, the anointed of the God of Jacob, and the sweet psalmist of Israel, said,

[2] The Spirit of the LORD spake by me, and his word *was* in my tongue.

[3] The God of Israel said, the Rock of Israel spake to me, He that ruleth over men *must be* just, ruling in the fear of God.

God wants righteous rulers to rule His people. (see Proverbs 29:2) David himself says and the Holy Bible confirms here that David's writings of the Psalms were not from him but from the Spirit of the LORD. The Spirit of the LORD **spoke by David.** (see Matthew 1:1; 10:20; Luke 12:12; 21:15; Hebrews 3:7) The Bible confirms the words of the Spirit (23:2). (see 1 Samuel 10:5 – 7)

_____

_____

_____

_____

_____

_____

WHICH WAY WENT THE SPIRIT OF THE LORD

1 Kings 22:24, 25, 27, 28 (KJV)

²⁴ But Zedekiah the son of Chenaanah went near, and smote Micaiah on the cheek, and said, Which way went the Spirit of the LORD from me to speak unto thee?

²⁵ And Micaiah said, Behold, thou shalt see in that day, when thou shalt go into an inner chamber to hide thyself.

²⁷ And say, Thus saith the king, Put this *fellow* in the prison, and feed him with bread of affliction and with water of affliction, until I come in peace.

²⁸ And Micaiah said, If thou return at all in peace, the LORD hath not spoken by me. And he said, Hearken, O people, every one of you.

Zedekiah blasphemed the Spirit of holy God implying that the Spirit of God was a man no better than him! Zedekiah ordered that the prophet of God be put into prison. His position of power in government could not **save** King Zedekiah. However, the man of God, Micaiah stood his ground and continued to speak in the name of the LORD.

_____

_____

_____

_____

THE SPIRIT... HATH TAKEN HIM (ELIJAH) UP

2 Kings 2:15 – 17 (KJV)

¹⁵ And when the sons of the prophets which *were* to view at Jericho saw him, they said, The spirit of Elijah doth rest on Elisha. And they came to meet him, and bowed themselves to the ground before him.

¹⁶ And they said unto him, Behold now, there be with thy servants fifty strong men; let them go, we pray thee, and seek thy master: lest peradventure the Spirit of the LORD hath taken him up, and cast him upon some mountain, or into some valley. And he said, Ye shall not send.

¹⁷ And when they urged him till he was ashamed, he said, Send. They sent therefore fifty men; and they sought three days, but found him not.

The sons of the prophets insisted they go search for Elijah. They spoke of the power of the Spirit to take him up or move Elijah. (see 1 Kings 18; Number 11:25)

_____

_____

_____

_____

_____

_____

_____

ALL HE (DAVID) HAD BY THE SPIRIT

1 Chronicles 28:11 – 13 (KJV)
[11] Then David gave to Solomon his son the pattern of the porch, and of the houses thereof, and of the treasuries thereof, and of the upper chambers thereof, and of the inner parlours thereof, and of the place of the mercy seat,
[12] And the pattern of all that he had by the spirit, of the courts of the house of the LORD, and of all the chambers round about, of the treasuries of the house of God, and of the treasuries of the dedicated things:
[13] Also for the courses of the priests and the Levites, and for all the work of the service of the house of the LORD, and for all the vessels of service in the house of the LORD.

David gave Solomon all the patterns for the house of God by the Spirit of the LORD! What do you need a pattern for from the One who has no beginning and no ending? What would happen if we waited and made all our choices by a transfer from the Spirit?
What was a vessel of service in the house of the LORD?

SPIRIT OF GOD CAME UPON AZARIAH

2 Chronicles 15:1 – 2, 4 – 5, 7 (KJV)
[1] And the Spirit of God came upon Azariah the son of Oded:
[2] And he went out to meet Asa, and said unto him, Hear ye me, Asa, and all Judah and Benjamin; The LORD *is* with you, while ye be with him; and if ye seek him, he will be found of you; but if ye forsake him, he will forsake you.
[4] But when they in their trouble did turn unto the LORD God of Israel, and sought him, he was found of them.
[5] And in those times *there was* no peace to him that went out, nor to him that came in, but great vexations *were* upon all the inhabitants of the countries.
[7] Be ye strong therefore, and let not your hands be weak: for your work shall be rewarded.

May we hold on to our confidence; for **great reward** comes to those who believe.
When we seek the LORD with all our heart, we will find Him in all His glory!

_____
_____
_____

date_____
WHICH WAY WENT THE SPIRIT OF THE LORD

2 Chronicles 18:23 – 27 (KJV)

²³ Then Zedekiah the son of Chenaanah came near, and smote Micaiah upon the cheek, and said, Which way went the Spirit of the LORD from me to speak unto thee?
²⁴ And Micaiah said, Behold, thou shalt see on that day when thou shalt go into an inner chamber to hide thyself.
²⁵ Then the king of Israel said, Take ye Micaiah, and carry him back to Amon the governor of the city, and to Joash the king's son;
²⁶ And say, Thus saith the king, Put this *fellow* in the prison, and feed him with bread of affliction and with water of affliction, until I return in peace.
²⁷ And Micaiah said, If thou certainly return in peace, *then* hath not the LORD spoken by me. And he said, Hearken, all ye people.

Zedekiah, a mean king of Israel, tried to protect himself from the prophecy. God will also fight your battle for you and He will win even if your enemy hides (2 Chronicles 18).

_____
_____
_____
_____

date_____
UPON JAHAZIEL...CAME THE SPIRIT

2 Chronicles 20:14 – 15 (KJV)

¹⁴ Then upon Jahaziel the son of Zechariah, the son of Benaiah, the son of Jeiel, the son of Mattaniah, a Levite of the sons of Asaph, came the Spirit of the LORD in the midst of the congregation;
¹⁵ And he said, Hearken ye, all Judah, and ye inhabitants of Jerusalem, and thou king Jehoshaphat, Thus saith the LORD unto you, Be not afraid nor dismayed by reason of this great multitude; for the battle *is* not yours, but God's.

Praise toward God caused God to raise His voice by a prophet Jahaziel, and announce "**Don't be afraid** of the enemy. Don't look around anxiously as if you have no hope; for the battle is not yours, but God's. You're not going to have to fight this one! **God will fight for you** and overpower your enemies." (20:1 – 27) (see Isaiah 41:10)

_____
_____
_____
_____
_____
_____
_____

date_____

SPIRIT OF GOD CAME UPON ZECHARIAH

2 Chronicles 24:18 – 20 (KJV)
¹⁸ And they left the house of the LORD God of their fathers, and served groves and idols: and wrath came upon Judah and Jerusalem for this their trespass.
¹⁹ Yet he sent prophets to them, to bring them again unto the LORD; and they testified against them: but they would not give ear.
²⁰ And the Spirit of God came upon Zechariah the son of Jehoiada the priest, which stood above the people, and said unto them, Thus saith God, Why transgress ye the commandments of the LORD, that ye cannot prosper? because ye have forsaken the LORD, he hath also forsaken you.

Did the LORD want them to prosper? (24:19) The Spirit of God spoke against those who had forsaken giving toward the house of God. The Spirit of God explained they were hindering themselves from receiving God's help (24:4 – 24). What has God told you to do before? What does God want you to do soon? (see Hebrews 7:8 – 10)

_____
_____
_____
_____
_____

date_____

GOOD SPIRIT TO INSTRUCT THEM

Nehemiah 9:18 – 21 (KJV)
¹⁸ Yea, when they had made them a molten calf, and said, This *is* thy God that brought thee up out of Egypt, and had wrought great provocations;
¹⁹ Yet thou in thy manifold mercies forsookest them not in the wilderness: the pillar of the cloud departed not from them by day, to lead them in the way; neither the pillar of fire by night, to shew them light, and the way wherein they should go.
²⁰ Thou gavest also thy good spirit to instruct them, and withheldest not thy manna from their mouth, and gavest them water for their thirst.
²¹ Yea, forty years didst thou sustain them in the wilderness, *so that* they lacked nothing; their clothes waxed not old, and their feet swelled not.

God sustained them by His mercy and we will be blessed by Him when we give mercy like He gave (Nehemiah 9). God's mercy is beyond human reasoning. (see Psalm 40:11)

_____
_____
_____
_____
_____

date_____
BY THY (GOD'S) SPIRIT IN THY PROPHETS

Nehemiah 9:28, 30 (KJV)
28 But after they had rest, they did evil again before thee: therefore leftest thou them in the hand of their enemies, so that they had the dominion over them: yet when they returned, and cried unto thee, thou heardest *them* from heaven; and many times didst thou deliver them according to thy mercies;
30 Yet many years didst thou forbear them, and testifiedst against them by thy spirit in thy prophets: yet would they not give ear: therefore gavest thou them into the hand of the people of the lands.

When I was young, I was rebellious and mean toward my mother because she was a Christian so I wanted nothing to do with her. But now we are both going to heaven because of faith in Jesus. God loved us and sent Jesus for us **before we loved Him according to His mercies,** the stuff we receive by His merit and not ours. (see 9:18 – 19; Romans 5:8; Genesis 32:10; Jeremiah 7:25) Who was the Spirit in His prophets?

_____
_____
_____
_____

date_____
BY HIS SPIRIT

Job 26:1, 7, 8, 10, 13, 14 (KJV)
1 But Job answered and said,
7 He stretcheth out the north over the empty place, *and* hangeth the earth upon nothing.
8 He bindeth up the waters in his thick clouds; and the cloud is not rent under them.
10 He hath compassed the waters with bounds, until the day and night come to an end.
13 By his spirit he hath garnished the heavens; his hand hath formed the crooked serpent.
14 Lo, these *are* parts of his ways: but how little a portion is heard of him? but the thunder of his power who can understand?

Job answered his critic (Bildad) by telling him about the omniscience of God, who made the aroma of the Buttercup and the scent of the skunk. God set the earth on her axis and expands the galaxies for a concert in the heavens. (see Joel 2:28 – 29) He does this by His breath (Genesis 1:3). Job gave God the glory for creation and God will take up for Job later (Job 42:7 – 8). Where do you need God to take up for you?

_____
_____
_____

SPIRIT OF GOD HATH MADE ME (ELIHU)

Job 33:1 – 7 (KJV)

[1] Wherefore, Job, I pray thee, hear my speeches, and hearken to all my words.
[2] Behold, now I have opened my mouth, my tongue hath spoken in my mouth.
[3] My words *shall be of* the uprightness of my heart: and my lips shall utter knowledge clearly.
[4] The Spirit of God hath made me, and the breath of the Almighty hath given me life.
[5] If thou canst answer me, set *thy words* in order before me, stand up.
[6] Behold, I *am* according to thy wish in God's stead: I also am formed out of the clay.
[7] Behold, my terror shall not make thee afraid, neither shall my hand be heavy upon thee.

Elihu praised God for life and breath as he spoke to Job. Elihu praised the Spirit of God for being his Maker. He wasn't humble but he also gave glory to God and **he wasn't scolded** when God took up for Job. Job's 3 friends didn't have good answers and they accused Job anyway. They didn't show mercy to Job but who did (42:7 – 10)?

_____
_____
_____

PROPHECY: THIS DAY HAVE I BEGOTTEN THEE
TODAY I (GOD) HAVE BEGOTTEN YOU

Psalm 2:7, 8 (KJV)

[7] I will declare the decree: the LORD hath said unto me, Thou *art* my Son; this day have I begotten thee.
[8] Ask of me, and I shall give *thee* the heathen *for* thine inheritance, and the uttermost parts of the earth *for* thy possession.

"For to which of the angels did He ever say: *"You are My Son, Today I have begotten You"*? And again: *"I will be to Him a Father, And He shall be to Me a Son"*? **Hebrews 1:5 (NKJV).** (also Isaiah 42:1; Matthew 3:17; 17:5; Mark 1:8 – 11; Luke 3:22; John 1:32; Acts 13:33; Hebrews 5:5; 2 Peter 1:17) (see 1 Peter 1:3; 2 Thessalonians 3:3; Luke 11:2)

If someone has the spiritual gift of prophecy, do they also automatically have the gift of discerning of spirits? (1 Corinthians 12)

_____
_____
_____
_____
_____

date_____

PROPHECY: PIERCED MY HANDS AND MY FEET
AND THEY CRUCIFIED HIM (JESUS)

Psalm 22:15 – 18 (KJV)
15 My strength is dried up like a potsherd; and my tongue cleaveth to my jaws; and thou hast brought me into the dust of death.
16 For dogs have compassed me: the assembly of the wicked have inclosed me: they pierced my hands and my feet.
17 I may tell all my bones: they look *and* stare upon me.
18 They part my garments among them, and cast lots upon my vesture.

"And they crucified him, and parted his garments, casting lots: that it might be fulfilled which was spoken by the prophet, They parted my garments among them, and upon my vesture did they cast lots" **Matthew 27:35 (KJV)**.
If 2 people have the ministry of teaching, will they both teach the same way? (see Luke 23:33 – 34; Hebrews 10:23; Ephesians 4:11 – 12)

_____
_____
_____
_____
_____

date_____

PROPHECY: NOT ONE OF THEM IS BROKEN
NOT ONE OF HIS BONES SHALL BE BROKEN

Psalm 34:18 – 20 (KJV)
18 The LORD *is* nigh unto them that are of a broken heart; and saveth such as be of a contrite spirit.
19 Many *are* the afflictions of the righteous: but the LORD delivereth him out of them all.
20 He keepeth all his bones: not one of them is broken.

"And he who has seen has testified, and his testimony is true; and he knows that he is telling the truth, so that you may believe. For these things were done that the Scripture should be fulfilled, *"Not one of His bones shall be broken."* And again another Scripture says, *"They shall look on Him whom they pierced"* **John 19:35 – 37 (NKJV).** (see 34:17; James 4:7; Romans 8:31; Zechariah 12:10)
The word Scripture is a direct reference to the Holy Bible spoken and written for us so we will hear before it happens and believe since we have already seen the prophecy.

_____
_____
_____
_____

PROPHECY: LIFTED UP HIS HEEL AGAINST ME
LIFTED UP HIS HEAL AGAINST ME (JESUS)

Psalm 41:9 – 12 (KJV)

⁹ Yea, mine own familiar friend, in whom I trusted, which did eat of my bread, hath lifted up *his* heel against me.

¹⁰ But thou, O LORD, be merciful unto me, and raise me up, that I may requite them.

¹¹ By this I know that thou favourest me, because mine enemy doth not triumph over me.

¹² And as for me, thou upholdest me in mine integrity, and settest me before thy face for ever.

"If you know these things, blessed are you if you do them. I do not speak concerning all of you. I know whom I have chosen; but that the Scripture may be fulfilled, *'He who eats bread with Me has lifted up his heel against Me.'* Now I tell you before it comes, that when it does come to pass, you may believe that I am *He*. Most assuredly, I say to you, he who receives whomever I send receives Me; and he who receives Me receives Him who sent Me'" **John 13:15, 17 – 20 (NKJV).** (see John 21:20 – 24; 1 Corinthians 1:9)

_____
_____

RENEW A RIGHT SPIRIT WITHIN ME (DAVID)

Psalm 51:1, 2, 7, 10 (KJV)

¹ Have mercy upon me, O God, according to thy lovingkindness: according unto the multitude of thy tender mercies blot out my transgressions.

² Wash me throughly from mine iniquity, and cleanse me from my sin.

⁷ Purge me with hyssop, and I shall be clean: wash me, and I shall be whiter than snow.

¹⁰ Create in me a clean heart, O God; and renew a right spirit within me.

The Lord puts no limits on His forgiveness for His people. David wanted wisdom. (see 1 Kings 3:5) Lord, create in me a heart for You! No limits on lovingkindness from God. He is love.

What is the difference between purge, cleanse and wash? What heart was David asking for in this Psalm? (see 51:17; 1 Samuel 13:14; Luke 15:21)

_____
_____
_____
_____
_____
_____
_____

date_____

TAKE NOT THY HOLY SPIRIT FROM ME

Psalm 51:11 – 15 (KJV)

[11] Cast me not away from thy presence; and take not thy holy spirit from me.

[12] Restore unto me the joy of thy salvation; and uphold me *with thy* free spirit.

[13] *Then* will I teach transgressors thy ways; and sinners shall be converted unto thee.

[14] Deliver me from bloodguiltiness, O God, thou God of my salvation: *and* my tongue shall sing aloud of thy righteousness.

[15] O Lord, open thou my lips; and my mouth shall shew forth thy praise.

David walked after the Spirit so when he knew he had sinned, he wanted to please God. so he asked, "Take not thy holy spirit from me."

Lord, I have no strength; but **uphold me Lord by the power of Your Spirit**. Lord, I am surrendered unto You. Cleanse me so I can abide in Your presence (1 John 1:7). David wanted the Spirit of God so he could praise God (51:11, 15). What was David's promise when God delivered him?

_____

_____

_____

_____

_____

date_____

SENDEST FORTH THY (LORD) SPIRIT

Psalm 104:1, 2, 3, 5, 30, 31 (KJV)

[1] Bless the LORD, O my soul. O LORD my God, thou art very great; thou art clothed with honour and majesty.

[2] Who coverest *thyself* with light as *with* a garment: who stretchest out the heavens like a curtain:

[3] Who layeth the beams of his chambers in the waters: who maketh the clouds his chariot: who walketh upon the wings of the wind:

[5] *Who* laid the foundations of the earth, *that* it should not be removed for ever.

[30] Thou sendest forth thy spirit, they are created: and thou renewest the face of the earth.

[31] The glory of the LORD shall endure for ever: the LORD shall rejoice in his works.

The Breath of life crowned creation when He made humankind (Hebrews 1).

_____

_____

_____

_____

_____

_____

date_____

FROM THY (LORD'S) SPIRIT?... THY PRESENCE?

Psalm 139:1 – 4, 7, 23, 24 (KJV)
¹ O LORD, thou hast searched me, and known *me*.
² Thou knowest my downsitting and mine uprising, thou understandest my thought afar off.
³ Thou compassest my path and my lying down, and art acquainted *with* all my ways.
⁴ For *there is* not a word in my tongue, *but*, lo, O LORD, thou knowest it altogether.
⁷ Whither shall I go from thy spirit? or whither shall I flee from thy presence?
²³ Search me, O God, and know my heart: try me, and know my thoughts:
²⁴ And see if *there be any* wicked way in me, and lead me in the way everlasting.

David is in the Presence (139:7) God is The Almighty! The moment we were saved we began to care! All mankind was made on the same level as Esther or John the Baptist (Acts 17:26). When we speak His words in faith, we speak Eternal Life into our earthly situation! Why did he ask about His Spirit and His presence together?

_____
_____
_____

date_____

THY (LORD'S) SPIRIT IS GOOD

Psalm 143:5, 8, 9, 10 (KJV)
⁵ I remember the days of old; I meditate on all thy works; I muse on the work of thy hands.
⁸ Cause me to hear thy lovingkindness in the morning; for in thee do I trust: cause me to know the way wherein I should walk; for I lift up my soul unto thee.
⁹ Deliver me, O LORD, from mine enemies: I flee unto thee to hide me.
¹⁰ Teach me to do thy will; for thou *art* my God: thy spirit *is* good; lead me into the land of uprightness.

The Psalmist (God's servant and soldier) prays for mercy (143:1), for direction (143:8), for deliverance (143:9), for teaching and guidance (143:10), for the end of trouble (143:11). "...thy spirit is good..." The Spirit of the LORD is good. Who said?

_____
_____
_____
_____
_____
_____
_____
_____
_____
_____

WAY OF THE SPIRIT

Ecclesiastes 11:1, 2, 4, 5 (KJV)
[1] Cast thy bread upon the waters: for thou shalt find it after many days.
[2] Give a portion to seven, and also to eight; for thou knowest not what evil shall be upon the earth.
[4] He that observeth the wind shall not sow; and he that regardeth the clouds shall not reap.
[5] As thou knowest not what *is* the way of the spirit, *nor* how the bones *do grow* in the womb of her that is with child: even so thou knowest not the works of God who maketh all.

The spirit of giving is of the Spirit of God (see John 3:1 – 8). We have no need to worry **if we have given away too much while believing we were serving God through giving.** His works were His spoken words and we have His written words. **God works His miracles in the spiritual realm first** before we see the physical answers.

_____
_____
_____
_____
_____
_____
_____

PROPHECY: BEHOLD, A VIRGIN SHALL CONCEIVE BEHOLD, THE VIRGIN SHALL BE WITH CHILD

Isaiah 7:3, 11 – 14 (KJV)
[3] Then said the LORD unto Isaiah, Go forth now to meet Ahaz, thou, and Shearjashub thy son, at the end of the conduit of the upper pool in the highway of the fuller's field;
[11] Ask thee a sign of the LORD thy God; ask it either in the depth, or in the height above.
[12] But Ahaz said, I will not ask, neither will I tempt the LORD.
[13] And he said, Hear ye now, O house of David; *Is it* a small thing for you to weary men, but will ye weary my God also?
[14] Therefore the Lord himself shall give you a sign; Behold, a virgin shall conceive, and bear a son, and shall call his name Immanuel.

"So all this was done that it might be fulfilled which was spoken by the Lord through the prophet, saying: *"Behold, the virgin shall be with child, and bear a Son, and they shall call His name Immanuel,"* which is translated, "God with us" **Matthew 1:22, 23 (NKJV).**

_____
_____

SPIRIT OF THE LORD

Isaiah 11:1, 2, 10 (KJV)
[1] And there shall come forth a rod out of the stem of Jesse, and a Branch shall grow out of his roots:
[2] And the spirit of the LORD shall rest upon him, the spirit of wisdom and understanding, the spirit of counsel and might, the spirit of knowledge and of the fear of the LORD;
[10] And in that day there shall be a root of Jesse, which shall stand for an ensign of the people; to it shall the Gentiles seek: and his rest shall be glorious.

The 7 characteristics of God are listed in verse 2 of this **prophecy:** the Spirit that rests on Him, or the Spirit of rest, is also the Spirit of strength and **pure reverence.** (see Matthew 3:16; John 1:32; Acts 17:23 – 31; Galatians 5:22 – 23, 1 Corinthians 12:8; Revelation 1:4, 11, 16; 3:1; 4:5; 5:6, 12; 8:1, 2, 3; 12:3; 13:1) (see Psalm 111:10; Luke 4:18)

_____
_____
_____
_____
_____
_____
_____

NOT OF MY (LORD'S) SPIRIT

Isaiah 30:1, 2, 7 (KJV)
[1] Woe to the rebellious children, saith the LORD, that take counsel, but not of me; and that cover with a covering, but not of my spirit, that they may add sin to sin:
[2] That walk to go down into Egypt, and have not asked at my mouth; to strengthen themselves in the strength of Pharaoh, and to trust in the shadow of Egypt!
[7] For the Egyptians shall help in vain, and to no purpose: therefore have I cried concerning this, Their strength *is* to sit still.

Will they wait and trust in God?
The Sword of the Spirit (the Lord's only weapon) is the word of God (Ephesians 6:17). Trusting in any defense but the LORD leaves us without defenses! But we may be still and trust in Him, and He will be exalted (Psalm 46:10)! They were rebellious, trusting in Pharaoh's might, rather than the Almighty God! (see Psalm 91:1; Isaiah 31:1; 2 Kings 18:21)

_____
_____
_____
_____

date_____

THE SPIRIT BE POURED UPON US

Isaiah 32:9, 10, 15, 17, 18 (KJV)

[9] Rise up, ye women that are at ease; hear my voice, ye careless daughters; give ear unto my speech.

[10] Many days and years shall ye be troubled, ye careless women: for the vintage shall fail, the gathering shall not come.

[15] Until the spirit be poured upon us from on high, and the wilderness be a fruitful field, and the fruitful field be counted for a forest.

[17] And the work of righteousness shall be peace; and the effect of righteousness quietness and assurance for ever.

[18] And my people shall dwell in a peaceable habitation, and in sure dwellings, and in quiet resting places;

They are waiting on the Spirit and seeking the effect of righteousness! (see Acts 1:8) God (through Isaiah the prophet) called on women. What would be the results?

_____

_____

_____

_____

_____

_____

date_____

HIS (LORD'S) SPIRIT

Isaiah 34:1, 16, 17 (KJV)

[1] Come near, ye nations, to hear; and hearken, ye people: let the earth hear, and all that is therein; the world, and all things that come forth of it.

[16] Seek ye out of the book of the LORD, and read: no one of these shall fail, none shall want her mate: for my mouth it hath commanded, and his spirit it hath gathered them.

[17] And he hath cast the lot for them, and his hand hath divided it unto them by line: they shall possess it for ever, from generation to generation shall they dwell therein.

Every **prophecy in the Book** of the LORD shall be fulfilled (37:32; 2 Kings 19:31). However, for those of us who stand firm with Israel, our wilderness will blossom. We will sing. He will strengthen and save us as if God is on our team **saying to the opposition, "Check mate!"** (Isaiah 35:1 – 4)! (see Isaiah 40:28)

_____

_____

_____

_____

_____

_____

WHO HAS DIRECTED THE SPIRIT OF THE LORD

Isaiah 40:12, 13, 18, 26, 28 (KJV)

¹² Who hath measured the waters in the hollow of his hand, and meted out heaven with the span, and comprehended the dust of the earth in a measure, and weighed the mountains in scales, and the hills in a balance?

¹³ Who hath directed the Spirit of the LORD, or *being* his counsellor hath taught him?

¹⁸ To whom then will ye liken God? or what likeness will ye compare unto him?

²⁶ Lift up your eyes on high, and behold who hath created these *things*, that bringeth out their host by number: he calleth them all by names by the greatness of his might, for that *he is* strong in power; not one faileth.

²⁸ Hast thou not known? hast thou not heard, *that* the everlasting God, the LORD, the Creator of the ends of the earth, fainteth not, neither is weary? *there is* no searching of his understanding.

The Spirit of the LORD is the all-powerful all-knowing Spirit of God. (see 41:10; 55:9)

_____
_____
_____

I (GOD) WILL PUT MY SPIRIT UPON HIM

Isaiah 42:1 – 3 (KJV)

¹ Behold my servant, whom I uphold; mine elect, *in whom* my soul delighteth; I have put my spirit upon him: he shall bring forth judgment to the Gentiles.

² He shall not cry, nor lift up, nor cause his voice to be heard in the street.

³ A bruised reed shall he not break, and the smoking flax shall he not quench: he shall bring forth judgment unto truth.

What is truth? Jesus brought our judgment (or punishment and penalty) upon Himself so we could be saved by grace through faith. God could have thundered His promise to the whole creation. But He spoke to and through an ordinary person named Isaiah.

In affect, we can say to judgment for sin, "Meet God's victory." (see Matthew 12:18)

_____
_____
_____
_____
_____
_____
_____

I WILL POUR MY (LORD'S) SPIRIT UPON THY SEED

Isaiah 44:1 – 4 (KJV)

¹ Yet now hear, O Jacob my servant; and Israel, whom I have chosen:

² Thus saith the LORD that made thee, and formed thee from the womb, *which* will help thee; Fear not, O Jacob, my servant; and thou, Jesurun, whom I have chosen.

³ For I will pour water upon him that is thirsty, and floods upon the dry ground: I will pour my spirit upon thy seed, and my blessing upon thine offspring:

⁴ And they shall spring up *as* among the grass, as willows by the water courses.

God is positioned to pour His Spirit on that seed you thought you couldn't see and on your child and they will spring up and speak. (see 45:8)

_____
_____
_____
_____
_____
_____
_____
_____
_____

HIS (GOD'S) SPIRIT, HATH SENT ME (ISAIAH)

Isaiah 48:12, 15 – 17 (KJV)

¹² Hearken unto me, O Jacob and Israel, my called; I *am* he; I *am* the first, I also *am* the last.

¹⁵ I, *even* I, have spoken; yea, I have called him: I have brought him, and he shall make his way prosperous.

¹⁶ Come ye near unto me, hear ye this; I have not spoken in secret from the beginning; from the time that it was, there *am* I: and now the Lord GOD, and his Spirit, hath sent me.

¹⁷ Thus saith the LORD, thy Redeemer, the Holy One of Israel; I *am* the LORD thy God which teacheth thee to profit, which leadeth thee by the way *that* thou shouldest go.

The prophet Isaiah declared the Lord God and His Spirit was the One who sent him.

Isaiah said, "Here I am" when He was called of the Lord GOD and His Spirit (6:8).

Jesus was here in Spirit before He came in flesh (John 1:1, 2, 14).

_____
_____
_____
_____
_____

PROPHECY: HE (JESUS) IS
BROUGHT AS A LAMB
HE (JESUS) WAS LED AS A
SHEEP

Isaiah 53:5 – 8 (KJV)

[5] But he *was* wounded for our transgressions, *he was* bruised for our iniquities: the chastisement of our peace *was* upon him; and with his stripes we are healed.

[6] All we like sheep have gone astray; we have turned every one to his own way; and the LORD hath laid on him the iniquity of us all.

[7] He was oppressed, and he was afflicted, yet he opened not his mouth: he is brought as a lamb to the slaughter, and as a sheep before her shearers is dumb, so he openeth not his mouth.

[8] He was taken from prison and from judgment: and who shall declare his generation? for he was cut off out of the land of the living: for the transgression of my people was he stricken.

"The place of the scripture which he read was this, He was led as a sheep to the slaughter; and like a lamb dumb before his shearer, so opened he not his mouth." **Acts 8:32 (KJV).**

_____
_____
_____

SPIRIT...SHALL LIFT UP A
STANDARD

Isaiah 59:17 – 19 (KJV)

[17] For he put on righteousness as a breastplate, and an helmet of salvation upon his head; and he put on the garments of vengeance *for* clothing, and was clad with zeal as a cloke.

[18] According to *their* deeds, accordingly he will repay, fury to his adversaries, recompence to his enemies; to the islands he will repay recompence.

[19] So shall they fear the name of the LORD from the west, and his glory from the rising of the sun. When the enemy shall come in like a flood, the Spirit of the LORD shall lift up a standard against him.

So the enemy has come against you but the **Spirit of the LORD is your army!** When the standard of the LORD comes on man, then through man, the Spirit will perform the impossible! When no one believed enough to ask, God pushed up His spiritual sleeves (prepared to fight for each of us). He established His own unbreakable covenant with His only begotten Son, Jesus, our Intercessor (7:14; 52:10; 59:16 or 53:12).

_____
_____
_____

date_____

MY (LORD) SPIRIT THAT IS UPON THEE

Isaiah 59:19 – 21 (KJV)

¹⁹ So shall they fear the name of the LORD from the west, and his glory from the rising of the sun. When the enemy shall come in like a flood, the Spirit of the LORD shall lift up a standard against him.

²⁰ And the Redeemer shall come to Zion, and unto them that turn from transgression in Jacob, saith the LORD.

²¹ As for me, this *is* my covenant with them, saith the LORD; My spirit that *is* upon thee, and my words which I have put in thy mouth, shall not depart out of thy mouth, nor out of the mouth of thy seed, nor out of the mouth of thy seed's seed, saith the LORD, from henceforth and for ever.

No one can take away His covenant! (7:14; 52:10) His Word is forever! The Spirit of God watches over His covenant! The Spirit of the LORD will come on His people and they will be redeemed (59:19, 20). His covenant remains as long as the earth remains!

_____
_____
_____
_____
_____

date_____

PROPHECY: SPIRIT OF THE LORD IS UPON ME (ISAIAH) THE SPIRIT OF THE LORD IS UPON ME (JESUS)

Isaiah 61:1 – 3 (KJV)

¹ The Spirit of the Lord GOD *is* upon me; because the LORD hath anointed me to preach good tidings unto the meek; he hath sent me to bind up the brokenhearted, to proclaim liberty to the captives, and the opening of the prison to *them that are* bound;

² To proclaim the acceptable year of the LORD, and the day of vengeance of our God; to comfort all that mourn;

³ To appoint unto them that mourn in Zion, to give unto them beauty for ashes, the oil of joy for mourning, the garment of praise for the spirit of heaviness; that they might be called trees of righteousness, the planting of the LORD, that he might be glorified.

"The Spirit of the LORD is upon Me, Because He has anointed Me To preach the gospel to the poor; He has sent Me to heal the brokenhearted, To proclaim liberty to the captives And recovery of sight to the blind, To set at liberty those who are oppressed," **Luke 4:18 (NKJV).**

_____
_____
_____
_____

date_____

THEY...VEXED HIS HOLY SPIRIT

Isaiah 63:9 – 10 (KJV)
⁹ In all their affliction he was afflicted, and the angel of his presence saved them: in his love and in his pity he redeemed them; and he bare them, and carried them all the days of old.
¹⁰ But they rebelled, and vexed his holy Spirit: therefore he was turned to be their enemy, *and* he fought against them.

But they fought against God and limited the power He wanted them to have and to implement through them all. So God fought against the rebellious as He had to do to save lives. All this so Jesus could come so we could be saved.

God was sad as He told the **testimonies of His own kindness** toward a rebellious people. Will God use His mercy and power again to rescue the rebellious? Yes.

_____
_____
_____
_____
_____
_____

date_____

PUT HIS HOLY SPIRIT WITHIN THEM

Isaiah 63:10 – 13 (KJV)
¹⁰ But they rebelled, and vexed his holy Spirit: therefore he was turned to be their enemy, *and* he fought against them.
¹¹ Then he remembered the days of old, Moses, *and* his people, *saying,* Where *is* he that brought them up out of the sea with the shepherd of his flock? where *is* he that put his holy Spirit within him?
¹² That led *them* by the right hand of Moses with his glorious arm, dividing the water before them, to make himself an everlasting name?
¹³ That led them through the deep, as an horse in the wilderness, *that* they should not stumble?

A shift takes place on earth when God remembers. (see Luke 22:19) One thought of God in our direction changes our world. We walk in the Spirit and we have tapped into His Spirit. Could the Spirit of God enter them in the Old Testament or only in the New?

_____
_____
_____
_____

THE SPIRIT OF THE LORD... GLORIOUS NAME

Isaiah 63:14 – 17 (KJV)

[14] As a beast goeth down into the valley, the Spirit of the LORD caused him to rest: so didst thou lead thy people, to make thyself a glorious name.

[15] Look down from heaven, and behold from the habitation of thy holiness and of thy glory: where *is* thy zeal and thy strength, the sounding of thy bowels and of thy mercies toward me? are they restrained?

[16] Doubtless thou *art* our father, though Abraham be ignorant of us, and Israel acknowledge us not: thou, O LORD, *art* our father, our redeemer; thy name *is* from everlasting.

[17] O LORD, why hast thou made us to err from thy ways, *and* hardened our heart from thy fear? Return for thy servants' sake, the tribes of thine inheritance.

God's name was His responsibility: **God led them by His rest**. As the sparrow, the beast did nothing. (see Luke 12:7) As we cannot out-give God, we cannot out-do His mercy.

_____
_____
_____
_____

THE SPIRIT ENTERED INTO ME (EZEKIEL)

Ezekiel 2:1 – 5 (KJV)

[1] And he said unto me, Son of man, stand upon thy feet, and I will speak unto thee.

[2] And the spirit entered into me when he spake unto me, and set me upon my feet, that I heard him that spake unto me.

[3] And he said unto me, Son of man, I send thee to the children of Israel, to a rebellious nation that hath rebelled against me: they and their fathers have transgressed against me, *even* unto this very day.

[4] For *they are* impudent children and stiffhearted. I do send thee unto them; and thou shalt say unto them, Thus saith the Lord GOD.

[5] And they, whether they will hear, or whether they will forbear, (for they *are* a rebellious house,) yet shall know that there hath been a prophet among them.

What instruction did God give Ezekiel? (2:4 – 5) God is love. Did you witness to someone you knew wouldn't listen to you? (see Luke 10:10 – 11; John 4:24; 1 John 4:6)

_____
_____
_____
_____

THE SPIRIT TOOK ME (EZEKIEL) UP

Ezekiel 3:10 – 12 (KJV)

[10] Moreover he said unto me, Son of man, all my words that I shall speak unto thee receive in thine heart, and hear with thine ears.

[11] And go, get thee to them of the captivity, unto the children of thy people, and speak unto them, and tell them, Thus saith the Lord GOD; whether they will hear, or whether they will forbear.

[12] Then the spirit took me up, and I heard behind me a voice of a great rushing, *saying*, Blessed *be* the glory of the LORD from his place.

Ezekiel has just been sent by the Spirit of the LORD to preach to his own people (who wouldn't listen) (3:4 – 27; 33:5 – 8, 32, 33). (see Acts 2:38 – 39)

_____

_____

_____

_____

_____

_____

_____

_____

SO THE SPIRIT LIFTED ME (EZEKIEL) UP

Ezekiel 3:14 – 17 (KJV)

[14] So the spirit lifted me up, and took me away, and I went in bitterness, in the heat of my spirit; but the hand of the LORD was strong upon me.

[15] Then I came to them of the captivity at Telabib, that dwelt by the river of Chebar, and I sat where they sat, and remained there astonished among them seven days.

[16] And it came to pass at the end of seven days, that the word of the LORD came unto me, saying,

[17] Son of man, I have made thee a watchman unto the house of Israel: therefore hear the word at my mouth, and give them warning from me.

All those who vote boldly for Jesus and the word of the LORD will be persecuted but the hundredfold is theirs (Luke 8:8; Mark 10:29 – 30). Ezekiel is overwhelmed by all things going on near and with him (see Luke 2:51).

_____

_____

_____

_____

THE SPIRIT ENTERED INTO ME (EZEKIEL)

Ezekiel 3:22 – 24 (KJV)

²² And the hand of the LORD was there upon me; and he said unto me, Arise, go forth into the plain, and I will there talk with thee.

²³ Then I arose, and went forth into the plain: and, behold, the glory of the LORD stood there, as the glory which I saw by the river of Chebar: and I fell on my face.

²⁴ Then the spirit entered into me, and set me upon my feet, and spake with me, and said unto me, Go, shut thyself within thine house.

Ezekiel's strength would come from the LORD. Ezekiel was not supposed to answer the rebellious accusers at this time; but the LORD would open his mouth when it was time (3:3; 1:3 – 28; 3:22 – 27). The Spirit entered and the instructions came! (see Number 11:29; 1 Samuel 10:10)

_____
_____
_____
_____
_____
_____
_____
_____
_____

THE SPIRIT LIFTED ME (EZEKIEL) UP

Ezekiel 8:2, 3, 12 (KJV)

² Then I beheld, and lo a likeness as the appearance of fire: from the appearance of his loins even downward, fire; and from his loins even upward, as the appearance of brightness, as the colour of amber.

³ And he put forth the form of an hand, and took me by a lock of mine head; and the spirit lifted me up between the earth and the heaven, and brought me in the visions of God to Jerusalem, to the door of the inner gate that looketh toward the north; where *was* the seat of the image of jealousy, which provoketh to jealousy.

¹² Then said he unto me, Son of man, hast thou seen what the ancients of the house of Israel do in the dark, every man in the chambers of his imagery? for they say, The LORD seeth us not; the LORD hath forsaken the earth.

The Spirit showed this preacher what the congregation did in secret (8:12). Would you like that preacher? Ezekiel visited his congregation, seeing them in the visions of God, while he sat with the elders of Judah in his house (8:1 – 17). (see 1:28; 2 Kings 6:12)

_____
_____
_____

THE SPIRIT LIFTED ME (EZEKIEL) UP

Ezekiel 11:1 – 3 (KJV)

[1] Moreover the spirit lifted me up, and brought me unto the east gate of the LORD'S house, which looketh eastward: and behold at the door of the gate five and twenty men; among whom I saw Jaazaniah the son of Azur, and Pelatiah the son of Benaiah, princes of the people.
[2] Then said he unto me, Son of man, these *are* the men that devise mischief, and give wicked counsel in this city:
[3] Which say, *It is* not near; let us build houses: this *city is* the caldron, and we *be* the flesh.

Ezekiel **sat in his home but his sight was set in internet space.** This unsuccessful-looking man of God was being led by the Spirit and through visions he knew who his enemies were!

_____
_____
_____
_____
_____
_____
_____
_____

THE SPIRIT OF THE LORD FELL UPON ME

Ezekiel 11:4 – 6, 13 (KJV)

[4] Therefore prophesy against them, prophesy, O son of man.
[5] And the Spirit of the LORD fell upon me, and said unto me, Speak; Thus saith the LORD; Thus have ye said, O house of Israel: for I know the things that come into your mind, *every one of* them.
[6] Ye have multiplied your slain in this city, and ye have filled the streets thereof with the slain.
[13] And it came to pass, when I prophesied, that Pelatiah the son of Benaiah died. Then fell I down upon my face, and cried with a loud voice, and said, Ah Lord GOD! wilt thou make a full end of the remnant of Israel?

God offers refuge in the Spirit to every person (11:14 – 17), The Spirit took over to show the truth to the prophet Ezekiel. When did the Spirit of the LORD help you? (see 1:28; John 16:13 – 15)

_____
_____
_____
_____
_____

NEW SPIRIT WITHIN YOU

Ezekiel 11:16, 18 – 20 (KJV)

¹⁶ Therefore say, Thus saith the Lord GOD; Although I have cast them far off among the heathen, and although I have scattered them among the countries, yet will I be to them as a little sanctuary in the countries where they shall come.

¹⁸ And they shall come thither, and they shall take away all the detestable things thereof and all the abominations thereof from thence.

¹⁹ And I will give them one heart, and I will put a new spirit within you; and I will take the stony heart out of their flesh, and will give them an heart of flesh:

²⁰ That they may walk in my statutes, and keep mine ordinances, and do them: and they shall be my people, and I will be their God.

From a hardened heart to a softened heart: They will come home with a new want-to in them from **the Holy Spirit in them**. God will cause this (Jeremiah 31:33; Psalm 51). Ezekiel 11:16 is 2 Chronicles 6 where Solomon dedicated the temple with prayer.

_____

_____

_____

_____

_____

SPIRIT...IN A VISION BY THE SPIRIT OF GOD

Ezekiel 11:22 – 25 (KJV)

²² Then did the cherubims lift up their wings, and the wheels beside them; and the glory of the God of Israel *was* over them above.

²³ And the glory of the LORD went up from the midst of the city, and stood upon the mountain which *is* on the east side of the city.

²⁴ Afterwards the spirit took me up, and brought me in a vision by the Spirit of God into Chaldea, to them of the captivity. So the vision that I had seen went up from me.

²⁵ Then I spake unto them of the captivity all the things that the LORD had shewed me.

Ezekiel had moved around in a vision but when the vision was taken up, (ended), he again saw the elders with him in his house and he prophesied to them! He told them what the LORD had **proven to him by the vision** (8:1; 11:25). (see 11:22, 24; Genesis 1:1 – 2; Genesis 15:5) What did the Spirit do?

_____

_____

_____

_____

_____

date_____
MY SPIRIT WITHIN YOU

Ezekiel 36:23, 25 – 27 (KJV)
²³ And I will sanctify my great name, which was profaned among the heathen, which ye have profaned in the midst of them; and the heathen shall know that I *am* the LORD, saith the Lord GOD, when I shall be sanctified in you before their eyes. ²⁵ Then will I sprinkle clean water upon you, and ye shall be clean: from all your filthiness, and from all your idols, will I cleanse you. ²⁶ A new heart also will I give you, and a new spirit will I put within you: and I will take away the stony heart out of your flesh, and I will give you an heart of flesh. ²⁷ And I will put my spirit within you, and cause you to walk in my statutes, and ye shall keep my judgments, and do *them.*

"will I…" God took full responsibility for choosing them! He was showing them His mercy and showing us His grace! When our spirit is one with His Spirit, we have a new spirit! We are abundantly pardoned! **He's on the throne.**

_____
_____
_____
_____
_____

date_____
CARRIED ME (EZEKIEL) OUT IN THE SPIRIT

Ezekiel 37:1 – 4 (KJV)
¹ The hand of the LORD was upon me, and carried me out in the spirit of the LORD, and set me down in the midst of the valley which *was* full of bones,
² And caused me to pass by them round about: and, behold, *there were* very many in the open valley; and, lo, *they were* very dry.
³ And he said unto me, Son of man, can these bones live? And I answered, O Lord GOD, thou knowest.
⁴ Again he said unto me, Prophesy upon these bones, and say unto them, O ye dry bones, hear the word of the LORD.

In the valley of dry bones is the place for the beginning of ministry! (Ephesians 4:12) Ezekiel is placed in a valley of dry bones so he may prophesy life and **watch it happen.** Resurrection demonstration. (see Revelation 21:10)

_____
_____
_____
_____
_____
_____

SHALL PUT MY SPIRIT IN YOU

Ezekiel 37:5 – 7, 10, 14 (KJV)
⁵ Thus saith the Lord GOD unto these bones; Behold, I will cause breath to enter into you, and ye shall live:
⁶ And I will lay sinews upon you, and will bring up flesh upon you, and cover you with skin, and put breath in you, and ye shall live; and ye shall know that I *am* the LORD.
⁷ So I prophesied as I was commanded: and as I prophesied, there was a noise, and behold a shaking, and the bones came together, bone to his bone.
¹⁰ So I prophesied as he commanded me, and the breath came into them, and they lived, and stood up upon their feet, an exceeding great army.
¹⁴ And shall put my spirit in you, and ye shall live, and I shall place you in your own land: then shall ye know that I the LORD have spoken *it*, and performed *it*, saith the LORD.

By His Spirit, He would make a way where there was no way and change the future!

_____
_____
_____
_____
_____
_____
_____

SO THE SPIRIT TOOK ME UP

Ezekiel 43:1, 2, 4 – 6 (KJV)
¹ Afterward he brought me to the gate, *even* the gate that looketh toward the east:
² And, behold, the glory of the God of Israel came from the way of the east: and his voice *was* like a noise of many waters: and the earth shined with his glory.
⁴ And the glory of the LORD came into the house by the way of the gate whose prospect *is* toward the east.
⁵ So the spirit took me up, and brought me into the inner court; and, behold, the glory of the LORD filled the house.
⁶ And I heard *him* speaking unto me out of the house; and the man stood by me.

The Man is Ezekiel's Guide. He is the pre-incarnate preeminent Christ, who took him on a tour of the temple. Who is your tour-guide? Who is your Helper?

_____
_____
_____
_____
_____
_____
_____

EXCELLENT SPIRIT

Daniel 5:12, 13, 15 (KJV)

¹² Forasmuch as an excellent spirit, and knowledge, and understanding, interpreting of dreams, and shewing of hard sentences, and dissolving of doubts, were found in the same Daniel, whom the king named Belteshazzar: now let Daniel be called, and he will shew the interpretation.

¹³ Then was Daniel brought in before the king. *And* the king spake and said unto Daniel, *Art* thou that Daniel, which *art* of the children of the captivity of Judah, whom the king my father brought out of Jewry?

¹⁵ And now the wise *men*, the astrologers, have been brought in before me, that they should read this writing, and make known unto me the interpretation thereof: but they could not shew the interpretation of the thing:

Daniel was brought in because someone heard of the Spirit who worked through him! Since they didn't know the name of the God of Daniel, they could only **describe Daniel.**

_____
_____
_____
_____
_____

EXCELLENT SPIRIT WAS IN HIM (DANIEL)

Daniel 6:1 – 4 (KJV)

¹ It pleased Darius to set over the kingdom an hundred and twenty princes, which should be over the whole kingdom;

² And over these three presidents; of whom Daniel *was* first: that the princes might give accounts unto them, and the king should have no damage.

³ Then this Daniel was preferred above the presidents and princes, because an excellent spirit *was* in him; and the king thought to set him over the whole realm.

⁴ Then the presidents and princes sought to find occasion against Daniel concerning the kingdom; but they could find none occasion nor fault; forasmuch as he *was* faithful, neither was there any error or fault found in him.

The nearer Daniel was to promotion, the more the enemy raged. If we discount the life that's under fire, we could be ignoring the true **prophet of God under persecution.**

_____
_____
_____
_____

date_____

PROPHECY: POUR OUT MY SPIRIT...MY SPIRIT FILLED WITH THE HOLY SPIRIT...THE SPIRIT
Joel 2:28 – 29 (KJV)

[28] And it shall come to pass afterward, *that* I will pour out my spirit upon all flesh; and your sons and your daughters shall prophesy, your old men shall dream dreams, your young men shall see visions:
[29] And also upon the servants and upon the handmaids in those days will I pour out my spirit.

"When the Day of Pentecost had fully come, they were all with one accord in one place.
And suddenly there came a sound from heaven, as of a rushing mighty wind, and it filled the whole house where they were sitting. Then there appeared to them divided tongues, as of fire, and *one* sat upon each of them. And they were all filled with the Holy Spirit and began to speak with other tongues, as the Spirit gave them utterance" **Acts 2:1 – 4 (NKJV)**. (Acts 2:17 – 18) God Himself made His Spirit available to them to be in them!
God's pitcher of the Spirit is perpetual! We are spending **time in the out-pouring.**

_____
_____
_____

date_____

IS THE SPIRIT OF THE LORD STRAITENED?

Micah 2:7 – 9 (KJV)

[7] O *thou that art* named the house of Jacob, is the spirit of the LORD straitened? *are* these his doings? do not my words do good to him that walketh uprightly?
[8] Even of late my people is risen up as an enemy: ye pull off the robe with the garment from them that pass by securely as men averse from war.
[9] The women of my people have ye cast out from their pleasant houses; from their children have ye taken away my glory for ever.

Justice comes from heaven when one is doing justly (6:8; Psalm 84:11). Giving mercy will overpower coming judgment (James 2:13). God is faithful and just. He will forgive anyone with a humble heart and remove them from the punishment to come because He will do what is right and righteous. "And now abide faith, hope, love, these three; but the greatest of these *is* love" **1 Corinthians 13:13 (NKJV)**.

_____
_____
_____
_____
_____

FULL OF POWER BY THE SPIRIT OF THE LORD

Micah 3:8 – 11 (KJV)

⁸ But truly I am full of power by the spirit of the LORD, and of judgment, and of might, to declare unto Jacob his transgression, and to Israel his sin.
⁹ Hear this, I pray you, ye heads of the house of Jacob, and princes of the house of Israel, that abhor judgment, and pervert all equity.
¹⁰ They build up Zion with blood, and Jerusalem with iniquity.
¹¹ The heads thereof judge for reward, and the priests thereof teach for hire, and the prophets thereof divine for money: yet will they lean upon the LORD, and say, *Is* not the LORD among us? none evil can come upon us.

Micah proclaimed the whole country would suffer because the leaders had turned corrupt! (see 1 Chronicles 28:12; Ezekiel 11:24; Matthew 6:24) If that happened today, how could each of us turn the results in the opposite direction?

PROPHECY: BETHLEHEM...OF JUDAH
BETHLEHEM ...OF JUDEA... JUDAH

Micah 5:1 – 2 (KJV)

¹ Now gather thyself in troops, O daughter of troops: he hath laid siege against us: they shall smite the judge of Israel with a rod upon the cheek.
² But thou, Bethlehem Ephratah, *though* thou be little among the thousands of Judah, *yet* out of thee shall he come forth unto me *that is* to be ruler in Israel; whose goings forth *have been* from of old, from everlasting.

"So they said to him, "In Bethlehem of Judea, for thus it is written by the prophet: *'But you, Bethlehem, in the land of Judah, Are not the least among the rulers of Judah; For out of you shall come a Ruler Who will shepherd My people Israel.'"* **Matthew 2:5 – 6 (NKJV).**
Little or large: where is the Leader coming from?
In each of these, who is speaking and what's the setting?

date_____

SO MY SPIRIT REMAINETH AMONG YOU

Haggai 2:1 – 5 (KJV)

¹ In the seventh *month*, in the one and twentieth *day* of the month, came the word of the LORD by the prophet Haggai, saying,

² Speak now to Zerubbabel the son of Shealtiel, governor of Judah, and to Joshua the son of Josedech, the high priest, and to the residue of the people, saying,

³ Who *is* left among you that saw this house in her first glory? and how do ye see it now? *is it* not in your eyes in comparison of it as nothing?

⁴ Yet now be strong, O Zerubbabel, saith the LORD; and be strong, O Joshua, son of Josedech, the high priest; and be strong, all ye people of the land, saith the LORD, and work: for I *am* with you, saith the LORD of hosts:

⁵ *According to* the word that I covenanted with you when ye came out of Egypt, so my spirit remaineth among you: fear ye not.

Their future would be limited without the obedience to finish the house of the LORD!

_____

_____

_____

_____

date_____

BUT BY MY SPIRIT, SAITH THE LORD OF HOSTS

Zechariah 4:2 – 4, 6 (KJV)

² And said unto me, What seest thou? And I said, I have looked, and behold a candlestick all *of* gold, with a bowl upon the top of it, and his seven lamps thereon, and seven pipes to the seven lamps, which *are* upon the top thereof:

³ And two olive trees by it, one upon the right *side* of the bowl, and the other upon the left *side* thereof.

⁴ So I answered and spake to the angel that talked with me, saying, What *are* these, my lord?

⁶ Then he answered and spake unto me, saying, This *is* the word of the LORD unto Zerubbabel, saying, Not by might, nor by power, but by my spirit, saith the LORD of hosts.

The prophet's encouraging words told the people they would finish (not by man's effort, strength or power) but they would finish by the Spirit of the LORD.

_____

_____

_____

_____

_____

_____

_____

PROPHECY: WHOM THEY HAVE PIERCED
WHOM (JESUS) THEY PIERCED
Zechariah 12:10 (KJV)

¹⁰ And I will pour upon the house of David, and upon the inhabitants of Jerusalem, the spirit of grace and of supplications: and they shall look upon me whom they have pierced, and they shall mourn for him, as one mourneth for *his* only *son*, and shall be in bitterness for him, as one that is in bitterness for *his* firstborn.

They will look and then they will know He is the Source of grace. He says, "I've got this! Don't turn back because of opposition! You will prevail!" They could go forward without being afraid of the reactions or the talk of others! When they spoke the Truth continually, they would win. **God defends** His people **by His Word.** (see Psalm 122:6)
"And again another Scripture says, *"They shall look on Him whom they pierced"* **John 19:37 (NKJV).** (see Joel 2:28; Luke 2:21 – 35; Hebrews 4:16)

_____
_____
_____
_____
_____
_____

WITH CHILD (JESUS) OF THE HOLY GHOST

Matthew 1:17 – 19 (KJV)
¹⁷ So all the generations from Abraham to David *are* fourteen generations; and from David until the carrying away into Babylon *are* fourteen generations; and from the carrying away into Babylon unto Christ *are* fourteen generations.
¹⁸ Now the birth of Jesus Christ was on this wise: When as his mother Mary was espoused to Joseph, before they came together, she was found with child of the Holy Ghost.
¹⁹ Then Joseph her husband, being a just *man*, and not willing to make her a publick example, was minded to put her away privily.

Joseph didn't believe her. The devil heard and thought he had won! But God stood in the gap for one – and He will do it again for you! (Psalm 27:10) With God nothing is impossible! How unbelievable is your solution? God can and will help you.

_____
_____
_____
_____
_____
_____

IS OF THE HOLY GHOST

Matthew 1:20 – 23 (KJV)
[20] But while he thought on these things, behold, the angel of the Lord appeared unto him in a dream, saying, Joseph, thou son of David, fear not to take unto thee Mary thy wife: for that which is conceived in her is of the Holy Ghost.
[21] And she shall bring forth a son, and thou shalt call his name JESUS: for he shall save his people from their sins.
[22] Now all this was done, that it might be fulfilled which was spoken of the Lord by the prophet, saying,
[23] Behold, a virgin shall be with child, and shall bring forth a son, and they shall call his name Emmanuel, which being interpreted is, God with us.

(Isaiah 7:14) God took up for her! Why was this "in a dream"? The devil couldn't see the angel of the Lord in Joseph's dream; so when Joseph ran to Mary's house, again the devil thought he had won! God will **seal your victory** and make you **unstoppable.**

_____
_____
_____
_____
_____
_____

BETHLEHEM OF JUDAEA

Matthew 2:1, 4, 5, 6 (KJV)
[1] Now when Jesus was born in Bethlehem of Judaea in the days of Herod the king, behold, there came wise men from the east to Jerusalem,
[4] And when he had gathered all the chief priests and scribes of the people together, he demanded of them where Christ should be born.
[5] And they said unto him, In Bethlehem of Judaea: for thus it is written by the prophet,
[6] And thou Bethlehem, _in_ the land of Juda, art not the least among the princes of Juda: for out of thee shall come a Governor, that shall rule my people Israel.

(Micah 5:1 – 2) King Herod knew the chief priests and scribes would know the Scriptures. The prophecies concerning Jesus were unstoppable, being **sent by God.**
Many prophets of God foretold that the Messiah would grow up in Nazareth; so much so that it was "spoken" but not written in the Torah because it was understood! (2:23)

_____
_____
_____
_____

date_____

BAPTIZE YOU WITH THE HOLY GHOST

Matthew 3:1, 2, 8, 10, 11 (KJV)
[1] In those days came John the Baptist, preaching in the wilderness of Judaea, [2] And saying, Repent ye: for the kingdom of heaven is at hand.
[8] Bring forth therefore fruits meet for repentance:
[10] And now also the axe is laid unto the root of the trees: therefore every tree which bringeth not forth good fruit is hewn down, and cast into the fire.
[11] I indeed baptize you with water unto repentance: but he that cometh after me is mightier than I, whose shoes I am not worthy to bear: he shall baptize you with the Holy Ghost, and *with* fire:

Fire purifies. When anyone believes, he or she is baptized into what truth they believe! Did Jesus baptize John? Was John greater than the people he baptized? (Matthew 3)
To be a part of John's gospel, did the people have to believe, repent and be baptized?
Everything Jesus did was being an Example. Can you give some examples of Jesus?

_____
_____
_____

date_____

SAW THE SPIRIT OF GOD DESCENDING

Matthew 3:15 – 17 (KJV)
[15] And Jesus answering said unto him, Suffer *it to be so* now: for thus it becometh us to fulfil all righteousness. Then he suffered him.
[16] And Jesus, when he was baptized, went up straightway out of the water: and, lo, the heavens were opened unto him, and he saw the Spirit of God descending like a dove, and lighting upon him:
[17] And lo a voice from heaven, saying, This is my beloved Son, in whom I am well pleased.

When God saved us through our faith in Jesus, God affirmed us as if He (our heavenly Father) was saying each of us, "You are accepted because I Am pleased with you." (see 17:5; Psalm 2:7; Isaiah 11:2, 42:1: Mark 1:11; Luke 3:22; John 1:32; Acts 13:33; Ephesians 1:6, 12, 14; Hebrews 1:5; 5:5; 2 Peter 1:17) Whose words or opinion are most important to you?

_____
_____
_____
_____

date_____

THE SPIRIT INTO THE WILDERNESS

Matthew 4:1, 2, 3, 4, 10 (KJV)

¹ Then was Jesus led up of the Spirit into the wilderness to be tempted of the devil.

² And when he had fasted forty days and forty nights, he was afterward an hungred.

³ And when the tempter came to him, he said, If thou be the Son of God, command that these stones be made bread.

⁴ But he answered and said, It is written, Man shall not live by bread alone, but by every word that proceedeth out of the mouth of God.

¹⁰ Then saith Jesus unto him, Get thee hence, Satan: for it is written, Thou shalt worship the Lord thy God, and him only shalt thou serve.

Jesus showed us how to answer the tempter (Satan). Jesus went to the wilderness physically and we will too! The one in the wilderness is in ministry training! (see Psalm 37:4) Is the Spirit resting on us individually? (1 Peter 4:14)

_____
_____
_____
_____
_____

date_____

THE SPIRIT...SPEAKETH IN YOU!

Matthew 10:18 – 20, 31 – 32 (KJV)

¹⁸ And ye shall be brought before governors and kings for my sake, for a testimony against them and the Gentiles.

¹⁹ But when they deliver you up, take no thought how or what ye shall speak: for it shall be given you in that same hour what ye shall speak.

²⁰ For it is not ye that speak, but the Spirit of your Father which speaketh in you.

³¹ Fear ye not therefore, ye are of more value than many sparrows.

³² Whosoever therefore shall confess me before men, him will I confess also before my Father which is in heaven.

Can we even imagine having Jesus before the Father being in agreement with our prayer? Jesus said, "He that receives anyone I send, is receiving Me" and "The one who is believing on Me is also believing on the One who sent Me" (John 13:20 and 12:44). Did Jesus say the Spirit would speak when you speak in faith in Him? (10:19 – 20)

_____
_____
_____
_____

I (GOD) WILL PUT MY SPIRIT UPON HIM

Matthew 12:15 – 21 (KJV)
15 But when Jesus knew *it*, he withdrew himself from thence: and great multitudes followed him, and he healed them all;
16 And charged them that they should not make him known:
17 That it might be fulfilled which was spoken by Esaias the prophet, saying,
18 Behold my servant, whom I have chosen; my beloved, in whom my soul is well pleased: I will put my spirit upon him, and he shall shew judgment to the Gentiles.
19 He shall not strive, nor cry; neither shall any man hear his voice in the streets.
20 A bruised reed shall he not break, and smoking flax shall he not quench, till he send forth judgment unto victory.
21 And in his name shall the Gentiles trust.

His judgment led to the truth, the **victory of assurance (Isaiah 42:1 – 3).** (see Isaiah 53:10 – 11; Luke 4:18)

_____
_____
_____
_____

BY THE SPIRIT OF GOD... KINGDOM OF GOD

Matthew 12:23 – 25, 27, 28 (KJV)
23 And all the people were amazed, and said, Is not this the son of David?
24 But when the Pharisees heard *it*, they said, This *fellow* doth not cast out devils, but by Beelzebub the prince of the devils.
25 And Jesus knew their thoughts, and said unto them, Every kingdom divided against itself is brought to desolation; and every city or house divided against itself shall not stand:
27 And if I by Beelzebub cast out devils, by whom do your children cast *them* out? therefore they shall be your judges.
28 But if I cast out devils by the Spirit of God, then the kingdom of God is come unto you.

The Spirit of God is empowering the kingdom of God (Matthew 12:28). We cast out devils in only His name (by the cross) of Jesus Christ (Acts 19:13 – 19).

_____
_____
_____
_____
_____

date_____
BLASPHEMY AGAINST THE HOLY GHOST

Matthew 12:28 – 31 (KJV)

²⁸ But if I cast out devils by the Spirit of God, then the kingdom of God is come unto you.

²⁹ Or else how can one enter into a strong man's house, and spoil his goods, except he first bind the strong man? and then he will spoil his house.

³⁰ He that is not with me is against me; and he that gathereth not with me scattereth abroad.

³¹ Wherefore I say unto you, All manner of sin and blasphemy shall be forgiven unto men: but the blasphemy *against* the *Holy* Ghost shall not be forgiven unto men.

We wouldn't want a book like this one if you blasphemed against the Holy Ghost. So we who has been saved did not and do not speak against the Holy Ghost. (see 1 Corinthians 12:3) Jesus died for every person; for the sins of each one. We believed on Jesus when we were quickened by the Holy Spirit.

_____
_____
_____
_____
_____
_____
_____

date_____
SPEAKETH AGAINST THE HOLY GHOST

Matthew 12:31 – 34 (KJV)

³¹ Wherefore I say unto you, All manner of sin and blasphemy shall be forgiven unto men: but the blasphemy *against* the *Holy* Ghost shall not be forgiven unto men.

³² And whosoever speaketh a word against the Son of man, it shall be forgiven him: but whosoever speaketh against the Holy Ghost, it shall not be forgiven him, neither in this world, neither in the *world* to come.

³³ Either make the tree good, and his fruit good; or else make the tree corrupt, and his fruit corrupt: for the tree is known by *his* fruit.

³⁴ O generation of vipers, how can ye, being evil, speak good things? for out of the abundance of the heart the mouth speaketh.

The Holy Ghost has shown every person he or she has sinned, but if the person says "No" to Him, then that one isn't forgiven, because that person has rejected Christ's forgiveness. This is the **only** unpardonable sin. Every individual has a **choice of surrender**.

_____
_____
_____
_____

DAVID IN SPIRIT CALL HIM (CHRIST) LORD

Matthew 22:37 – 39, 41 – 44 (KJV)
³⁷ Jesus said unto him, Thou shalt love the Lord thy God with all thy heart, and with all thy soul, and with all thy mind.
³⁸ This is the first and great commandment.
³⁹ And the second *is* like unto it, Thou shalt love thy neighbour as thyself.
⁴¹ While the Pharisees were gathered together, Jesus asked them,
⁴² Saying, What think ye of Christ? whose son is he? They say unto him, *The Son* of David.
⁴³ He saith unto them, How then doth David in spirit call him Lord, saying,
⁴⁴ The LORD said unto my Lord, Sit thou on my right hand, till I make thine enemies thy footstool?

All the law hangs on these commands of love from the **Spirit of the law of love according to Jesus** (Galatians 5:14; Romans 13:8 – 10; Hebrews 3:7; 4:7).

_____

_____

_____

_____

_____

_____

THAT IT MIGHT BE FULFILLED

Matthew 27:32 – 35 (KJV)
³² And as they came out, they found a man of Cyrene, Simon by name: him they compelled to bear his cross.
³³ And when they were come unto a place called Golgotha, that is to say, a place of a skull,
³⁴ They gave him vinegar to drink mingled with gall: and when he had tasted *thereof,* he would not drink.
³⁵ And they crucified him, and parted his garments, casting lots: that it might be fulfilled which was spoken by the prophet, They parted my garments among them, and upon my vesture did they cast lots.

(Psalm 22:15 – 18) As Jesus hung on the cross at Calvary, His body was so torn, His bones were visible (Leviticus 16:3 – 34; 1 Peter 2:24). If someone paid for your dinner, would you try to pay for again or say "Thank you"?

_____

_____

_____

_____

_____

_____

_____

GO YE...OF THE HOLY GHOST

Matthew 28:16 – 20 (KJV)

¹⁶ Then the eleven disciples went away into Galilee, into a mountain where Jesus had appointed them.

¹⁷ And when they saw him, they worshipped him: but some doubted.

¹⁸ And Jesus came and spake unto them, saying, All power is given unto me in heaven and in earth.

¹⁹ Go ye therefore, and teach all nations, baptizing them in the name of the Father, and of the Son, and of the Holy Ghost:

²⁰ Teaching them to observe all things whatsoever I have commanded you: and, lo, I am with you alway, *even* unto the end of the world. Amen.

We are disciples and we go and give to make more disciples at home and around the globe; to obey the words of Jesus. We continue in love to make His paths straight (3:3).

Now Mark's Gospel will also tell us of the beginning of the story of Jesus:

_____
_____
_____
_____
_____
_____
_____

BAPTIZE YOU WITH THE HOLY GHOST

Mark 1:2, 5 – 8 (KJV)

² As it is written in the prophets, Behold, I send my messenger before thy face, which shall prepare thy way before thee.

⁵ And there went out unto him all the land of Judaea, and they of Jerusalem, and were all baptized of him in the river of Jordan, confessing their sins.

⁶ And John was clothed with camel's hair, and with a girdle of a skin about his loins; and he did eat locusts and wild honey;

⁷ And preached, saying, There cometh one mightier than I after me, the latchet of whose shoes I am not worthy to stoop down and unloose.

⁸ I indeed have baptized you with water: but he shall baptize you with the Holy Ghost.

Jesus is the Baptizer with the Holy Ghost (Acts 1:4 – 5). We pray to preach so others will look for Jesus... to teach, so others will want to know His Word...to serve, so others will want to know His love...to decrease, so the name of Jesus will increase.

_____
_____
_____
_____

THE HEAVENS OPENED, AND THE SPIRIT

Mark 1:8 – 11 (KJV)

⁸ I indeed have baptized you with water: but he shall baptize you with the Holy Ghost.

⁹ And it came to pass in those days, that Jesus came from Nazareth of Galilee, and was baptized of John in Jordan.

¹⁰ And straightway coming up out of the water, he saw the heavens opened, and the Spirit like a dove descending upon him:

¹¹ And there came a voice from heaven, *saying*, Thou art my beloved Son, in whom I am well pleased.

Jesus went public (1:28). The inauguration of Jesus must have been a sight to behold; as if God **laid hands on Jesus** and gave Him His **blessing** (John 16:14, 15). Now when we were saved, we also received the blessing of our Father. (see Matthew 3:17; 6:9) What was Jesus teaching when He insisted on being baptized?

_____
_____
_____
_____
_____
_____
_____

THE SPIRIT DRIVETH… WILDERNESS

Mark 1:12 – 15 (KJV)

¹² And immediately the Spirit driveth him into the wilderness.

¹³ And he was there in the wilderness forty days, tempted of Satan; and was with the wild beasts; and the angels ministered unto him.

¹⁴ Now after that John was put in prison, Jesus came into Galilee, preaching the gospel of the kingdom of God,

¹⁵ And saying, The time is fulfilled, and the kingdom of God is at hand: repent ye, and believe the gospel.

How to repent? We accept **the blame and apologize** (1:15). All Christians are tempted at their most vulnerable place and time. The test endured is the test that toughens (1:13)! When we enter our prayer closet and shut the door, the devil gets nervous because he knows Jesus sees our faith! (Matthew 6:5 – 8; 1 John 5:14 – 15)

_____
_____
_____
_____
_____
_____
_____

PERCEIVED IN HIS SPIRIT

Mark 2:5 – 9 (KJV)
⁵ When Jesus saw their faith, he said unto the sick of the palsy, Son, thy sins be forgiven thee.
⁶ But there were certain of the scribes sitting there, and reasoning in their hearts,
⁷ Why doth this *man* thus speak blasphemies? who can forgive sins but God only?
⁸ And immediately when Jesus perceived in his spirit that they so reasoned within themselves, he said unto them, Why reason ye these things in your hearts?
⁹ Whether is it easier to say to the sick of the palsy, *Thy* sins be forgiven thee; or to say, Arise, and take up thy bed, and walk?

Jesus heard their words in their hearts as clearly as if they had spoken their words out loud. They were only thinking and Jesus heard them. He hears our heart's prayer anywhere and every time. Can Jesus still hear our prayers from our heart today?

_____
_____
_____
_____
_____

AGAINST THE HOLY GHOST

Mark 3:14, 15, 28, 29, 30 (KJV)
¹⁴ And he ordained twelve, that they should be with him, and that he might send them forth to preach,
¹⁵ And to have power to heal sicknesses, and to cast out devils:
²⁸ Verily I say unto you, All sins shall be forgiven unto the sons of men, and blasphemies wherewith soever they shall blaspheme:
²⁹ But he that shall blaspheme against the Holy Ghost hath never forgiveness, but is in danger of eternal damnation:
³⁰ Because they said, He hath an unclean spirit.

The throne of grace is still standing for the kneeling heart! God has a family by His Spirit! (3:31 – 35) (see John 17:20)! He is waiting for anyone to open their heart since that's why He came (Revelation 3:20; Luke 19:10).

_____
_____
_____
_____
_____
_____

date_____

HE (JESUS) SIGHED DEEPLY IN HIS SPIRIT

Mark 8:9 – 12 (KJV)

9 And they that had eaten were about four thousand: and he sent them away.
10 And straightway he entered into a ship with his disciples, and came into the parts of Dalmanutha.
11 And the Pharisees came forth, and began to question with him, seeking of him a sign from heaven, tempting him.
12 And he sighed deeply in his spirit, and saith, Why doth this generation seek after a sign? verily I say unto you, There shall no sign be given unto this generation.

They were seeing Jesus the Christ – the Sign of the LORD – without seeing Him! A new eternity begins for all who will believe on Him, the **Sign, the One who was born of a virgin.**

date_____

DAVID…SAID BY THE HOLY GHOST

Mark 12:35 – 37 (KJV)

35 And Jesus answered and said, while he taught in the temple, How say the scribes that Christ is the Son of David?
36 For David himself said by the Holy Ghost, The LORD said to my Lord, Sit thou on my right hand, till I make thine enemies thy footstool.
37 David therefore himself calleth him Lord; and whence is he *then* his son? And the common people heard him gladly.

In the Old Testament who spoke by the Holy Ghost? David heard from the Holy Ghost then (B.C.). We hear in our spirit, the **voice of the Comforter!**
Who is the voice of Jesus? Who is the voice of the Holy Ghost?

NOT YE THAT SPEAK, BUT THE HOLY GHOST

Mark 13:8 – 11 (KJV)

8 For nation shall rise against nation, and kingdom against kingdom: and there shall be earthquakes in divers places, and there shall be famines and troubles: these *are* the beginnings of sorrows.

9 But take heed to yourselves: for they shall deliver you up to councils; and in the synagogues ye shall be beaten: and ye shall be brought before rulers and kings for my sake, for a testimony against them.

10 And the gospel must first be published among all nations.

11 But when they shall lead *you*, and deliver you up, take no thought beforehand what ye shall speak, neither do ye premeditate: but whatsoever shall be given you in that hour, that speak ye: for it is not ye that speak, but the Holy Ghost.

The Holy Ghost shall explain what to say! (Luke 12:11 – 12; 21:14– 15; Matthew 10:18 – 20) When we **say what He said, God has already answered.** (Jeremiah 33:3)!

_____
_____
_____
_____
_____

FILLED WITH THE HOLY GHOST

Luke 1:5, 6, 13 – 15 (KJV)

5 There was in the days of Herod, the king of Judaea, a certain priest named Zacharias, of the course of Abia: and his wife *was* of the daughters of Aaron, and her name *was* Elisabeth.

6 And they were both righteous before God, walking in all the commandments and ordinances of the Lord blameless.

13 But the angel said unto him, Fear not, Zacharias: for thy prayer is heard; and thy wife Elisabeth shall bear thee a son, and thou shalt call his name John.

14 And thou shalt have joy and gladness; and many shall rejoice at his birth.

15 For he shall be great in the sight of the Lord, and shall drink neither wine nor strong drink; and he shall be filled with the Holy Ghost, even from his mother's womb.

Before John was born, the parents of John were **living letters of righteous living in their public and private lives. Your 'nitch' in the earth is in being you for God.**

_____
_____
_____
_____

date_____

IN THE SPIRIT AND POWER OF ELIAS (ELIJAH)

Luke 1:17, 18, 24, 25 (KJV)

[17] And he shall go before him in the spirit and power of Elias, to turn the hearts of the fathers to the children, and the disobedient to the wisdom of the just; to make ready a people prepared for the Lord.

[18] And Zacharias said unto the angel, Whereby shall I know this? for I am an old man, and my wife well stricken in years.

[24] And after those days his wife Elisabeth conceived, and hid herself five months, saying,

[25] Thus hath the Lord dealt with me in the days wherein he looked on *me*, to take away my reproach among men.

Your prayers are heard! Now as for Jesus: How can Jesus be God? God the Spirit put on a coat of flesh and came to earth placing **the Spirit having heaven's blood** in the womb of Mary a virgin so she would give birth to the **sinless-forever Child and His name is Jesus** (1:34 – 35). When Jesus was conceived, where was the Holy Ghost?

date_____

HOLY GHOST SHALL COME UPON THEE (MARY)

Luke 1:30 – 35 (KJV)

[30] And the angel said unto her, Fear not, Mary: for thou hast found favour with God.

[31] And, behold, thou shalt conceive in thy womb, and bring forth a son, and shalt call his name JESUS.

[32] He shall be great, and shall be called the Son of the Highest: and the Lord God shall give unto him the throne of his father David:

[33] And he shall reign over the house of Jacob for ever; and of his kingdom there shall be no end.

[34] Then said Mary unto the angel, How shall this be, seeing I know not a man?

[35] And the angel answered and said unto her, The Holy Ghost shall come upon thee, and the power of the Highest shall overshadow thee: therefore also that holy thing which shall be born of thee shall be called the Son of God.

We call His name JESUS! The name above every name is born! (2:16; Philippians 2:9)

ELISABETH WAS FILLED WITH THE HOLY GHOST

Luke 1:39 – 42, 44 (KJV)

[39] And Mary arose in those days, and went into the hill country with haste, into a city of Juda;

[40] And entered into the house of Zacharias, and saluted Elisabeth.

[41] And it came to pass, that, when Elisabeth heard the salutation of Mary, the babe leaped in her womb; and Elisabeth was filled with the Holy Ghost:

[42] And she spake out with a loud voice, and said, Blessed *art* thou among women, and blessed *is* the fruit of thy womb.

[44] For, lo, as soon as the voice of thy salutation sounded in mine ears, the babe leaped in my womb for joy.

When Elisabeth **recognized the One** in Mary's womb, **she was filled** with the Holy Ghost. How could she be filled with the Holy Ghost before Pentecost (Acts 2:4, 17)? What did Elisabeth know before she saw Mary? (see 1 Corinthians 12:8)

_____
_____
_____
_____
_____
_____

ZACHARIAS WAS FILLED WITH THE HOLY GHOST

Luke 1:59, 63, 67 – 70 (KJV)

[59] And it came to pass, that on the eighth day they came to circumcise the child; and they called him Zacharias, after the name of his father.

[63] And he asked for a writing table, and wrote, saying, His name is John. And they marvelled all.

[67] And his father Zacharias was filled with the Holy Ghost, and prophesied, saying,

[68] Blessed *be* the Lord God of Israel; for he hath visited and redeemed his people,

[69] And hath raised up an horn of salvation for us in the house of his servant David;

[70] As he spake by the mouth of his holy prophets, which have been since the world began:

Zacharias was filled and prophesied **after he wrote** the word as he had been told.

Who was filled with the Holy Ghost and yet not saved, not indwelled? John the Baptist (1:15). John did none of this in his strength. He is a person before he is born!

_____
_____
_____

HOLY GHOST WAS UPON HIM (SIMEON) :25

Luke 2:21, 22, 25 (KJV)

²¹ And when eight days were accomplished for the circumcising of the child, his name was called JESUS, which was so named of the angel before he was conceived in the womb.
²² And when the days of her purification according to the law of Moses were accomplished, they brought him to Jerusalem, to present *him* to the Lord;
²⁵ And, behold, there was a man in Jerusalem, whose name *was* Simeon; and the same man *was* just and devout, waiting for the consolation of Israel: and the Holy Ghost was upon him.

God's timing. How did Simeon know? Simeon was **often in the temple** waiting for the Messiah, Jesus, and he **saw them bringing Baby Jesus into the church house. We belong** to the house of the Firstborn – the Lord Jesus (2:7 – 20).

REVEALED UNTO HIM (SIMEON) BY THE HOLY GHOST :26

Luke 2:24 – 27 (KJV)

²⁴ And to offer a sacrifice according to that which is said in the law of the Lord, A pair of turtledoves, or two young pigeons.
²⁵ And, behold, there was a man in Jerusalem, whose name *was* Simeon; and the same man *was* just and devout, waiting for the consolation of Israel: and the Holy Ghost was upon him.
²⁶ And it was revealed unto him by the Holy Ghost, that he should not see death, before he had seen the Lord's Christ.
²⁷ And he came by the Spirit into the temple: and when the parents brought in the child Jesus, to do for him after the custom of the law,

BABY JESUS WAS BORN! (2:1 – 7)! Simeon knew JESUS, the Lord's Christ, (The Consolation, the Redemption of Israel, Jesus, the Messiah Himself), by the Holy Ghost (2:25). What do you want to know that you can't know by your own strength?

HE (SIMEON) CAME BY THE SPIRIT INTO THE TEMPLE :27

Luke 2:25 – 30 (KJV)

²⁵ And, behold, there was a man in Jerusalem, whose name *was* Simeon; and the same man *was* just and devout, waiting for the consolation of Israel: and the Holy Ghost was upon him.

²⁶ And it was revealed unto him by the Holy Ghost, that he should not see death, before he had seen the Lord's Christ.

²⁷ And he came by the Spirit into the temple: and when the parents brought in the child Jesus, to do for him after the custom of the law,

²⁸ Then took he him up in his arms, and blessed God, and said,

²⁹ Lord, now lettest thou thy servant depart in peace, according to thy word:

³⁰ For mine eyes have seen thy salvation,

God promised to show His Salvation (Psalm 91:16) and Simeon waited and **Simeon saw Him.** (see Hebrews 4:12 – 13; Luke 10:38 – 42; John 12:7) Is anything too hard for God!

———————————————
———————————————
———————————————
———————————————
———————————————

(JESUS) WILL BAPTIZE YOU WITH THE HOLY GHOST

Luke 3:2, 3, 15, 16 (KJV)

² Annas and Caiaphas being the high priests, the word of God came unto John the son of Zacharias in the wilderness.

³ And he came into all the country about Jordan, preaching the baptism of repentance for the remission of sins;

¹⁵ And as the people were in expectation, and all men mused in their hearts of John, whether he were the Christ, or not;

¹⁶ John answered, saying unto *them* all, I indeed baptize you with water; but one mightier than I cometh, the latchet of whose shoes I am not worthy to unloose: he shall baptize you with the Holy Ghost and with fire:

Change is the fruit of repentance! The time is now! (3:8 – 10; Acts 19:4; John 3:17) Who said "and with fire" and what name is he usually called today?

———————————————
———————————————
———————————————
———————————————
———————————————
———————————————
———————————————
———————————————

THE HOLY GHOST DESCENDED

Luke 3:18 – 22 (KJV)
[18] And many other things in his exhortation preached he unto the people.
[19] But Herod the tetrarch, being reproved by him for Herodias his brother Philip's wife, and for all the evils which Herod had done,
[20] Added yet this above all, that he shut up John in prison.
[21] Now when all the people were baptized, it came to pass, that Jesus also being baptized, and praying, the heaven was opened,
[22] And the Holy Ghost descended in a bodily shape like a dove upon him, and a voice came from heaven, which said, Thou art my beloved Son; in thee I am well pleased.

The heavens opened **as Jesus** prayed. The Holy Ghost took on **visual** shape, came down and **affirmed only** Jesus as the Beloved Son of God when **He** was baptized. (see Genesis 11:5; Matthew 3:17; John 10:27) You have been affirmed by your Father in heaven!

_____
_____
_____
_____
_____

FULL OF THE HOLY GHOST... LED BY THE SPIRIT

Luke 4:1 – 4 (KJV)
[1] And Jesus being full of the Holy Ghost returned from Jordan, and was led by the Spirit into the wilderness,
[2] Being forty days tempted of the devil. And in those days he did eat nothing: and when they were ended, he afterward hungered.
[3] And the devil said unto him, If thou be the Son of God, command this stone that it be made bread.
[4] And Jesus answered him, saying, It is written, That man shall not live by bread alone, but by every word of God

Who led Jesus into the wilderness? Is Jesus our example?
Is there a difference between the Spirit and the Holy Ghost? (see 2:25 – 27) What kind of words will we say by the Spirit? What was the Weapon Jesus used? (4:4)

_____
_____
_____
_____
_____
_____
_____
_____

date_____
POWER OF THE SPIRIT

Luke 4:8, 12, 13, 14 (KJV)

⁸ And Jesus answered and said unto him, Get thee behind me, Satan: for it is written, Thou shalt worship the Lord thy God, and him only shalt thou serve.

¹² And Jesus answering said unto him, It is said, Thou shalt not tempt the Lord thy God.

¹³ And when the devil had ended all the temptation, he departed from him for a season.

¹⁴ And Jesus returned in the power of the Spirit into Galilee: and there went out a fame of him through all the region round about.

Jesus came by demonstration! **The most powerful force** for us **is the written Word spoken.** (see Deuteronomy 6:13, 16; Matthew 28:18 – 20) Jesus passed the test of integrity and came back to the people in the power of the Spirit.

Every **minister with His Spirit** will be tested for strength and endurance.

_____

_____

_____

_____

_____

_____

date_____
THE SPIRIT OF THE LORD IS UPON ME (JESUS)

Luke 4:15 – 19, 21 (KJV)

¹⁵ And he taught in their synagogues, being glorified of all.

¹⁶ And he came to Nazareth, where he had been brought up: and, as his custom was, he went into the synagogue on the sabbath day, and stood up for to read.

¹⁷ And there was delivered unto him the book of the prophet Esaias. And when he had opened the book, he found the place where it was written,

¹⁸ The Spirit of the Lord *is* upon me, because he hath anointed me to preach the gospel to the poor; he hath sent me to heal the brokenhearted, to preach deliverance to the captives, and recovering of sight to the blind, to set at liberty them that are bruised,

¹⁹ To preach the acceptable year of the Lord.

²¹ And he began to say unto them, This day is this scripture fulfilled in your ears.

(Isaiah 61:1 – 3) "...he found..." He read the Word with purpose! The Spirit of the Lord was on Jesus and He spoke gracious words! (see 2:25; 10:38 – 42)! Upon who?

_____

_____

WENT UPON THE HOUSETOP

Luke 5:17 – 20 (KJV)

[17] And it came to pass on a certain day, as he was teaching, that there were Pharisees and doctors of the law sitting by, which were come out of every town of Galilee, and Judaea, and Jerusalem: and the power of the Lord was *present* to heal them.

[18] And, behold, men brought in a bed a man which was taken with a palsy: and they sought *means* to bring him in, and to lay *him* before him.

[19] And when they could not find by what *way* they might bring him in because of the multitude, they went upon the housetop, and let him down through the tiling with *his* couch into the midst before Jesus.

[20] And when he saw their faith, he said unto him, Man, thy sins are forgiven thee.

The crowd of people was an obstacle for the four friends, but we have any-time access to Jesus by the Spirit. He will show you things to come and things you have never seen before (John 16:13; Mark 2:12; Matthew 9:8; 10:27). What will you ask Jesus today?

_____

_____

_____

_____

MERCIFUL...FORGIVEN

Luke 6:35 – 39 (KJV)

[35] But love ye your enemies, and do good, and lend, hoping for nothing again; and your reward shall be great, and ye shall be the children of the Highest: for he is kind unto the unthankful and *to* the evil.

[36] Be ye therefore merciful, as your Father also is merciful.

[37] Judge not, and ye shall not be judged: condemn not, and ye shall not be condemned: forgive, and ye shall be forgiven:

[38] Give, and it shall be given unto you; good measure, pressed down, and shaken together, and running over, shall men give into your bosom. For with the same measure that ye mete withal it shall be measured to you again.

[39] And he spake a parable unto them, Can the blind lead the blind? shall they not both fall into the ditch?

We are different. He is merciful. We are merciful. We forgive. He loves. We love.

_____

_____

_____

_____

_____

date_____

THY FAITH HATH SAVED THEE; GO IN PEACE

Luke 7:40 – 43, 47, 50 (KJV)

[40] And Jesus answering said unto him, Simon, I have somewhat to say unto thee. And he saith, Master, say on.

[41] There was a certain creditor which had two debtors: the one owed five hundred pence, and the other fifty.

[42] And when they had nothing to pay, he frankly forgave them both. Tell me therefore, which of them will love him most?

[43] Simon answered and said, I suppose that *he*, to whom he forgave most. And he said unto him, Thou hast rightly judged.

[47] Wherefore I say unto thee, Her sins, which are many, are forgiven; for she loved much: but to whom little is forgiven, *the same* loveth little.

[50] And he said to the woman, Thy faith hath saved thee; go in peace.

Forgiveness causes us to act forgiven to the degree of known forgiveness (7:47)!

_____
_____
_____
_____
_____
_____

date_____

FOR I (JESUS) PERCEIVE THAT VIRTUE

Luke 8:45 – 48 (KJV)

[45] And Jesus said, Who touched me? When all denied, Peter and they that were with him said, Master, the multitude throng thee and press *thee*, and sayest thou, Who touched me?

[46] And Jesus said, Somebody hath touched me: for I perceive that virtue is gone out of me.

[47] And when the woman saw that she was not hid, she came trembling, and falling down before him, she declared unto him before all the people for what cause she had touched him, and how she was healed immediately.

[48] And he said unto her, Daughter, be of good comfort: thy faith hath made thee whole; go in peace.

The word "whole" means that she was well physically, emotionally and spiritually! She could "go in peace" because the **illness would not return a second time.** (see Nahum 1:9) How is the word 'virtue' translated in other versions of the Bible?

_____
_____
_____
_____
_____

WHAT MANNER OF SPIRIT YE ARE OF

Luke 9:52 – 56 (KJV)

52 And sent messengers before his face: and they went, and entered into a village of the Samaritans, to make ready for him.

53 And they did not receive him, because his face was as though he would go to Jerusalem.

54 And when his disciples James and John saw *this*, they said, Lord, wilt thou that we command fire to come down from heaven, and consume them, even as Elias did?

55 But he turned, and rebuked them, and said, Ye know not what manner of spirit ye are of.

56 For the Son of man is not come to destroy men's lives, but to save *them*. And they went to another village.

When we make decisions with the wisdom of Jesus, we draw nearer to Him (see Matthew 7:4; John 3:17; 10:10; 1 Kings 18) How do we know what Spirit we are reacting from?

_____
_____
_____
_____
_____
_____

JESUS REJOICED IN SPIRIT

Luke 10:21, 30, 33, 37 (KJV)

21 In that hour Jesus rejoiced in spirit, and said, I thank thee, O Father, Lord of heaven and earth, that thou hast hid these things from the wise and prudent, and hast revealed them unto babes: even so, Father; for so it seemed good in thy sight.

30 And Jesus answering said, A certain *man* went down from Jerusalem to Jericho, and fell among thieves, which stripped him of his raiment, and wounded *him*, and departed, leaving *him* half dead.

33 But a certain Samaritan, as he journeyed, came where he was: and when he saw him, he had compassion *on him*,

37 And he said, He that shewed mercy on him. Then said Jesus unto him, Go, and do thou likewise.

To give mercy and to forgive can only come from a heart like Jesus. When we got saved we inherited the heart like His (10:25 – 37). Mercy defeats judgment (23:34; James 2:13).

_____
_____
_____
_____
_____
_____

GIVE THE HOLY SPIRIT TO THEM THAT ASK

Luke 11:2, 3, 4, 11 – 13 (KJV)

2 And he said unto them, When ye pray, say, Our Father which art in heaven, Hallowed be thy name. Thy kingdom come. Thy will be done, as in heaven, so in earth.

3 Give us day by day our daily bread.

4 And forgive us our sins; for we also forgive every one that is indebted to us. And lead us not into temptation; but deliver us from evil.

11 If a son shall ask bread of any of you that is a father, will he give him a stone? or if *he ask* a fish, will he for a fish give him a serpent?

12 Or if he shall ask an egg, will he offer him a scorpion?

13 If ye then, being evil, know how to give good gifts unto your children: how much more shall *your* heavenly Father give the Holy Spirit to them that ask him?

Your heavenly Father has no need to wait and earn anything since He has everything. He doesn't get weary. He will grant His Spirit to you when you ask (11:1 – 13; 1 John 5:14).

_____

_____

_____

_____

_____

AGAINST THE HOLY GHOST

Luke 12:4, 7 – 10 (KJV)

4 And I say unto you my friends, Be not afraid of them that kill the body, and after that have no more that they can do.

7 But even the very hairs of your head are all numbered. Fear not therefore: ye are of more value than many sparrows.

8 Also I say unto you, Whosoever shall confess me before men, him shall the Son of man also confess before the angels of God:

9 But he that denieth me before men shall be denied before the angels of God.

10 And whosoever shall speak a word against the Son of man, it shall be forgiven him: but unto him that blasphemeth against the Holy Ghost it shall not be forgiven.

Jesus told us how to get God's attention: Jesus said when we acknowledge Him or take a stand for Him, He will Himself stand before **Heaven** on our behalf. (see John 15:8; Matthew 5:16; 10:32; Ecclesiastes 11:2 – 3; Acts 26:24 – 27)

_____

_____

_____

_____

THE HOLY GHOST SHALL TEACH YOU

Luke 12:11 – 12 (KJV)
[11] And when they bring you unto the synagogues, and *unto* magistrates, and powers, take ye no thought how or what thing ye shall answer, or what ye shall say:
[12] For the Holy Ghost shall teach you in the same hour what ye ought to say.

The Holy Ghost is the Spirit of our Father! (Matthew 10:18 – 29) When we are talking for Him, **He is taking up for us** no matter what happens in this life. (see 21:14; Matthew 10:20; Mark 13:11; 2 Samuel 23:2)! Jesus gave them a super safety net telling them to want only what was already theirs (12:13 – 15). Do you suppose Jesus was protecting them from some worry?

_____
_____
_____
_____
_____
_____
_____
_____
_____

WOMAN, THOU ART LOOSED

Luke 13:11 – 13, 18 – 19 (KJV)
[11] And, behold, there was a woman which had a spirit of infirmity eighteen years, and was bowed together, and could in no wise lift up *herself*.
[12] And when Jesus saw her, he called *her to him*, and said unto her, Woman, thou art loosed from thine infirmity.
[13] And he laid *his* hands on her: and immediately she was made straight, and glorified God.
[18] Then said he, Unto what is the kingdom of God like? and whereunto shall I resemble it?
[19] It is like a grain of mustard seed, which a man took, and cast into his garden; and it grew, and waxed a great tree; and the fowls of the air lodged in the branches of it.

The spirit of infirmity hinders us all at times. The infirmity was stopping her from looking up and reaching up to her full potential (John 4:34 – 35; 6:37 – 40).

_____
_____
_____
_____
_____
_____

THOU (YOU) SHALT BE BLESSED

Luke 14:11 – 14 (KJV)

¹¹ For whosoever exalteth himself shall be abased; and he that humbleth himself shall be exalted.

¹² Then said he also to him that bade him, When thou makest a dinner or a supper, call not thy friends, nor thy brethren, neither thy kinsmen, nor *thy* rich neighbours; lest they also bid thee again, and a recompence be made thee.

¹³ But when thou makest a feast, call the poor, the maimed, the lame, the blind:

¹⁴ And thou shalt be blessed; for they cannot recompense thee: for thou shalt be recompensed at the resurrection of the just.

Whom we serve shows us where we are going and how high.

_____
_____
_____
_____
_____
_____
_____
_____
_____

ALL THAT I HAVE IS THINE

Luke 15:27 – 31 (KJV)

²⁷ And he said unto him, Thy brother is come; and thy father hath killed the fatted calf, because he hath received him safe and sound.

²⁸ And he was angry, and would not go in: therefore came his father out, and intreated him.

²⁹ And he answering said to *his* father, Lo, these many years do I serve thee, neither transgressed I at any time thy commandment: and yet thou never gavest me a kid, that I might make merry with my friends:

³⁰ But as soon as this thy son was come, which hath devoured thy living with harlots, thou hast killed for him the fatted calf.

³¹ And he said unto him, Son, thou art ever with me, and all that I have is thine.

We are heirs **through and with** Jesus Christ. (see 15:15 - 39) What have we missed because we didn't ask the Father, our Father in heaven?

_____
_____
_____
_____
_____

date_____
FAITHFUL

Luke 16:10, 11. 12, 14, 15 (KJV)
[10] He that is faithful in that which is least is faithful also in much: and he that is unjust in the least is unjust also in much.

[11] If therefore ye have not been faithful in the unrighteous mammon, who will commit to your trust the true *riches*?

[12] And if ye have not been faithful in that which is another man's, who shall give you that which is your own?

[14] And the Pharisees also, who were covetous, heard all these things: and they derided him.

[15] And he said unto them, Ye are they which justify yourselves before men; but God knoweth your hearts: for that which is highly esteemed among men is abomination in the sight of God.

God is pleased when we remove ourselves from the anxiety of distractions!

_____
_____
_____
_____
_____
_____
_____
_____

date_____
GIVING HIM (JESUS) THANKS

Luke 17:12 – 19 (KJV)
[12] And as he entered into a certain village, there met him ten men that were lepers, which stood afar off:

[13] And they lifted up *their* voices, and said, Jesus, Master, have mercy on us.

[14] And when he saw *them*, he said unto them, Go shew yourselves unto the priests. And it came to pass, that, as they went, they were cleansed.

[15] And one of them, when he saw that he was healed, turned back, and with a loud voice glorified God,

[16] And fell down on *his* face at his feet, giving him thanks: and he was a Samaritan.

[17] And Jesus answering said, Were there not ten cleansed? but where *are* the nine?

[18] There are not found that returned to give glory to God, save this stranger.

[19] And he said unto him, Arise, go thy way: thy faith hath made thee whole.

This one gave thanks to Jesus. What are the benefits of being thankful?

_____
_____
_____
_____
_____
_____

WHAT WILT THOU THAT I (JESUS) SHALL DO...?

Luke 18:38 – 42 (KJV)

[38] And he cried, saying, Jesus, *thou* Son of David, have mercy on me.

[39] And they which went before rebuked him, that he should hold his peace: but he cried so much the more, *Thou* Son of David, have mercy on me.

[40] And Jesus stood, and commanded him to be brought unto him: and when he was come near, he asked him,

[41] Saying, What wilt thou that I shall do unto thee? And he said, Lord, that I may receive my sight.

[42] And Jesus said unto him, Receive thy sight: thy faith hath saved thee.

Jesus had just prophesied His beating and His death and His resurrection to life on the 3rd day (18:32 – 33). **He advertised Jesus** and Jesus asked him, "What do you want Me to do for you?" **What will you say** when Jesus asked you that question? (see 1 Kings 3:5)

_____

_____

_____

_____

_____

_____

_____

MY (JESUS)...HOUSE OF PRAYER

Luke 19:41, 45, 46, 48 (KJV)

[41] And when he was come near, he beheld the city, and wept over it,

[45] And he went into the temple, and began to cast out them that sold therein, and them that bought;

[46] Saying unto them, It is written, My house is the house of prayer: but ye have made it a den of thieves.

[48] And could not find what they might do: for all the people were very attentive to hear him.

Jesus wept. So much was going on all at the same time: While some of the leaders looked for a way to destroy Jesus, He prepared to die for their sin, but not for theirs only, but for ours also. While they were yelling, "Crucify Him!" our sin was yelling the same thing! Jesus died for all (19:47).

_____

_____

_____

_____

_____

_____

_____

date_____

GAVE THEE (JESUS) THIS AUTHORITY

Luke 20:1, 2, 3, 4, 7, 8 (KJV)

¹ And it came to pass, *that* on one of those days, as he taught the people in the temple, and preached the gospel, the chief priests and the scribes came upon *him* with the elders,

² And spake unto him, saying, Tell us, by what authority doest thou these things? or who is he that gave thee this authority?

³ And he answered and said unto them, I will also ask you one thing; and answer me:

⁴ The baptism of John, was it from heaven, or of men?

⁷ And they answered, that they could not tell whence *it was*.

⁸ And Jesus said unto them, Neither tell I you by what authority I do these things.

Jesus was in the temple every day preaching the gospel of the kingdom to the government and the people? Who gave Jesus His authority? Who gave John his authority?

_____
_____
_____
_____
_____

date_____

I WILL GIVE YOU...WISDOM

Luke 21:12 – 15 (KJV)

¹² But before all these, they shall lay their hands on you, and persecute *you*, delivering *you* up to the synagogues, and into prisons, being brought before kings and rulers for my name's sake.

¹³ And it shall turn to you for a testimony.

¹⁴ Settle *it* therefore in your hearts, not to meditate before what ye shall answer:

¹⁵ For I will give you a mouth and wisdom, which all your adversaries shall not be able to gainsay nor resist.

God wants us to influence the world (Matthew 5:16; 9:8; 1 Peter 2:12; 4:11, 14)! Jesus declared when **they hear us, they hear our voice with** the words of the Holy Ghost. (see 2 Samuel 23:2)

_____
_____
_____
_____
_____
_____
_____
_____
_____
_____
_____

date_____
REMEMBRANCE OF ME (JESUS)

Luke 22:40 – 45 (KJV)
40 And when he was at the place, he said unto them, Pray that ye enter not into temptation.

41 And he was withdrawn from them about a stone's cast, and kneeled down, and prayed,

42 Saying, Father, if thou be willing, remove this cup from me: nevertheless not my will, but thine, be done.

43 And there appeared an angel unto him from heaven, strengthening him.

44 And being in an agony he prayed more earnestly: and his sweat was as it were great drops of blood falling down to the ground.

45 And when he rose up from prayer, and was come to his disciples, he found them sleeping for sorrow,

Jesus knew His Father would need to forsake Him in order for us to be accepted in Him. Jesus sowed seeds of agony so we could reap the harvest of love! (22:27; Isaiah 53)

_____
_____
_____
_____
_____
_____

date_____
FATHER, FORGIVE THEM

Luke 23:11, 12, 32 – 34 (KJV)
11 And Herod with his men of war set him at nought, and mocked *him*, and arrayed him in a gorgeous robe, and sent him again to Pilate.

12 And the same day Pilate and Herod were made friends together: for before they were at enmity between themselves.

32 And there were also two other, malefactors, led with him to be put to death.

33 And when they were come to the place, which is called Calvary, there they crucified him, and the malefactors, one on the right hand, and the other on the left.

34 Then said Jesus, Father, forgive them; for they know not what they do. And they parted his raiment, and cast lots.

We are **more like Jesus** when we forgive those who are or have been cruel to us. When did Jesus (our Example) say, "Father, forgive them" and who was He referring to?

_____
_____
_____
_____
_____

PROMISE OF MY (JESUS) FATHER

Luke 24:45 – 49 (KJV)
[45] Then opened he their understanding, that they might understand the scriptures,
[46] And said unto them, Thus it is written, and thus it behoved Christ to suffer, and to rise from the dead the third day:
[47] And that repentance and remission of sins should be preached in his name among all nations, beginning at Jerusalem.
[48] And ye are witnesses of these things.
[49] And, behold, I send the promise of my Father upon you: but tarry ye in the city of Jerusalem, until ye be endued with power from on high.

The word *endued* means to be clothed inside and out! When the Spirit of God comes upon us, we will know and those near us will also know! (see 1 Samuel 10:6; Acts 1:8)
God gave us the story of His Son from **4 different perspectives since His thoughts are far above ours.** We needed all 4 and 4 is the number that means cover the earth.

_____
_____
_____
_____
_____

IN THE BEGINNING WAS THE WORD…MADE FLESH

John 1:1, 11, 12, 13, 14 (KJV)
[1] In the beginning was the Word, and the Word was with God, and the Word was God.
[11] He came unto his own, and his own received him not.
[12] But as many as received him, to them gave he power to become the sons of God, *even* to them that believe on his name:
[13] Which were born, not of blood, nor of the will of the flesh, nor of the will of man, but of God.
[14] And the Word was made flesh, and dwelt among us, (and we beheld his glory, the glory as of the only begotten of the Father,) full of grace and truth.

God sent Himself, the Spirit, wrapped in skin, so we could **believe on His name** (Jesus) and be born of Spirit and **continue** in a body **as His witnesses.** Through believing on **His name**, we have received **His fullness** (1:12 – 17). (see Matthew 17:1 – 5)

_____
_____
_____
_____
_____

date_____

I (JOHN THE BAPTIST) SAW THE SPIRIT

John 1:29 – 32 (KJV)

²⁹ The next day John seeth Jesus coming unto him, and saith, Behold the Lamb of God, which taketh away the sin of the world.

³⁰ This is he of whom I said, After me cometh a man which is preferred before me: for he was before me.

³¹ And I knew him not: but that he should be made manifest to Israel, therefore am I come baptizing with water.

³² And John bare record, saying, I saw the Spirit descending from heaven like a dove, and it abode upon him.

John the Baptist explained his ministry in one sentence: why he did what he did. He was watching for the Spirit! **He was humble and bold** and now he is in heaven.

_____
_____
_____
_____
_____
_____
_____
_____
_____

date_____

HE (JESUS)...BAPTIZETH WITH THE HOLY GHOST

John 1:33 – 37 (KJV)

³³ And I knew him not: but he that sent me to baptize with water, the same said unto me, Upon whom thou shalt see the Spirit descending, and remaining on him, the same is he which baptizeth with the Holy Ghost.

³⁴ And I saw, and bare record that this is the Son of God.

³⁵ Again the next day after John stood, and two of his disciples;

³⁶ And looking upon Jesus as he walked, he saith, Behold the Lamb of God!

³⁷ And the two disciples heard him speak, and they followed Jesus.

The Spirit first! Who baptizes us with the Holy Ghost? The Holy Spirit, Jesus or God? The Spirit remaining on Jesus was John's proof that **Jesus was and is the Baptizer with the Holy Ghost**. Are you a disciple and preacher like John? Are you a disciple and follower of Jesus? How could you follow Jesus more closely?

_____
_____
_____
_____

FILLED THEM UP TO THE BRIM

John 2:7 – 10 (KJV)

[7] Jesus saith unto them, Fill the waterpots with water. And they filled them up to the brim.
[8] And he saith unto them, Draw out now, and bear unto the governor of the feast. And they bare *it*.
[9] When the ruler of the feast had tasted the water that was made wine, and knew not whence it was: (but the servants which drew the water knew;) the governor of the feast called the bridegroom,
[10] And saith unto him, Every man at the beginning doth set forth good wine; and when men have well drunk, then that which is worse: *but* thou hast kept the good wine until now.

God created that water too! Jesus made unleavened and aged wine (at the same time) from His water **without yeast and time.** What do you need **in one hour**?

_____
_____
_____
_____
_____
_____
_____

BORN OF WATER AND OF THE SPIRIT

John 3:3 – 5 (KJV)

[3] Jesus answered and said unto him, Verily, verily, I say unto thee, Except a man be born again, he cannot see the kingdom of God.
[4] Nicodemus saith unto him, How can a man be born when he is old? can he enter the second time into his mother's womb, and be born?
[5] Jesus answered, Verily, verily, I say unto thee, Except a man be born of water and *of* the Spirit, he cannot enter into the kingdom of God.

Who does Jesus tell Nicodemus about? To see means to be in or to enter the kingdom of God! To *see* and to *enter* are inseparable (3:3, 5). Can he go back and enter the second time into his mother's womb?
Born of water and born of Spirit are 2 different things! How can one grown man have two births? What is the second birth?

_____
_____
_____
_____
_____
_____
_____

BORN OF THE SPIRIT

John 3:5 – 8 (KJV)
⁵ Jesus answered, Verily, verily, I say unto thee, Except a man be born of water and *of* the Spirit, he cannot enter into the kingdom of God.

⁶ That which is born of the flesh is flesh; and that which is born of the Spirit is spirit.

⁷ Marvel not that I said unto thee, Ye must be born again.

⁸ The wind bloweth where it listeth, and thou hearest the sound thereof, but canst not tell whence it cometh, and whither it goeth: so is every one that is born of the Spirit.

The wind was made by God to divide the Red Sea so God's people could leave Pharaoh and worship God. Jesus used the wind to demonstrate the Spirit. Jesus witnessed by talking about the weather and **talking about the Spirit**. (see 1 John 5:4 – 5) Why did Jesus mention the Spirit? Why did Jesus mention the sound of the wind?

_____

_____

_____

_____

_____

_____

_____

_____

WHOSOEVER BELIEVETH IN HIM (JESUS)

John 3:13 – 17 (KJV)
¹³ And no man hath ascended up to heaven, but he that came down from heaven, *even* the Son of man which is in heaven.

¹⁴ And as Moses lifted up the serpent in the wilderness, even so must the Son of man be lifted up:

¹⁵ That whosoever believeth in him should not perish, but have eternal life.

¹⁶ For God so loved the world, that he gave his only begotten Son, that whosoever believeth in him should not perish, but have everlasting life.

¹⁷ For God sent not his Son into the world to condemn the world; but that the world through him might be saved.

He came to pursue each of us, so we could be saved, receive His Spirit and glorify God.

Jesus used the true story of the serpent on a pole to explain His death when He became sin for each of us and died on His cross. (Numbers 21:4 – 9; 2 Corinthians 5:21)

_____

_____

_____

_____

GOD GIVETH NOT THE SPIRIT BY MEASURE

John 3:27, 31 – 35 (KJV)

²⁷ John answered and said, A man can receive nothing, except it be given him from heaven.

³¹ He that cometh from above is above all: he that is of the earth is earthly, and speaketh of the earth: he that cometh from heaven is above all.

³² And what he hath seen and heard, that he testifieth; and no man receiveth his testimony.

³³ He that hath received his testimony hath set to his seal that God is true.

³⁴ For he whom God hath sent speaketh the words of God: for God giveth not the Spirit by measure *unto him*.

³⁵ The Father loveth the Son, and hath given all things into his hand.

No one can be a house for only part of the Spirit, seeing that **Jesus** is above all. (see 16:13; Romans 8:32; Ephesians 4:10)

_____
_____
_____
_____
_____
_____
_____
_____

GIFT...GIVE...GIVEN THEE LIVING WATER

John 4:4, 7, 10, 11 (KJV)

⁴ And he must needs go through Samaria.

⁷ There cometh a woman of Samaria to draw water: Jesus saith unto her, Give me to drink.

¹⁰ Jesus answered and said unto her, If thou knewest the gift of God, and who it is that saith to thee, Give me to drink; thou wouldest have asked of him, and he would have given thee living water.

¹¹ The woman saith unto him, Sir, thou hast nothing to draw with, and the well is deep: from whence then hast thou that living water?

A partnership of faith increases faith, activates power and accelerates answers. The Living Water Jesus spoke of, was His Spirit, who created **the first water.** Jesus **began witnessing** by **teaching about the water and the Spirit.** (see Ezekiel 47:9; Matthew 5:16)

_____
_____
_____
_____
_____
_____

FATHER IN SPIRIT AND IN TRUTH

John 4:13 – 15, 21, 23 (KJV)

¹³ Jesus answered and said unto her, Whosoever drinketh of this water shall thirst again:

¹⁴ But whosoever drinketh of the water that I shall give him shall never thirst; but the water that I shall give him shall be in him a well of water springing up into everlasting life.

¹⁵ The woman saith unto him, Sir, give me this water, that I thirst not, neither come hither to draw.

²¹ Jesus saith unto her, Woman, believe me, the hour cometh, when ye shall neither in this mountain, nor yet at Jerusalem, worship the Father.

²³ But the hour cometh, and now is, when the true worshippers shall worship the Father in spirit and in truth: for the Father seeketh such to worship him.

The Father is seeking those who will live their worship! The woman didn't understand the Spirit but she understood thirst and water. Was His word sufficient? (see 6:34)

_____
_____
_____
_____
_____

GOD IS A SPIRIT...WORSHIP

John 4:24, 25, 26, 28, 29 (KJV)

²⁴ God *is* a Spirit: and they that worship him must worship *him* in spirit and in truth.

²⁵ The woman saith unto him, I know that Messias cometh, which is called Christ: when he is come, he will tell us all things.

²⁶ Jesus saith unto her, I that speak unto thee am *he*.

²⁸ The woman then left her waterpot, and went her way into the city, and saith to the men,

²⁹ Come, see a man, which told me all things that ever I did: is not this the Christ?

We worship only God. Worshipping in spirit and in truth is the picture of us being **willing to do anything to stay in His presence.** God is fighting on our behalf as we sacrifice our time for worship. Did Jesus accomplish His purpose for that day?

Jesus just called the first evangelist to Samaria (4:42). He talked about water and she believed for Living Water. (see 7:37 – 39; 17:8; Proverbs 4:23; 1 John 5:4 – 5)

_____
_____
_____
_____

ALSO DOETH THE SON LIKEWISE

John 5:17, 19 – 21 (KJV)

¹⁷ But Jesus answered them, My Father worketh hitherto, and I work.

¹⁹ Then answered Jesus and said unto them, Verily, verily, I say unto you, The Son can do nothing of himself, but what he seeth the Father do: for what things soever he doeth, these also doeth the Son likewise.

²⁰ For the Father loveth the Son, and sheweth him all things that himself doeth: and he will shew him greater works than these, that ye may marvel.

²¹ For as the Father raiseth up the dead, and quickeneth *them*; even so the Son quickeneth whom he will.

Jesus did what He saw the Father do. Jesus gave witness He Himself was equal with God, who wants to amaze you. The works are to amaze us, to prove who Jesus is and guide us into a place of faith. (see John 10:38; Mark 5:20; Genesis 18:17) How and where can we get into a place of faith?

_____

_____

_____

_____

_____

_____

SPIRIT THAT QUICKENETH

John 6:35, 42, 43, 47, 63 (KJV)

³⁵ And Jesus said unto them, I am the bread of life: he that cometh to me shall never hunger; and he that believeth on me shall never thirst.

⁴² And they said, Is not this Jesus, the son of Joseph, whose father and mother we know? how is it then that he saith, I came down from heaven?

⁴³ Jesus therefore answered and said unto them, Murmur not among yourselves.

⁴⁷ Verily, verily, I say unto you, He that believeth on me hath everlasting life.

⁶³ It is the spirit that quickeneth; the flesh profiteth nothing: the words that I speak unto you, *they* are spirit, and *they* are life.

As we ingest food, particles of the food become part of our body-DNA as particles feed us from inside. When we open our heart for Jesus to come in, the principles of His Spirit become part of our spirit-DNA from inside (verses 35 – 58). (see Ephesians 1:13)

_____

_____

_____

_____

_____

_____

date_____
THE SPIRIT...THE HOLY GHOST WAS NOT YET GIVEN

John 7:37 – 39 (KJV)

³⁷ In the last day, that great *day* of the feast, Jesus stood and cried, saying, If any man thirst, let him come unto me, and drink.

³⁸ He that believeth on me, as the scripture hath said, out of his belly shall flow rivers of living water.

³⁹ (But this spake he of the Spirit, which they that believe on him should receive: for the Holy Ghost was not yet *given*; because that Jesus was not yet glorified.)

When we believe on Him, we have received the Spirit of the defender (7:38 – 39; 9:35; 12:7). The overflow of the Spirit came after Jesus was glorified. **Only Jesus could bring the Spirit of God** and be the first house of the Holy Ghost. Why wasn't He speaking about the Holy Ghost then (7:39)? Does the Spirit indwell us when Jesus baptizes us with the Holy Ghost (Acts 1:5; 11:16)? When were the people baptized by Jesus with the Holy Ghost (Acts 2:4, 17, 18, 38)? Why does the Bible use the word 'given' here (Acts 11:17)?

———————————————
———————————————
———————————————
———————————————

date_____
CONTINUE IN MY (JESUS') WORD

John 8:29 – 32 (KJV)

²⁹ And he that sent me is with me: the Father hath not left me alone; for I do always those things that please him.

³⁰ As he spake these words, many believed on him.

³¹ Then said Jesus to those Jews which believed on him, If ye continue in my word, *then* are ye my disciples indeed;

³² And ye shall know the truth, and the truth shall make you free.

Jesus encouraged them to delight in the Word as He told them of the benefits and the promotion of verse 32. (see Joshua 1:8; Psalm 1:1 – 3; Ephesians 6:17; John 5:17 – 21).

Do you think His word is the word of God, the words God said, the words the Holy Ghost, the written word, the spoken written words? (see 2 Peter 1:21; Mark 12:36; Hebrews 1:2)

———————————————
———————————————
———————————————
———————————————
———————————————
———————————————
———————————————
———————————————

WHO IS HE, LORD

John 9:10 – 11, 35 – 38(KJV)

[10] Therefore said they unto him, How were thine eyes opened?

[11] He answered and said, A man that is called Jesus made clay, and anointed mine eyes, and said unto me, Go to the pool of Siloam, and wash: and I went and washed, and I received sight.

[35] Jesus heard that they had cast him out; and when he had found him, he said unto him, Dost thou believe on the Son of God?

[36] He answered and said, Who is he, Lord, that I might believe on him?

[37] And Jesus said unto him, Thou hast both seen him, and it is he that talketh with thee.

[38] And he said, Lord, I believe. And he worshipped him.

Jesus made it His business to go after the castaway – just one. Have you ever been unwanted? Jesus understands. Have you ever been an outcast? Jesus will visit you. When you visit the rejected, the **power of heaven meets you** there (Matthew 25:35 – 40).

_____

_____

_____

_____

_____

HEAR MY (JESUS') VOICE

John 10:25 – 29 (KJV)

[25] Jesus answered them, I told you, and ye believed not: the works that I do in my Father's name, they bear witness of me.

[26] But ye believe not, because ye are not of my sheep, as I said unto you.

[27] My sheep hear my voice, and I know them, and they follow me:

[28] And I give unto them eternal life; and they shall never perish, neither shall any *man* pluck them out of my hand.

[29] My Father, which gave *them* me, is greater than all; and no *man* is able to pluck *them* out of my Father's hand.

In the Old Testament, Elijah the prophet became depressed and the voice of God spoke to him in **the same still small voice.** He speaks to us, by **the Spirit of Jesus,** as Jesus said (10:27; 1 Kings 19:12).

_____

_____

_____

_____

_____

_____

_____

date_____

PROPHESIED THAT JESUS SHOULD DIE

John 11:48 – 52 (KJV)

[48] If we let him thus alone, all *men* will believe on him: and the Romans shall come and take away both our place and nation.

[49] And one of them, *named* Caiaphas, being the high priest that same year, said unto them, Ye know nothing at all,

[50] Nor consider that it is expedient for us, that one man should die for the people, and that the whole nation perish not.

[51] And this spake he not of himself: but being high priest that year, he prophesied that Jesus should die for that nation;

[52] And not for that nation only, but that also he should gather together in one the children of God that were scattered abroad.

A bounty was placed on the life of Jesus, who made Himself the **Fugitive who refused to run away.** Who knew Jesus would die? (11:47 – 57) (see James 1:1)

_____
_____
_____
_____
_____

date_____

JESUS...COMING...HOSANNA

John 12:3, 7, 12, 13 (KJV)

[3] Then took Mary a pound of ointment of spikenard, very costly, and anointed the feet of Jesus, and wiped his feet with her hair: and the house was filled with the odour of the ointment.

[7] Then said Jesus, Let her alone: against the day of my burying hath she kept this.

[12] On the next day much people that were come to the feast, when they heard that Jesus was coming to Jerusalem,

[13] Took branches of palm trees, and went forth to meet him, and cried, Hosanna: Blessed *is* the King of Israel that cometh in the name of the Lord.

Jesus was fulfilling prophecies (12:9 – 19; Zechariah 9:9; Psalm 118:24 – 28). She gave up her savings for Jesus and Jesus took up for her (12:3, 7). When we praise Him, **victory is already on the way. The next Sunday morning, Jesus would arise from the dead forever. Hosanna!** We can never praise Him too much!

_____
_____
_____
_____
_____

HE (JESUS) WAS COME FROM GOD

John 13:3 – 5, 15, 18, 19 (KJV)
³ Jesus knowing that the Father had given all things into his hands, and that he was come from God, and went to God;

⁴ He riseth from supper, and laid aside his garments; and took a towel, and girded himself.

⁵ After that he poureth water into a bason, and began to wash the disciples' feet, and to wipe *them* with the towel wherewith he was girded.

¹⁵ For I have given you an example, that ye should do as I have done to you.

¹⁸ I speak not of you all: I know whom I have chosen: but that the scripture may be fulfilled, He that eateth bread with me hath lifted up his heel against me.

¹⁹ Now I tell you before it come, that, when it is come to pass, ye may believe that I am *he*.

(Psalm 41:9) Jesus set aside His strength and made Himself low! He told before too.

HE (JESUS) WAS TROUBLED IN SPIRIT

John 13:20 – 25 (KJV)
²⁰ Verily, verily, I say unto you, He that receiveth whomsoever I send receiveth me; and he that receiveth me receiveth him that sent me.

²¹ When Jesus had thus said, he was troubled in spirit, and testified, and said, Verily, verily, I say unto you, that one of you shall betray me.

²² Then the disciples looked one on another, doubting of whom he spake.

²³ Now there was leaning on Jesus' bosom one of his disciples, whom Jesus loved.

²⁴ Simon Peter therefore beckoned to him, that he should ask who it should be of whom he spake.

²⁵ He then lying on Jesus' breast saith unto him, Lord, who is it?

Peter asked "him" (John) to ask Jesus on his behalf. Can you imagine this? You are also the one "whom Jesus loved." (see 21:20 – 24; Ephesians 4:30; Romans 5:5, 8:38 – 39) None of our acts could cause God to stop loving any of us (3:16; 1 Corinthians 13:7).

LOVE...AS I (JESUS) HAVE LOVED YOU

John 13:31, 32, 34, 35 (KJV)
[31] Therefore, when he was gone out, Jesus said, Now is the Son of man glorified, and God is glorified in him.
[32] If God be glorified in him, God shall also glorify him in himself, and shall straightway glorify him.
[34] A new commandment I give unto you, That ye love one another; as I have loved you, that ye also love one another.
[35] By this shall all *men* know that ye are my disciples, if ye have love one to another.

We show we love Him as we love those of the household of faith (13:20; 4:24). As we sow seeds of love, time, caring, helping, we will reap the multiplied **harvests of heaven (Galatians 6:7 – 10).** (see Genesis 8:22)
How serious do you think Jesus was when He commanded, "Love one another; as I have loved you...?" (see 2 Corinthians 6:16 – 18; Ephesians 5:25)

_____
_____
_____
_____
_____
_____

ANOTHER COMFORTER

John 14:3, 7, 14, 15, 16 (KJV)
[3] And if I go and prepare a place for you, I will come again, and receive you unto myself; that where I am, *there* ye may be also.
[7] If ye had known me, ye should have known my Father also: and from henceforth ye know him, and have seen him.
[14] If ye shall ask any thing in my name, I will do *it*.
[15] If ye love me, keep my commandments.
[16] And I will pray the Father, and he shall give you another Comforter, that he may abide with you for ever;

Jesus was the first Comforter come in the flesh and when He left here, He sent another **Comforter just like Himself.** Jesus is with us and the Spirit in us! (see 5:17 – 19)
We always want to listen to the Daddy we believe loves us! (14:15; 1 John 3:2)

_____
_____
_____
_____
_____
_____
_____

EVEN THE SPIRIT OF TRUTH... WITH YOU...IN YOU

John 14:17 – 20 (KJV)

¹⁷ *Even* the Spirit of truth; whom the world cannot receive, because it seeth him not, neither knoweth him: but ye know him; for he dwelleth with you, and shall be in you.

¹⁸ I will not leave you comfortless: I will come to you.

¹⁹ Yet a little while, and the world seeth me no more; but ye see me: because I live, ye shall live also.

²⁰ At that day ye shall know that I *am* in my Father, and ye in me, and I in you.

The relationship between us and Him is undeniable and unmatchable (14:17, 20).

Each follower of Jesus is an extension of His ministry! The Spirit is in the house! The desire to obey Him is a **proof we love Him**. Only the Spirit could live with and in each of us all at the same time! The Spirit in us is the Spirit poured out. He will fill one available individual or many. Why did He say "and shall be in you?" (see 6:53 – 57)

_____
_____
_____
_____
_____

COMFORTER, WHICH IS THE HOLY GHOST

John 14:21, 23, 25 – 27 (KJV)

²¹ He that hath my commandments, and keepeth them, he it is that loveth me: and he that loveth me shall be loved of my Father, and I will love him, and will manifest myself to him.

²³ Jesus answered and said unto him, If a man love me, he will keep my words: and my Father will love him, and we will come unto him, and make our abode with him.

²⁵ These things have I spoken unto you, being *yet* present with you.

²⁶ But the Comforter, *which is* the Holy Ghost, whom the Father will send in my name, he shall teach you all things, and bring all things to your remembrance, whatsoever I have said unto you.

²⁷ Peace I leave with you, my peace I give unto you: not as the world giveth, give I unto you. Let not your heart be troubled, neither let it be afraid.

Through the Holy Ghost, Jesus is the Comforter! Now we speak in His name! (see 16:7)

_____
_____
_____
_____

COMFORTER...TESTIFY OF ME (JESUS)

John 15:15, 18, 25 – 27 (KJV)

¹⁵ Henceforth I call you not servants; for the servant knoweth not what his lord doeth: but I have called you friends; for all things that I have heard of my Father I have made known unto you.

¹⁸ If the world hate you, ye know that it hated me before *it hated* you.

²⁵ But *this cometh to pass*, that the word might be fulfilled that is written in their law, They hated me without a cause.

²⁶ But when the Comforter is come, whom I will send unto you from the Father, *even* the Spirit of truth, which proceedeth from the Father, he shall testify of me:

²⁷ And ye also shall bear witness, because ye have been with me from the beginning.

Jesus shows us how to love others His way. (see Psalm 69:4). The Spirit will testify from the words of Jesus: The Spirit shall speak for Jesus. He will point us to Jesus forever. The Comforter will take the side of Jesus so we'll know who is speaking. (see 1 John 4:1 – 5)

_____

_____

_____

THE COMFORTER...I (JESUS) WILL SEND HIM

John 16:4 – 7 (KJV)

⁴ But these things have I told you, that when the time shall come, ye may remember that I told you of them. And these things I said not unto you at the beginning, because I was with you.

⁵ But now I go my way to him that sent me; and none of you asketh me, Whither goest thou?

⁶ But because I have said these things unto you, sorrow hath filled your heart.

⁷ Nevertheless I tell you the truth; It is expedient for you that I go away: for if I go not away, the Comforter will not come unto you; but if I depart, I will send him unto you.

Every time we are near the Comforter, we are in the presence of Jesus!
The Comforter shows the world what His justice looks like! (Jeremiah 31:31 – 34)
Are you dreaming **as big as God** wants you to dream, in Jesus name? (Acts 1:8)

_____

_____

_____

_____

SPIRIT OF TRUTH...WILL GUIDE YOU

John 16:13, 14, 15, 27 (KJV)
¹³ Howbeit when he, the Spirit of truth, is come, he will guide you into all truth: for he shall not speak of himself; but whatsoever he shall hear, *that* shall he speak: and he will shew you things to come.
¹⁴ He shall glorify me: for he shall receive of mine, and shall shew *it* unto you.
¹⁵ All things that the Father hath are mine: therefore said I, that he shall take of mine, and shall shew *it* unto you.
²⁷ For the Father himself loveth you, because ye have loved me, and have believed that I came out from God.

Father God initiates. (see 14:10) Lord, let me be speaking only words You want to say through me. (see Acts 16:5 – 8; Luke 12:12; 21:15)

_____
_____
_____
_____
_____
_____
_____
_____

LIFE ETERNAL...KNOW... GOD, AND JESUS

John 17:1 – 4, 17, 20 (KJV)
¹ These words spake Jesus, and lifted up his eyes to heaven, and said, Father, the hour is come; glorify thy Son, that thy Son also may glorify thee:
² As thou hast given him power over all flesh, that he should give eternal life to as many as thou hast given him.
³ And this is life eternal, that they might know thee the only true God, and Jesus Christ, whom thou hast sent.
⁴ I have glorified thee on the earth: I have finished the work which thou gavest me to do.
¹⁷ Sanctify them through thy truth: thy word is truth.
²⁰ Neither pray I for these alone, but for them also which shall believe on me through their word;

Jesus entered the end of His commission of suffering on earth (Luke 11:2; Matthew 3:15). He prayed this prayer the night before He would be nailed to His cross.

_____
_____
_____
_____
_____

PETER THEN DENIED AGAIN

John 18:17, 25 – 27 (KJV)

¹⁷ Then saith the damsel that kept the door unto Peter, Art not thou also *one* of this man's disciples? He saith, I am not.

²⁵ And Simon Peter stood and warmed himself. They said therefore unto him, Art not thou also *one* of his disciples? He denied *it*, and said, I am not.

²⁶ One of the servants of the high priest, being *his* kinsman whose ear Peter cut off, saith, Did not I see thee in the garden with him?

²⁷ Peter then denied again: and immediately the cock crew.

Jesus had told Peter that Satan wanted to sift him but He had prayed for him and for us too. (see John 17) Jesus told Peter to comfort others when his fears were gone (Luke 22:31 – 32). Jesus would go alone because He (the One) came to die for us all. What would your ministry of comfort look like? (2 Corinthians 1:3 – 7)

JESUS KNOWING THAT ALL THINGS

John 19:25, 26, 27, 28 (KJV)

²⁵ Now there stood by the cross of Jesus his mother, and his mother's sister, Mary the *wife* of Cleophas, and Mary Magdalene.

²⁶ When Jesus therefore saw his mother, and the disciple standing by, whom he loved, he saith unto his mother, Woman, behold thy son!

²⁷ Then saith he to the disciple, Behold thy mother! And from that hour that disciple took her unto his own *home*.

²⁸ After this, Jesus knowing that all things were now accomplished, that the scripture might be fulfilled, saith, I thirst.

Jesus cares for His mother as the Apostle John was **appointed from the cross**. Where were you appointed? When we serve someone with **out-of-the-ordinary** service, we will make them **thirsty to know** the love of Jesus. (see Isaiah 53)

_____
_____
_____
_____
_____
_____
_____

_____
_____
_____
_____
_____
_____
_____

THEY (ROMANS)…PIERCED HIS (JESUS) SIDE

John 19:33 – 37 (KJV)

33 But when they came to Jesus, and saw that he was dead already, they brake not his legs:

34 But one of the soldiers with a spear pierced his side, and forthwith came there out blood and water.

35 And he that saw *it* bare record, and his record is true: and he knoweth that he saith true, that ye might believe.

36 For these things were done, that the scripture should be fulfilled, A bone of him shall not be broken.

37 And again another scripture saith, They shall look on him whom they pierced.

(Psalm 34:20; Zechariah 12:10) Jesus was beaten so His bones would not be broken (but all His bones were visible) and His side was pierced with a spear by the Romans. The blood and water from His side was the spiritual birth of the church of His body!

RECEIVE YE THE HOLY GHOST

John 20:21, 22, 23 (KJV)

21 Then said Jesus to them again, Peace *be* unto you: as *my* Father hath sent me, even so send I you.

22 And when he had said this, he breathed on *them*, and saith unto them, Receive ye the Holy Ghost:

23 Whose soever sins ye remit, they are remitted unto them; *and* whose soever *sins* ye retain, they are retained.

His disciples were **witnessing for Him** when they forgave others and themselves. They believed, and received the Holy Ghost **before they were filled** with the Holy Ghost (Acts 2:1 – 4). Is it necessary to believe on Jesus before we receive the Holy Ghost? Is it necessary to receive or be baptized with the Holy Ghost before (or at the same time) we can be filled with the Holy Ghost? Why or why not? Who was the first person filled with the Holy Ghost? (Luke 1:41) And Jesus will come to you again! (20:19 – 31)

date_____

LOVEST THOU ME...FEED MY LAMBS

John 21:12, 15 – 17 (KJV)

¹² Jesus saith unto them, Come *and* dine. And none of the disciples durst ask him, Who art thou? knowing that it was the Lord.

¹⁵ So when they had dined, Jesus saith to Simon Peter, Simon, *son* of Jonas, lovest thou me more than these? He saith unto him, Yea, Lord; thou knowest that I love thee. He saith unto him, Feed my lambs.

¹⁶ He saith to him again the second time, Simon, *son* of Jonas, lovest thou me? He saith unto him, Yea, Lord; thou knowest that I love thee. He saith unto him, Feed my sheep.

¹⁷ He saith unto him the third time, Simon, *son* of Jonas, lovest thou me? Peter was grieved because he said unto him the third time, Lovest thou me? And he said unto him, Lord, thou knowest all things; thou knowest that I love thee. Jesus saith unto him, Feed my sheep.

We can never go wrong **giving** ourselves away to **honor the name of Jesus.**

_____
_____
_____
_____
_____

date_____

HE (JESUS) THROUGH THE HOLY GHOST :2

Acts 1:1 – 4 (KJV)

¹ The former treatise have I made, O Theophilus, of all that Jesus began both to do and teach,

² Until the day in which he was taken up, after that he through the Holy Ghost had given commandments unto the apostles whom he had chosen:

³ To whom also he shewed himself alive after his passion by many infallible proofs, being seen of them forty days, and speaking of the things pertaining to the kingdom of God:

⁴ And, being assembled together with *them*, commanded them that they should not depart from Jerusalem, but wait for the promise of the Father, which, *saith he*, ye have heard of me.

The same Spirit who filled all these men and women gathered together, also fills you!

_____
_____
_____
_____
_____
_____
_____
_____

PROMISE...BAPTIZED WITH THE HOLY GHOST :5

Acts 1:3 – 5 (KJV)

³ To whom also he shewed himself alive after his passion by many infallible proofs, being seen of them forty days, and speaking of the things pertaining to the kingdom of God:
⁴ And, being assembled together with *them*, commanded them that they should not depart from Jerusalem, but wait for the promise of the Father, which, *saith he*, ye have heard of me.
⁵ For John truly baptized with water; but ye shall be baptized with the Holy Ghost not many days hence.

Jesus told them to wait for the promise and they would surely be baptized with the Holy Ghost in a few days! We are Christians, **extensions of Christ through the Holy Ghost.**

_____
_____
_____
_____
_____
_____
_____
_____
_____

RECEIVE POWER, AFTER THE HOLY GHOST :8

Acts 1:5 – 9 (KJV)

⁵ For John truly baptized with water; but ye shall be baptized with the Holy Ghost not many days hence.
⁶ When they therefore were come together, they asked of him, saying, Lord, wilt thou at this time restore again the kingdom to Israel?
⁷ And he said unto them, It is not for you to know the times or the seasons, which the Father hath put in his own power.
⁸ But ye shall receive power, after that the Holy Ghost is come upon you: and ye shall be witnesses unto me both in Jerusalem, and in all Judaea, and in Samaria, and unto the uttermost part of the earth.
⁹ And when he had spoken these things, while they beheld, he was taken up; and a cloud received him out of their sight.

What does the phrase "come upon" mean? (see Matthew 6:13; 12:28 – 29; Luke 11:20)

_____
_____
_____
_____

date_____

HOLY GHOST BY THE MOUTH OF DAVID SPAKE

Acts 1:16, 20 – 22 (KJV)

¹⁶ Men *and* brethren, this scripture must needs have been fulfilled, which the Holy Ghost by the mouth of David spake before concerning Judas, which was guide to them that took Jesus.
²⁰ For it is written in the book of Psalms, Let his habitation be desolate, and let no man dwell therein: and his bishoprick let another take.
²¹ Wherefore of these men which have companied with us all the time that the Lord Jesus went in and out among us,
²² Beginning from the baptism of John, unto that same day that he was taken up from us, must one be ordained to be a witness with us of his resurrection.

Jesus told the 11 and they have spread the word to hundreds of people and over 120 are waiting in the upper room (1:1, 12). Who is speaking the sermon in these verses and where was he?

date_____

FILLED WITH THE HOLY GHOST...AS THE SPIRIT

Acts 2:1 – 4 (KJV)

¹ And when the day of Pentecost was fully come, they were all with one accord in one place.
² And suddenly there came a sound from heaven as of a rushing mighty wind, and it filled all the house where they were sitting.
³ And there appeared unto them cloven tongues like as of fire, and it sat upon each of them.
⁴ And they were all filled with the Holy Ghost, and began to speak with other tongues, as the Spirit gave them utterance.

(Joel 2:28, 29) The gift of the Holy Ghost was poured out on all those waiting (1:4 – 5, 8; 10:45). A lotta fireworks! (see 1 Peter 1:20 – 21; John 14:12, 17) How many in the upper room received the Holy Ghost? (1:5/11:16; 2:4/10:47; 11:15/10:44; 10:45/11:17; 15:8/2:4) (see Luke 24:49) The Spirit in Jesus is now in every one of them.

POUR OUT OF MY SPIRIT...MY SPIRIT

Acts 2:14 – 18 (KJV)
14 But Peter, standing up with the eleven, lifted up his voice, and said unto them, Ye men of Judaea, and all *ye* that dwell at Jerusalem, be this known unto you, and hearken to my words:

15 For these are not drunken, as ye suppose, seeing it is *but* the third hour of the day.

16 But this is that which was spoken by the prophet Joel;

17 And it shall come to pass in the last days, saith God, I will pour out of my Spirit upon all flesh: and your sons and your daughters shall prophesy, and your young men shall see visions, and your old men shall dream dreams:

18 And on my servants and on my handmaidens I will pour out in those days of my Spirit; and they shall prophesy:

They were **filled for the assignment** and indwelled (Hebrews 9:14)? They saw what God said (2:11). When was the Holy Ghost given? (2:1) (see John 7:39; Psalm 107:20)

————————————————
————————————————
————————————————
————————————————
————————————————

THE PROMISE OF THE HOLY GHOST

Acts 2:29 – 33 (KJV)
29 Men *and* brethren, let me freely speak unto you of the patriarch David, that he is both dead and buried, and his sepulchre is with us unto this day.

30 Therefore being a prophet, and knowing that God had sworn with an oath to him, that of the fruit of his loins, according to the flesh, he would raise up Christ to sit on his throne;

31 He seeing this before spake of the resurrection of Christ, that his soul was not left in hell, neither his flesh did see corruption.

32 This Jesus hath God raised up, whereof we all are witnesses.

33 Therefore being by the right hand of God exalted, and having received of the Father the promise of the Holy Ghost, he hath shed forth this, which ye now see and hear.

David spoke by the Holy Ghost. David knew God would raise the Messiah from the dead.
Did they all or some receive? Could they all receive the same or just some? (1:14; 2:4)

————————————————
————————————————
————————————————
————————————————
————————————————

date_____

THE GIFT OF THE HOLY GHOST

Acts 2:34 – 39 (KJV)

34 For David is not ascended into the heavens: but he saith himself, The LORD said unto my Lord, Sit thou on my right hand,

35 Until I make thy foes thy footstool.

36 Therefore let all the house of Israel know assuredly, that God hath made that same Jesus, whom ye have crucified, both Lord and Christ.

37 Now when they heard *this*, they were pricked in their heart, and said unto Peter and to the rest of the apostles, Men *and* brethren, what shall we do?

38 Then Peter said unto them, Repent, and be baptized every one of you in the name of Jesus Christ for the remission of sins, and ye shall receive the gift of the Holy Ghost.

39 For the promise is unto you, and to your children, and to all that are afar off, *even* as many as the Lord our God shall call.

The promise of the gift is for all. Why? God wants to do more through us! (Genesis 10)

_____

_____

_____

_____

_____

date_____

GOD HATH SPOKEN BY... HOLY PROPHETS

Acts 3:19 – 22 (KJV)

19 Repent ye therefore, and be converted, that your sins may be blotted out, when the times of refreshing shall come from the presence of the Lord;

20 And he shall send Jesus Christ, which before was preached unto you:

21 Whom the heaven must receive until the times of restitution of all things, which God hath spoken by the mouth of all his holy prophets since the world began.

22 For Moses truly said unto the fathers, A prophet shall the Lord your God raise up unto you of your brethren, like unto me; him shall ye hear in all things whatsoever he shall say unto you.

Peter was preaching. The Holy Ghost was preaching the gospel through the prophets like Moses! As we purpose to get nearer to Him, He will get nearer to us. Where did he say the times of refreshing would come from? (3:19) What one promise had God made to all? (Joel 2:28 – 29; Acts 2:1 – 4; 17 – 18)

_____

_____

_____

_____

PETER, FILLED WITH THE HOLY GHOST

Acts 4:7, 8, 10, 11, 12 (KJV)

⁷ And when they had set them in the midst, they asked, By what power, or by what name, have ye done this?

⁸ Then Peter, filled with the Holy Ghost, said unto them, Ye rulers of the people, and elders of Israel,

¹⁰ Be it known unto you all, and to all the people of Israel, that by the name of Jesus Christ of Nazareth, whom ye crucified, whom God raised from the dead, *even* by him doth this man stand here before you whole.

¹¹ This is the stone which was set at nought of you builders, which is become the head of the corner.

¹² Neither is there salvation in any other: for there is none other name under heaven given among men, whereby we must be saved.

All glory belongs to Jesus. Have you been rejected? Jesus was rejected and He understands in the deepest way how you feel today. (see Hebrews 4:15; Acts 7:9)

_____
_____
_____
_____
_____
_____

FILLED WITH THE HOLY GHOST

Acts 4:29 – 32 (KJV)

²⁹ And now, Lord, behold their threatenings: and grant unto thy servants, that with all boldness they may speak thy word,

³⁰ By stretching forth thine hand to heal; and that signs and wonders may be done by the name of thy holy child Jesus.

³¹ And when they had prayed, the place was shaken where they were assembled together; and they were all filled with the Holy Ghost, and they spake the word of God with boldness.

³² And the multitude of them that believed were of one heart and of one soul: neither said any *of them* that ought of the things which he possessed was his own; but they had all things common.

We can pray the same prayer when we are threatened.

The congregation of thousands became unselfish all at the same time. How?

_____
_____
_____
_____
_____
_____

date_____

THE HOLY GHOST...THE SPIRIT OF THE LORD

Acts 5:3, 7, 8, 9, 18 (KJV)

³ But Peter said, Ananias, why hath Satan filled thine heart to lie to the Holy Ghost, and to keep back *part* of the price of the land?

⁷ And it was about the space of three hours after, when his wife, not knowing what was done, came in.

⁸ And Peter answered unto her, Tell me whether ye sold the land for so much? And she said, Yea, for so much.

⁹ Then Peter said unto her, How is it that ye have agreed together to tempt the Spirit of the Lord? behold, the feet of them which have buried thy husband *are* at the door, and shall carry thee out.

¹⁸ And laid their hands on the apostles, and put them in the common prison.

The Holy Ghost defended the church! The same thing happened to them because they were in agreement with Satan to destroy the church; but **grace is an indestructible seed.**

_____
_____
_____
_____
_____
_____
_____

date_____

WITNESSES...THE HOLY GHOST

Acts 5:22, 28, 29, 32 (KJV)

²² But when the officers came, and found them not in the prison, they returned, and told,

²⁸ Saying, Did not we straitly command you that ye should not teach in this name? and, behold, ye have filled Jerusalem with your doctrine, and intend to bring this man's blood upon us.

²⁹ Then Peter and the *other* apostles answered and said, We ought to obey God rather than men.

³² And we are his witnesses of these things; and *so is* also the Holy Ghost, whom God hath given to them that obey him.

The Holy Ghost was the Witness. Peter testified before the most powerful governing body of that day. The apostles rejoiced to suffer for the name of Jesus (5:41).

_____
_____
_____
_____
_____
_____
_____
_____

FULL OF THE HOLY GHOST AND WISDOM

Acts 6:1 – 3 (KJV)
[1] And in those days, when the number of the disciples was multiplied, there arose a murmuring of the Grecians against the Hebrews, because their widows were neglected in the daily ministration.
[2] Then the twelve called the multitude of the disciples *unto them*, and said, It is not reason that we should leave the word of God, and serve tables.
[3] Wherefore, brethren, look ye out among you seven men of honest report, full of the Holy Ghost and wisdom, whom we may appoint over this business.

A life with a mature reputation of character and under the influence of the Holy Ghost and a desire for God's wisdom were prerequisites for caring for widows. (see Galatians 5:22) How did God describe the way the Spirit-transfer happens? (Numbers 27:18 – 23)

_____
_____
_____
_____
_____
_____
_____

FULL OF FAITH AND OF THE HOLY GHOST

Acts 6:4 – 7 (KJV)
[4] But we will give ourselves continually to prayer, and to the ministry of the word.
[5] And the saying pleased the whole multitude: and they chose Stephen, a man full of faith and of the Holy Ghost, and Philip, and Prochorus, and Nicanor, and Timon, and Parmenas, and Nicolas a proselyte of Antioch:
[6] Whom they set before the apostles: and when they had prayed, they laid *their* hands on them.
[7] And the word of God increased; and the number of the disciples multiplied in Jerusalem greatly; and a great company of the priests were obedient to the faith.

Increase came when **unity was restored through serving.** One of the ministers chosen was Stephen.

_____
_____
_____
_____
_____
_____
_____
_____

NOT ABLE TO RESIST THE... SPIRIT

Acts 6:8 – 10 (KJV)

[8] And Stephen, full of faith and power, did great wonders and miracles among the people.

[9] Then there arose certain of the synagogue, which is called *the synagogue* of the Libertines, and Cyrenians, and Alexandrians, and of them of Cilicia and of Asia, disputing with Stephen.

[10] And they were not able to resist the wisdom and the spirit by which he spake.

An army couldn't successfully debate him because they were arguing with the Spirit of our Father, who was **Stephen's Backup.** Stephen didn't have to talk to them; but as long as he wanted to, **the Spirit was present (Luke 21:12 – 15).** Stephen preaches:

_____
_____
_____
_____
_____
_____
_____
_____
_____
_____

RESIST THE HOLY GHOST

Acts 7:45 – 51 (KJV)

[45] Which also our fathers that came after brought in with Jesus into the possession of the Gentiles, whom God drave out before the face of our fathers, unto the days of David;

[46] Who found favour before God, and desired to find a tabernacle for the God of Jacob.

[47] But Solomon built him an house.

[48] Howbeit the most High dwelleth not in temples made with hands; as saith the prophet,

[49] Heaven *is* my throne, and earth *is* my footstool: what house will ye build me? saith the Lord: or what *is* the place of my rest?

[50] Hath not my hand made all these things?

[51] Ye stiffnecked and uncircumcised in heart and ears, ye do always resist the Holy Ghost: as your fathers *did*, so *do* ye.

Stephen told them **their ancestors wouldn't put their trust in the Spirit of God.** The people rejected Stephen (the messenger for God) and **they rejected Jesus.**

_____
_____
_____
_____

FULL OF THE HOLY GHOST

Acts 7:52 – 55 (KJV)

⁵² Which of the prophets have not your fathers persecuted? and they have slain them which shewed before of the coming of the Just One; of whom ye have been now the betrayers and murderers:

⁵³ Who have received the law by the disposition of angels, and have not kept *it*.

⁵⁴ When they heard these things, they were cut to the heart, and they gnashed on him with *their* teeth.

⁵⁵ But he, being full of the Holy Ghost, looked up stedfastly into heaven, and saw the glory of God, and Jesus standing on the right hand of God,

Stephen was martyred for his sermon. The impact of **Stephen's suffering and sermon and death, softened** the hardened heart of Saul, who would **never forget Stephen.**

We also **impact the hearts** of those who come to Jesus **after we are in heaven**.

_____
_____
_____
_____
_____
_____

PRAYED...RECEIVE THE HOLY GHOST :15

Acts 8:5, 12, 14 – 16 (KJV)

⁵ Then Philip went down to the city of Samaria, and preached Christ unto them.

¹² But when they believed Philip preaching the things concerning the kingdom of God, and the name of Jesus Christ, they were baptized, both men and women.

¹⁴ Now when the apostles which were at Jerusalem heard that Samaria had received the word of God, they sent unto them Peter and John:

¹⁵ Who, when they were come down, prayed for them, that they might receive the Holy Ghost:

¹⁶ (For as yet he was fallen upon none of them: only they were baptized in the name of the Lord Jesus.)

What was Philip doing in Samaria? What does it mean "received the word of God"? Had the Holy Ghost entered or "fallen upon" or come upon everyone of them?

_____
_____
_____
_____
_____
_____

date_____

HANDS...RECEIVED THE HOLY GHOST :17

Acts 8:14 – 17 (KJV)

¹⁴ Now when the apostles which were at Jerusalem heard that Samaria had received the word of God, they sent unto them Peter and John:

¹⁵ Who, when they were come down, prayed for them, that they might receive the Holy Ghost:

¹⁶ (For as yet he was fallen upon none of them: only they were baptized in the name of the Lord Jesus.)

¹⁷ Then laid they *their* hands on them, and they received the Holy Ghost.

Those who had received the Holy Ghost could have been baptized in water again, this time in the name of the Lord Jesus and the first time, in the baptism of John (19:1 – 5)!

_____
_____
_____
_____
_____
_____
_____
_____
_____
_____
_____

date_____

HANDS...THE HOLY GHOST WAS GIVEN :18

Acts 8:17 – 19 (KJV)

¹⁷ Then laid they *their* hands on them, and they received the Holy Ghost.

¹⁸ And when Simon saw that through laying on of the apostles' hands the Holy Ghost was given, he offered them money,

¹⁹ Saying, Give me also this power, that on whomsoever I lay hands, he may receive the Holy Ghost.

Did they all receive? What did Simon see? Was Simon's heart visible? Did Simon receive the Holy Ghost? Was Simon humble? Was Simon seeking to please God or himself? (see 1 John 3:3; Matthew 5:1 – 3; Proverbs 16:18) What does Simon's story teach us?

_____
_____
_____
_____
_____
_____
_____
_____
_____
_____
_____

date_____
MAY RECEIVE THE HOLY GHOST :19

Acts 8:18 – 22 (KJV)

18 And when Simon saw that through laying on of the apostles' hands the Holy Ghost was given, he offered them money,

19 Saying, Give me also this power, that on whomsoever I lay hands, he may receive the Holy Ghost.

20 But Peter said unto him, Thy money perish with thee, because thou hast thought that the gift of God may be purchased with money.

21 Thou hast neither part nor lot in this matter: for thy heart is not right in the sight of God.

22 Repent therefore of this thy wickedness, and pray God, if perhaps the thought of thine heart may be forgiven thee.

Peter's saying Simon they didn't do this in their own strength. Did the Holy Ghost come upon all of them? What did Simon see? (see 16:31)

_____
_____
_____
_____
_____
_____
_____
_____

date_____
THE SPIRIT SAID UNTO PHILIP :29

Acts 8:29 – 33 (KJV)

29 Then the Spirit said unto Philip, Go near, and join thyself to this chariot.

30 And Philip ran thither to *him*, and heard him read the prophet Esaias, and said, Understandest thou what thou readest?

31 And he said, How can I, except some man should guide me? And he desired Philip that he would come up and sit with him.

32 The place of the scripture which he read was this, He was led as a sheep to the slaughter; and like a lamb dumb before his shearer, so opened he not his mouth:

33 In his humiliation his judgment was taken away: and who shall declare his generation? for his life is taken from the earth.

(Isaiah 53:7 – 8) Who will declare Him 'Lord'? Philip explained Esaias (Isaiah) was telling us about Jesus, the Messiah who came to take away sin permanently since we believe in Jesus, God's Son. (see 13:37; Romans 10:9 – 10; 1 Corinthians 12:3)

_____
_____
_____
_____

date_____

SPIRIT OF THE LORD CAUGHT AWAY PHILIP :39

Acts 8:35 – 39 (KJV)

³⁵ Then Philip opened his mouth, and began at the same scripture, and preached unto him Jesus.

³⁶ And as they went on *their* way, they came unto a certain water: and the eunuch said, See, *here is* water; what doth hinder me to be baptized?

³⁷ And Philip said, If thou believest with all thine heart, thou mayest. And he answered and said, I believe that Jesus Christ is the Son of God.

³⁸ And he commanded the chariot to stand still: and they went down both into the water, both Philip and the eunuch; and he baptized him.

³⁹ And when they were come up out of the water, the Spirit of the Lord caught away Philip, that the eunuch saw him no more: and he went on his way rejoicing.

The man in the chariot was **saved through the word of prophecy**! (see 1 John 4:15)

_____
_____
_____
_____
_____

date_____

SIGHT, AND BE FILLED WITH THE HOLY GHOST

Acts 9:13 – 17 (KJV)

¹³ Then Ananias answered, Lord, I have heard by many of this man, how much evil he hath done to thy saints at Jerusalem:

¹⁴ And here he hath authority from the chief priests to bind all that call on thy name.

¹⁵ But the Lord said unto him, Go thy way: for he is a chosen vessel unto me, to bear my name before the Gentiles, and kings, and the children of Israel:

¹⁶ For I will shew him how great things he must suffer for my name's sake.

¹⁷ And Ananias went his way, and entered into the house; and putting his hands on him said, Brother Saul, the Lord, *even* Jesus, that appeared unto thee in the way as thou camest, hath sent me, that thou mightest receive thy sight, and be filled with the Holy Ghost.

Ananias was sent on assignment to one person. Have you ever been afraid to do what God said? Who is the one person you are praying Jesus to talk to? (see 18:9 – 10)

_____
_____
_____
_____

date_____
COMFORT OF THE HOLY GHOST

Acts 9:20, 29 – 31 (KJV)
²⁰ And straightway he preached Christ in the synagogues, that he is the Son of God.
²⁹ And he spake boldly in the name of the Lord Jesus, and disputed against the Grecians: but they went about to slay him.
³⁰ *Which* when the brethren knew, they brought him down to Caesarea, and sent him forth to Tarsus.
³¹ Then had the churches rest throughout all Judaea and Galilee and Samaria, and were edified; and walking in the fear of the Lord, and in the comfort of the Holy Ghost, were multiplied.

When we live and teach the truth, the Holy Ghost will also guide us and be the Captain of our peace in the midst of life's storms. The people of the church were all encouraged and increased (9:20 – 31; Matthew 5:19; Colossians 3:15; 1 Corinthians 3:7) and the churches were multiplied. Is there a difference between the words increase and multiply?

_____
_____
_____
_____
_____

date_____
THE SPIRIT SAID

Acts 10:17, 19, 20, 21 (KJV)
¹⁷ Now while Peter doubted in himself what this vision which he had seen should mean, behold, the men which were sent from Cornelius had made enquiry for Simon's house, and stood before the gate,
¹⁹ While Peter thought on the vision, the Spirit said unto him, Behold, three men seek thee.
²⁰ Arise therefore, and get thee down, and go with them, doubting nothing: for I have sent them.
²¹ Then Peter went down to the men which were sent unto him from Cornelius; and said, Behold, I am he whom ye seek: what *is* the cause wherefore ye are come?

"…while…While…" God was working **in both houses** at the same time to accomplish His will! "…sent…sent…" The Spirit sent a word of knowledge and Cornelius sent a **team** to Peter. He went to one man, Cornelius and everyone was gathered in the house:

_____
_____
_____
_____
_____

ANOINTED JESUS...WITH THE HOLY GHOST

Acts 10:34 – 38 (KJV)
[34] Then Peter opened *his* mouth, and said, Of a truth I perceive that God is no respecter of persons:
[35] But in every nation he that feareth him, and worketh righteousness, is accepted with him.
[36] The word which *God* sent unto the children of Israel, preaching peace by Jesus Christ: (he is Lord of all:)
[37] That word, *I say*, ye know, which was published throughout all Judaea, and began from Galilee, after the baptism which John preached;
[38] How God anointed Jesus of Nazareth with the Holy Ghost and with power: who went about doing good, and healing all that were oppressed of the devil; for God was with him.

God was with Jesus, and Jesus was God. Jesus was always full of the Holy Ghost and anointed (see John 1:1 – 14; 10:30 – 33; 15:8; Genesis 4:7). Jesus demonstrated John 1:1!

_____
_____
_____
_____
_____
_____

HOLY GHOST FELL ON ALL THEM

Acts 10:40 – 44 (KJV)
[40] Him God raised up the third day, and shewed him openly;
[41] Not to all the people, but unto witnesses chosen before of God, *even* to us, who did eat and drink with him after he rose from the dead.
[42] And he commanded us to preach unto the people, and to testify that it is he which was ordained of God *to be* the Judge of quick and dead.
[43] To him give all the prophets witness, that through his name whosoever believeth in him shall receive remission of sins.
[44] While Peter yet spake these words, the Holy Ghost fell on all them which heard the word.

They believed and heard: Hearts were stirred when Peter preached who Jesus was and what Jesus did and what would be done in His name and the Day of Pentecost returned; and the Holy Ghost entered "all them which heard the word" (2:1 – 4; 8:16; 15:8).

_____
_____
_____
_____
_____
_____

date_____

POURED OUT THE GIFT OF THE HOLY GHOST

Acts 10:44 – 47 (KJV)
⁴⁴ While Peter yet spake these words, the Holy Ghost fell on all them which heard the word.

⁴⁵ And they of the circumcision which believed were astonished, as many as came with Peter, because that on the Gentiles also was poured out the gift of the Holy Ghost.

⁴⁶ For they heard them speak with tongues, and magnify God. Then answered Peter,

⁴⁷ Can any man forbid water, that these should not be baptized, which have received the Holy Ghost as well as we?

God loves every person the same! The Jewish people were surprised this time when **the gift of** the Holy Ghost was poured out on the Gentiles. The phrase "the gift of the Holy Ghost" is used only one other time in Acts 2:38. Can we describe the acts of the gift of the Holy Ghost? What's the difference in "poured out the gift of the Holy Ghost" in verse 45 and "received the Holy Ghost" in verse 47? Who poured out and who received?

_____
_____
_____
_____

date_____

RECEIVED THE HOLY GHOST AS WELL AS WE

Acts 10:45 – 48 (KJV)
⁴⁵ And they of the circumcision which believed were astonished, as many as came with Peter, because that on the Gentiles also was poured out the gift of the Holy Ghost.

⁴⁶ For they heard them speak with tongues, and magnify God. Then answered Peter,

⁴⁷ Can any man forbid water, that these should not be baptized, which have received the Holy Ghost as well as we?

⁴⁸ And he commanded them to be baptized in the name of the Lord. Then prayed they him to tarry certain days.

Jesus did it again! The One who gave the gift is God! There's a difference between pouring a cup of water to give to another to drink and drinking a cup of water ourselves. God had said, "I will pour out My Spirit on all..." (Joel 2:28). They received the Holy Ghost and then they were baptized in water. (see 8:17; 10:47; 19:2) Then what did Peter mean when he said "as well as we" (1:5; 2:4; 10:47; 11:16)?

_____
_____
_____
_____

THE SPIRIT BADE ME GO WITH THEM

Acts 11:4, 11 – 14 (KJV)

⁴ But Peter rehearsed *the matter* from the beginning, and expounded *it* by order unto them, saying,

¹¹ And, behold, immediately there were three men already come unto the house where I was, sent from Caesarea unto me

¹² And the Spirit bade me go with them, nothing doubting. Moreover these six brethren accompanied me, and we entered into the man's house:

¹³ And he shewed us how he had seen an angel in his house, which stood and said unto him, Send men to Joppa, and call for Simon, whose surname is Peter;

¹⁴ Who shall tell thee words, whereby thou and all thy house shall be saved.

Saved=born of Spirit. All angels from heaven will always exalt Jesus! (Galatians 1:3 – 10) Peter continued telling what happened when he came to the house of Cornelius:

_____
_____
_____
_____
_____
_____

HOLY GHOST FELL ON THEM, AS ON US

Acts 11:13 – 15 (KJV)

¹³ And he shewed us how he had seen an angel in his house, which stood and said unto him, Send men to Joppa, and call for Simon, whose surname is Peter;

¹⁴ Who shall tell thee words, whereby thou and all thy house shall be saved.

¹⁵ And as I began to speak, the Holy Ghost fell on them, as on us at the beginning.

Could they be **filled and baptized** with the Holy Spirit **at the same time**? All who believed on Jesus, have believed through the witness of these few apostles (John 17:20). Jesus said each of us are the salt that makes others **thirsty for the Water of Life** (Matthew 5:13; Acts 1:4 – 8; 2:1 – 4; 2:17 – 18; 10:44 – 47; 15:8; Joel 2:28). Was Pentecost a day or a daily thought, in the mind of God? Why did Peter say "the Holy Ghost fell on them, as on us?" And who was Peter talking about?

_____
_____
_____
_____
_____

BAPTIZED WITH THE HOLY GHOST

Acts 11:16 – 18, 20 (KJV)

[16] Then remembered I the word of the Lord, how that he said, John indeed baptized with water; but ye shall be baptized with the Holy Ghost.

[17] Forasmuch then as God gave them the like gift as he did unto us, who believed on the Lord Jesus Christ; what was I, that I could withstand God?

[18] When they heard these things, they held their peace, and glorified God, saying, Then hath God also to the Gentiles granted repentance unto life.

[20] And some of them were men of Cyprus and Cyrene, which, when they were come to Antioch, spake unto the Grecians, preaching the Lord Jesus.

They were also filled and baptized with the Holy Ghost at the same time! (1:5; 2:4; 10:44 – 47; 11:16) Is it possible to be filled with and baptized with the Holy Ghost at different times? What is "the word of the Lord" according to Peter? What is "the like gift?" Who do you think was the evangelist from Cyrene?

_____
_____
_____
_____
_____

FULL OF THE HOLY GHOST AND OF FAITH

Acts 11:20 – 24 (KJV)

[20] And some of them were men of Cyprus and Cyrene, which, when they were come to Antioch, spake unto the Grecians, preaching the Lord Jesus.

[21] And the hand of the Lord was with them: and a great number believed, and turned unto the Lord.

[22] Then tidings of these things came unto the ears of the church which was in Jerusalem: and they sent forth Barnabas, that he should go as far as Antioch.

[23] Who, when he came, and had seen the grace of God, was glad, and exhorted them all, that with purpose of heart they would cleave unto the Lord.

[24] For he was a good man, and full of the Holy Ghost and of faith: and much people was added unto the Lord.

Who saw the grace of God and encouraged all to remember who they are in Christ?

_____
_____
_____
_____
_____

SIGNIFIED BY THE SPIRIT

Acts 11:25 – 28 (KJV)

²⁵ Then departed Barnabas to Tarsus, for to seek Saul:

²⁶ And when he had found him, he brought him unto Antioch. And it came to pass, that a whole year they assembled themselves with the church, and taught much people. And the disciples were called Christians first in Antioch.

²⁷ And in these days came prophets from Jerusalem unto Antioch.

²⁸ And there stood up one of them named Agabus, and signified by the Spirit that there should be great dearth throughout all the world: which came to pass in the days of Claudius Caesar.

Signified and said aren't the same: The Spirit led Agabus to **prophesy** to warn the people so the church had the opportunity to send help. They did and were blessed (11:30; Romans 12:6). What two things did Paul and Barnabas do with the people at church?

_____
_____
_____
_____
_____
_____
_____

ARISE UP QUICKLY

Acts 12:5, 7, 8, 9 (KJV)

⁵ Peter therefore was kept in prison: but prayer was made without ceasing of the church unto God for him.

⁷ And, behold, the angel of the Lord came upon *him*, and a light shined in the prison: and he smote Peter on the side, and raised him up, saying, Arise up quickly. And his chains fell off from *his* hands.

⁸ And the angel said unto him, Gird thyself, and bind on thy sandals. And so he did. And he saith unto him, Cast thy garment about thee, and follow me.

⁹ And he went out, and followed him; and wist not that it was true which was done by the angel; but thought he saw a vision.

God is happy to make His people marvel (Mark 5:20; John 5:20). God is prepared to work quickly, right now for you. What was the church doing when an angel was sent to Peter? (12:5, 12)

_____
_____
_____
_____
_____
_____
_____

AND FASTED, THE HOLY GHOST SAID :2

Acts 13:1 – 3 (KJV)

[1] Now there were in the church that was at Antioch certain prophets and teachers; as Barnabas, and Simeon that was called Niger, and Lucius of Cyrene, and Manaen, which had been brought up with Herod the tetrarch, and Saul.

[2] As they ministered to the Lord, and fasted, the Holy Ghost said, Separate me Barnabas and Saul for the work whereunto I have called them.

[3] And when they had fasted and prayed, and laid *their* hands on them, they sent *them* away.

Paul and Barnabas were **set apart by God for a certain mission.** Were Paul and Barnabas more important to God at this point than when they **fulfilled their mission** to take supplies and support to Jerusalem (11:29, 30; 12:25)? (see 14:21 – 27**)**

_____
_____
_____
_____
_____
_____
_____
_____
_____

SENT FORTH BY THE HOLY GHOST :4

Acts 13:2 – 4 (KJV)

[2] As they ministered to the Lord, and fasted, the Holy Ghost said, Separate me Barnabas and Saul for the work whereunto I have called them.

[3] And when they had fasted and prayed, and laid *their* hands on them, they sent *them* away.

[4] So they, being sent forth by the Holy Ghost, departed unto Seleucia; and from thence they sailed to Cyprus.

Two of these five prophets and teachers were sent away for a mission by the Holy Ghost!

In the kingdom, there are many more sheep than shepherds (1 Corinthians 12:29)!

_____
_____
_____
_____
_____
_____
_____
_____
_____
_____
_____
_____

date_____

FILLED WITH THE HOLY GHOST :9

Acts 13:8 – 11 (KJV)

[8] But Elymas the sorcerer (for so is his name by interpretation) withstood them, seeking to turn away the deputy from the faith.

[9] Then Saul, (who also *is called* Paul,) filled with the Holy Ghost, set his eyes on him,

[10] And said, O full of all subtilty and all mischief, *thou* child of the devil, *thou* enemy of all righteousness, wilt thou not cease to pervert the right ways of the Lord?

[11] And now, behold, the hand of the Lord *is* upon thee, and thou shalt be blind, not seeing the sun for a season. And immediately there fell on him a mist and a darkness; and he went about seeking some to lead him by the hand.

Sorcery weakens the minds of people, slows the progress of their greatest potential and hinders them from the faith; but God's Word protects (Deuteronomy 18:9 – 18).

date_____

FILLED WITH JOY, AND WITH THE HOLY GHOST :52

Acts 13:44, 47, 48, 49, 52 (KJV)

[44] And the next sabbath day came almost the whole city together to hear the word of God.

[47] For so hath the Lord commanded us, *saying*, I have set thee to be a light of the Gentiles, that thou shouldest be for salvation unto the ends of the earth.

[48] And when the Gentiles heard this, they were glad, and glorified the word of the Lord: and as many as were ordained to eternal life believed.

[49] And the word of the Lord was published throughout all the region.

[52] And the disciples were filled with joy, and with the Holy Ghost.

No one is left out (13:47). How is their light still preaching to generations? (13:47 – 49) God loves to be glorified in us (13:48).

Grace will always abound (13:43)!

RECOMMENDED TO THE GRACE OF GOD

Acts 14:21 – 23, 25 – 27 (KJV)

²¹ And when they had preached the gospel to that city, and had taught many, they returned again to Lystra, and *to* Iconium, and Antioch,

²² Confirming the souls of the disciples, *and* exhorting them to continue in the faith, and that we must through much tribulation enter into the kingdom of God.

²³ And when they had ordained them elders in every church, and had prayed with fasting, they commended them to the Lord, on whom they believed.

²⁵ And when they had preached the word in Perga, they went down into Attalia:

²⁶ And thence sailed to Antioch, from whence they had been recommended to the grace of God for the work which they fulfilled.

²⁷ And when they were come, and had gathered the church together, they rehearsed all that God had done with them, and how he had opened the door of faith unto the Gentiles.

Apostleship wasn't easy but Paul and Barnabas never gave up (14:19 – 27).

_____
_____
_____
_____

GIVING THEM (GENTILES) THE HOLY GHOST

Acts 15:7, 8, 11 (KJV)

⁷ And when there had been much disputing, Peter rose up, and said unto them, Men *and* brethren, ye know how that a good while ago God made choice among us, that the Gentiles by my mouth should hear the word of the gospel, and believe.

⁸ And God, which knoweth the hearts, bare them witness, giving them the Holy Ghost, even as *he did* unto us;

¹¹ But we believe that through the grace of the Lord Jesus Christ we shall be saved, even as they.

They have the Holy Ghost too. David worshipped God. His heart's desire was to build the house of God and he was the only one called a man after God's own heart (15:1 – 28; 7:46). (see John 14:1 – 3) Why did Peter say "a good while ago"? (15:7; 10:1 – 47) What did Peter mean by his words "even as he [God] did unto us"? (15:8; 2:1 – 4, 17 – 18; Joel 2:28 – 29) (see 7:46; 11:21 – 23; 14:9, 33; 2 Samuel 7:11)

_____
_____
_____
_____

GOOD TO THE HOLY GHOST, AND TO US

Acts 15:13 – 16, 28 (KJV)

[13] And after they had held their peace, James answered, saying, Men *and* brethren, hearken unto me:

[14] Simeon hath declared how God at the first did visit the Gentiles, to take out of them a people for his name.

[15] And to this agree the words of the prophets; as it is written,

[16] After this I will return, and will build again the tabernacle of David, which is fallen down; and I will build again the ruins thereof, and I will set it up:

[28] For it seemed good to the Holy Ghost, and to us, to lay upon you no greater burden than these necessary things;

The Holy Ghost confirms the message and the name of Jesus. The Holy Ghost was teaching the disciples to keep their faith **in Christ alone.** The letter of burden was sent to the churches to **remove a burden** and to remind them of the heart of David (15:11 – 30).

_____

_____

_____

_____

FORBIDDEN OF THE HOLY GHOST

Acts 16:4 – 7 (KJV)

[4] And as they went through the cities, they delivered them the decrees for to keep, that were ordained of the apostles and elders which were at Jerusalem.

[5] And so were the churches established in the faith, and increased in number daily.

[6] Now when they had gone throughout Phrygia and the region of Galatia, and were forbidden of the Holy Ghost to preach the word in Asia,

[7] After they were come to Mysia, they assayed to go into Bithynia: but the Spirit suffered them not.

When you are afraid something will happen, what can you do to stop it? To begin prophecy is always encouraging or a warning to edify people. However, when unclean spirits cause us to be afraid, we can speak and prophesy against them one at a time or in a group. We can command them up close or far away. We are defeating them when we speak against them in faith in the blood of Jesus and the Word and all in Jesus' name.

_____

_____

_____

_____

BUT THE SPIRIT SUFFERED THEM NOT

Acts 16:7, 9, 10, 13 (KJV)

[7] After they were come to Mysia, they assayed to go into Bithynia: but the Spirit suffered them not.

[9] And a vision appeared to Paul in the night; There stood a man of Macedonia, and prayed him, saying, Come over into Macedonia, and help us.

[10] And after he had seen the vision, immediately we endeavoured to go into Macedonia, assuredly gathering that the Lord had called us for to preach the gospel unto them.

[13] And on the sabbath we went out of the city by a river side, where prayer was wont to be made; and we sat down, and spake unto the women which resorted *thither.*

As they were led by the Holy Ghost, churches were strengthened in the faith. In verse 4, who wrote and sent "the decrees," (bylaws, the letter of burden), for the churches? God is involved in the timing, direction and location of the missionary team the Holy Ghost **sealed and sent out**? (13:4) (see Joshua 6:25; 2 Corinthians 1:22)

_____

_____

_____

DWELLETH NOT IN TEMPLES MADE WITH HANDS

Acts 17:3, 24 – 27 (KJV)

[3] Opening and alleging, that Christ must needs have suffered, and risen again from the dead; and that this Jesus, whom I preach unto you, is Christ.

[24] God that made the world and all things therein, seeing that he is Lord of heaven and earth, dwelleth not in temples made with hands;

[25] Neither is worshipped with men's hands, as though he needed any thing, seeing he giveth to all life, and breath, and all things;

[26] And hath made of one blood all nations of men for to dwell on all the face of the earth, and hath determined the times before appointed, and the bounds of their habitation;

[27] That they should seek the Lord, if haply they might feel after him, and find him, though he be not far from every one of us:

God made you in His image (Genesis 1:27; John 14:17). Paul's sermon on Mars' Hill was life changing (17:22). What temples does God want to dwell in? (1 Corinthians 3:16)

_____

_____

_____

HAD BELIEVED THROUGH GRACE

Acts 18:24 – 28 (KJV)

²⁴ And a certain Jew named Apollos, born at Alexandria, an eloquent man, *and* mighty in the scriptures, came to Ephesus.

²⁵ This man was instructed in the way of the Lord; and being fervent in the spirit, he spake and taught diligently the things of the Lord, knowing only the baptism of John.

²⁶ And he began to speak boldly in the synagogue: whom when Aquila and Priscilla had heard, they took him unto *them*, and expounded unto him the way of God more perfectly.

²⁷ And when he was disposed to pass into Achaia, the brethren wrote, exhorting the disciples to receive him: who, when he was come, helped them much which had believed through grace:

²⁸ For he mightily convinced the Jews, *and that* publickly, shewing by the scriptures that Jesus was Christ.

When did Apollos begin to help the Christians and how did he do it?

_____
_____
_____
_____
_____

RECEIVED THE HOLY GHOST

Acts 19:1 – 5 (KJV)

¹ And it came to pass, that, while Apollos was at Corinth, Paul having passed through the upper coasts came to Ephesus: and finding certain disciples,

² He said unto them, Have ye received the Holy Ghost since ye believed? And they said unto him, We have not so much as heard whether there be any Holy Ghost.

³ And he said unto them, Unto what then were ye baptized? And they said, Unto John's baptism.

⁴ Then said Paul, John verily baptized with the baptism of repentance, saying unto the people, that they should believe on him which should come after him, that is, on Christ Jesus.

⁵ When they heard *this*, they were baptized in the name of the Lord Jesus.

Who asked, "Unto what then were ye baptized?" Did the Apostle Paul believe receiving the Holy Ghost was a requirement to believe? (see Acts 13:24 – 25)

_____
_____
_____
_____
_____

THE HOLY GHOST CAME ON THEM

Acts 19:5 – 7 (KJV)
[5] When they heard *this*, they were baptized in the name of the Lord Jesus.
[6] And when Paul had laid *his* hands upon them, the Holy Ghost came on them; and they spake with tongues, and prophesied.
[7] And all the men were about twelve.

Why did Paul ask, "Unto what then were ye baptized" (19:1 – 5)? What did he mean when he asked if they had, "received the Holy Ghost" (19:1 – 5)? (see 8:15, 17; 10:47) What happened when they **heard Christ Jesus had already come**? (19:5) (see 18:24 – 28) Did Paul want them to receive the Holy Ghost? (19:1 – 2) (see 9:17)

Who sent Paul to Ephesus where he heard this discussion? Who sent these (1:8; 8:14; 9:6, 11; 10:3 – 5, 13, 19 – 20, 28, 30; 11:11 – 17; 13:2 – 3; 16:9; John 3:16 – 17; 20:21)?

PAUL PURPOSED IN THE SPIRIT

Acts 19:17, 18, 20 – 22 (KJV)
[17] And this was known to all the Jews and Greeks also dwelling at Ephesus; and fear fell on them all, and the name of the Lord Jesus was magnified.
[18] And many that believed came, and confessed, and shewed their deeds.
[20] So mightily grew the word of God and prevailed.
[21] After these things were ended, Paul purposed in the spirit, when he had passed through Macedonia and Achaia, to go to Jerusalem, saying, After I have been there, I must also see Rome.
[22] So he sent into Macedonia two of them that ministered unto him, Timotheus and Erastus; but he himself stayed in Asia for a season.

Paul had made his plans waiting for the Spirit to lead his spirit in the way of the Lord. (see John 17:21) How important is it to plan our steps and reason by the Spirit?

_____
_____
_____
_____
_____
_____
_____

THE HOLY GHOST WITNESSETH

Acts 20:20 – 24 (KJV)
²⁰ *And* how I kept back nothing that was profitable *unto you*, but have shewed you, and have taught you publickly, and from house to house,
²¹ Testifying both to the Jews, and also to the Greeks, repentance toward God, and faith toward our Lord Jesus Christ.
²² And now, behold, I go bound in the spirit unto Jerusalem, not knowing the things that shall befall me there:
²³ Save that the Holy Ghost witnesseth in every city, saying that bonds and afflictions abide me.
²⁴ But none of these things move me, neither count I my life dear unto myself, so that I might finish my course with joy, and the ministry, which I have received of the Lord Jesus, to testify the gospel of the grace of God.

The Holy Ghost confirmed Paul's ministry of suffering as Jesus had said (9:13 – 17).

HOLY GHOST HATH MADE YOU OVERSEERS

Acts 20:28, 29, 31, 32 (KJV)
²⁸ Take heed therefore unto yourselves, and to all the flock, over the which the Holy Ghost hath made you overseers, to feed the church of God, which he hath purchased with his own blood.
²⁹ For I know this, that after my departing shall grievous wolves enter in among you, not sparing the flock.
³¹ Therefore watch, and remember, that by the space of three years I ceased not to warn every one night and day with tears.
³² And now, brethren, I commend you to God, and to the word of his grace, which is able to build you up, and to give you an inheritance among all them which are sanctified.

Spiritual gifts were given to feed the flock! (see John 21:17) We are overseers, **promoted by the Holy Ghost**, feeding the church of God (Matthew 4:4; John 21:15). (see 1 Timothy 3) What is an overseer? Whose the Promoter? (Psalm 75:7)

_____
_____
_____
_____
_____

date_____

SAID...THROUGH THE SPIRIT

Acts 21:4 – 7 (KJV)

⁴ And finding disciples, we tarried there seven days: who said to Paul through the Spirit, that he should not go up to Jerusalem.

⁵ And when we had accomplished those days, we departed and went our way; and they all brought us on our way, with wives and children, till *we were* out of the city: and we kneeled down on the shore, and prayed.

⁶ And when we had taken our leave one of another, we took ship; and they returned home again.

⁷ And when we had finished *our* course from Tyre, we came to Ptolemais, and saluted the brethren, and abode with them one day.

The missionaries leave their families to go to tell the world about Jesus. How could the people believe in Jesus if they haven't heard His name? How will they hear without a preacher? How will they preach Jesus unless they are sent? (Romans 10:14)

date_____

THUS SAITH THE HOLY GHOST

Acts 21:9 – 12 (KJV)

⁹ And the same man had four daughters, virgins, which did prophesy.

¹⁰ And as we tarried *there* many days, there came down from Judaea a certain prophet, named Agabus.

¹¹ And when he was come unto us, he took Paul's girdle, and bound his own hands and feet, and said, Thus saith the Holy Ghost, So shall the Jews at Jerusalem bind the man that owneth this girdle, and shall deliver *him* into the hands of the Gentiles.

¹² And when we heard these things, both we, and they of that place, besought him not to go up to Jerusalem.

The prophecy confirmed the word of the Lord; the word the Spirit had told Paul through the disciples earlier (20:23). Paul received confirmation from the disciples too (21:4). God will continue to confirm His word to our heart also.

WHY PERSECUTEST THOU ME?

Acts 22:7 – 11 (KJV)
7 And I fell unto the ground, and heard a voice saying unto me, Saul, Saul, why persecutest thou me?
8 And I answered, Who art thou, Lord? And he said unto me, I am Jesus of Nazareth, whom thou persecutest.
9 And they that were with me saw indeed the light, and were afraid; but they heard not the voice of him that spake to me.
10 And I said, What shall I do, Lord? And the Lord said unto me, Arise, and go into Damascus; and there it shall be told thee of all things which are appointed for thee to do.
11 And when I could not see for the glory of that light, being led by the hand of them that were with me, I came into Damascus.

Paul told his testimony, his story of before and after the day he encountered Jesus (22:4, 12 – 21). What is your testimony?

_____
_____
_____
_____
_____
_____

THY (THE LORD'S) MARTYR STEPHEN

Acts 22:18 – 21 (KJV)
18 And saw him saying unto me, Make haste, and get thee quickly out of Jerusalem: for they will not receive thy testimony concerning me.
19 And I said, Lord, they know that I imprisoned and beat in every synagogue them that believed on thee:
20 And when the blood of thy martyr Stephen was shed, I also was standing by, and consenting unto his death, and kept the raiment of them that slew him.
21 And he said unto me, Depart: for I will send thee far hence unto the Gentiles.

Paul was saying, "Lord these people know my past. They know the person I was and they will not believe me." (8:1 – 3; 22:4, 12 – 21) (see Exodus 3) Are you afraid people will remember your past? Paul was afraid, but God didn't remember his past nor our past. We are not guilty in His sight. (see Jeremiah 31:34)

_____
_____
_____
_____
_____

date_____

BUT IF A SPIRIT OR AN ANGEL

Acts 23:6 – 9 (KJV)

[6] But when Paul perceived that the one part were Sadducees, and the other Pharisees, he cried out in the council, Men *and* brethren, I am a Pharisee, the son of a Pharisee: of the hope and resurrection of the dead I am called in question.

[7] And when he had so said, there arose a dissension between the Pharisees and the Sadducees: and the multitude was divided.

[8] For the Sadducees say that there is no resurrection, neither angel, nor spirit: but the Pharisees confess both.

[9] And there arose a great cry: and the scribes *that were* of the Pharisees' part arose, and strove, saying, We find no evil in this man: but if a spirit or an angel hath spoken to him, let us not fight against God.

Paul was in court as he used division like a military leader; and was rescued (23:27).

_____
_____
_____
_____
_____
_____
_____
_____

date_____

REASONED OF RIGHTEOUSNESS

Acts 24:24 – 27 (KJV)

[24] And after certain days, when Felix came with his wife Drusilla, which was a Jewess, he sent for Paul, and heard him concerning the faith in Christ.

[25] And as he reasoned of righteousness, temperance, and judgment to come, Felix trembled, and answered, Go thy way for this time; when I have a convenient season, I will call for thee.

[26] He hoped also that money should have been given him of Paul, that he might loose him: wherefore he sent for him the oftener, and communed with him.

[27] But after two years Porcius Festus came into Felix' room: and Felix, willing to shew the Jews a pleasure, left Paul bound.

Paul gave his testimony of faith in Jesus and Paul was left in prison. How does this remind you of Joseph in Genesis chapter 39 – 40?

_____
_____
_____
_____
_____
_____
_____

date_____
AFFIRMED

Acts 25:14, 19, 25, 27 (KJV)

¹⁴ And when they had been there many days, Festus declared Paul's cause unto the king, saying, There is a certain man left in bonds by Felix:

¹⁹ But had certain questions against him of their own superstition, and of one Jesus, which was dead, whom Paul affirmed to be alive.

²⁵ But when I found that he had committed nothing worthy of death, and that he himself hath appealed to Augustus, I have determined to send him.

²⁷ For it seemeth to me unreasonable to send a prisoner, and not withal to signify the crimes *laid* against him.

Festus, the new governor, repeated Paul's witness to the king saying Jesus is alive! Paul was in prison on purpose – to preach the gospel to the governors. Some times the most unlikely place is the safest (25:1 – 5).

_____
_____
_____
_____
_____
_____
_____
_____
_____

date_____
FOR THIS PURPOSE

Acts 26:15 – 19 (KJV)

¹⁵ And I said, Who art thou, Lord? And he said, I am Jesus whom thou persecutest.

¹⁶ But rise, and stand upon thy feet: for I have appeared unto thee for this purpose, to make thee a minister and a witness both of these things which thou hast seen, and of those things in the which I will appear unto thee;

¹⁷ Delivering thee from the people, and *from* the Gentiles, unto whom now I send thee,

¹⁸ To open their eyes, *and* to turn *them* from darkness to light, and *from* the power of Satan unto God, that they may receive forgiveness of sins, and inheritance among them which are sanctified by faith that is in me.

¹⁹ Whereupon, O king Agrippa, I was not disobedient unto the heavenly vision:

Saul/Paul tells the details. What list of purposes did Jesus say were for Saul/Paul? (1:8; 9:5 – 15) Can we be a witness for a short time? Can we be a witness for a life time?

_____
_____
_____
_____
_____

date_____

THE ANGEL OF GOD...SAYING FEAR NOT

Acts 27:21 – 24, 44 (KJV)

²¹ But after long abstinence Paul stood forth in the midst of them, and said, Sirs, ye should have hearkened unto me, and not have loosed from Crete, and to have gained this harm and loss.
²² And now I exhort you to be of good cheer: for there shall be no loss of *any man's* life among you, but of the ship.
²³ For there stood by me this night the angel of God, whose I am, and whom I serve,
²⁴ Saying, Fear not, Paul; thou must be brought before Caesar: and, lo, God hath given thee all them that sail with thee.
⁴⁴ And the rest, some on boards, and some on *broken pieces* of the ship. And so it came to pass, that they escaped all safe to land.

God gave them grace, but Paul is in a storm he didn't cause. He had warned them but they didn't listen. Have you been there?

_____
_____
_____
_____
_____
_____
_____

date_____

HOLY GHOST BY ESAIAS (ISAIAH)...SAYING

Acts 28:25 – 28 (KJV)

²⁵ And when they agreed not among themselves, they departed, after that Paul had spoken one word, Well spake the Holy Ghost by Esaias the prophet unto our fathers,
²⁶ Saying, Go unto this people, and say, Hearing ye shall hear, and shall not understand; and seeing ye shall see, and not perceive:
²⁷ For the heart of this people is waxed gross, and their ears are dull of hearing, and their eyes have they closed; lest they should see with *their* eyes, and hear with *their* ears, and understand with *their* heart, and should be converted, and I should heal them.
²⁸ Be it known therefore unto you, that the salvation of God is sent unto the Gentiles, and *that* they will hear it.

Paul used the words of the prophet Esaias (Isaiah) to **build his case for grace** (Isaiah 6). Paul silenced his judges (28:1 – 9). He explained this was because of prophecy – a powerful and confirming testimony. (see Revelation 19:10)

_____
_____
_____
_____

date_____
SPIRIT OF HOLINESS

Romans 1:1 – 4 (KJV)
[1] Paul, a servant of Jesus Christ, called *to be* an apostle, separated unto the gospel of God,
[2] (Which he had promised afore by his prophets in the holy scriptures,)
[3] Concerning his Son Jesus Christ our Lord, which was made of the seed of David according to the flesh;
[4] And declared *to be* the Son of God with power, according to the spirit of holiness, by the resurrection from the dead:

The Spirit of holiness is His Spirit showing His work through us. (see 1 Corinthians 4:20 – 21) We receive the Spirit of holiness when we were born again and we want to please God. As surely as we couldn't earn God's power, we can't earn His holiness. (see Acts 3:1 – 12; Psalm 51:12; 1 Chronicles 16:29; 2 Chronicles 20:21; Psalm 29:1 – 2; 96:7 – 9)

_____
_____
_____
_____
_____
_____
_____
_____

date_____
THE HOLY GHOST WHICH IS GIVEN UNTO US

Romans 5:1 – 5 (KJV)
[1] Therefore being justified by faith, we have peace with God through our Lord Jesus Christ:
[2] By whom also we have access by faith into this grace wherein we stand, and rejoice in hope of the glory of God.
[3] And not only *so*, but we glory in tribulations also: knowing that tribulation worketh patience;
[4] And patience, experience; and experience, hope:
[5] And hope maketh not ashamed; because the love of God is shed abroad in our hearts by the Holy Ghost which is given unto us.

The love of God unites us to Him and the Holy Ghost is the seal of each salvation. We are justified in Him because He was the only One who could take away the penalty.

_____
_____
_____
_____
_____
_____
_____
_____

IN NEWNESS OF SPIRIT

Romans 7:4 – 7 (KJV)
[4] Wherefore, my brethren, ye also are become dead to the law by the body of Christ; that ye should be married to another, *even* to him who is raised from the dead, that we should bring forth fruit unto God.
[5] For when we were in the flesh, the motions of sins, which were by the law, did work in our members to bring forth fruit unto death.
[6] But now we are delivered from the law, that being dead wherein we were held; that we should serve in newness of spirit, and not *in* the oldness of the letter.
[7] What shall we say then? *Is* the law sin? God forbid. Nay, I had not known sin, but by the law: for I had not known lust, except the law had said, Thou shalt not covet.

Only by the Spirit do we serve the living God with the newness of His Spirit in us. Where does the newness of the Spirit come from? (Hebrews 9:12 – 14; Galatians 3:5)

_____
_____
_____
_____
_____

WALK...AFTER THE SPIRIT :1

Romans 8:1 – 3 (KJV)
[1] *There is* therefore now no condemnation to them which are in Christ Jesus, who walk not after the flesh, but after the Spirit.
[2] For the law of the Spirit of life in Christ Jesus hath made me free from the law of sin and death.
[3] For what the law could not do, in that it was weak through the flesh, God sending his own Son in the likeness of sinful flesh, and for sin, condemned sin in the flesh:

When we exhibit a genuine effort to do the right thing for our heavenly Father, we are walking in the Spirit! **Time with God is the** perfect **will of God** (Luke 10:38 – 32).
Walking in the Spirit is what we do with our day. We want to accomplish His purposes or do God's will in the earth not because we are perfect, but because **we are His.** (see Genesis 6:9; Psalm 37:4; John 4:34; 6:38 – 40; 10:10) Those who walk after the Spirit are those who walk not after the flesh.

_____
_____
_____
_____
_____

THE LAW OF THE SPIRIT OF LIFE IN CHRIST JESUS :2

Romans 8:1 – 4 (KJV)
¹ *There is* therefore now no condemnation to them which are in Christ Jesus, who walk not after the flesh, but after the Spirit.
² For the law of the Spirit of life in Christ Jesus hath made me free from the law of sin and death.
³ For what the law could not do, in that it was weak through the flesh, God sending his own Son in the likeness of sinful flesh, and for sin, condemned sin in the flesh:
⁴ That the righteousness of the law might be fulfilled in us, who walk not after the flesh, but after the Spirit.

We are under the law of the Spirit of life, and free, as we walk (living on purpose) after the Spirit! We are walking after the Spirit. As we lean on Him to guide our hearts, walking in the Spirit and we are in God's perfect will. As we go, we are showing God's Spirit in us and His calling on us (8:1, 4). What law is discussed in verse 2?

_____
_____
_____
_____
_____

AFTER THE SPIRIT THE THINGS OF THE SPIRIT :4

Romans 8:4 – 7 (KJV)
⁴ That the righteousness of the law might be fulfilled in us, who walk not after the flesh, but after the Spirit.
⁵ For they that are after the flesh do mind the things of the flesh; but they that are after the Spirit the things of the Spirit.
⁶ For to be carnally minded *is* death; but to be spiritually minded *is* life and peace.
⁷ Because the carnal mind *is* enmity against God: for it is not subject to the law of God, neither indeed can be.

We are walking in the Spirit as we purpose to dwell in the presence of God!
We walk in the Spirit and God is already saying, "Well done!" (8:1, 4, 5) As we step forward and refuse to look back we are walking with Jesus in the Spirit. We are only flesh but when we stir up **the Spirit in us** for His kingdom motives, **we are walking after the Spirit,** His Spirit and not our flesh.

_____
_____
_____
_____
_____

AFTER THE SPIRIT THE THINGS OF THE SPIRIT :5

Romans 8:5 – 7 (KJV)
5 For they that are after the flesh do mind the things of the flesh; but they that are after the Spirit the things of the Spirit.
6 For to be carnally minded *is* death; but to be spiritually minded *is* life and peace.
7 Because the carnal mind *is* enmity against God: for it is not subject to the law of God, neither indeed can be.

We've been saved and walking after the Spirit, the Spirit of God who abides in us through the faith He gave. His faith works through love (1 Corinthians 12:1 – 4).
We know we have turned from the flesh and we are spiritually minded. (see John 14:27; 1 Corinthians 2:13 – 16; 13:1 – 3) The things we do for love's sake are the things making Jesus visible to someone. These are the everlasting things, treasures in heaven.

_____

_____

_____

_____

_____

_____

IN THE SPIRIT...SPIRIT OF GOD DWELL IN YOU :9

Romans 8:7 – 9 (KJV)
7 Because the carnal mind *is* enmity against God: for it is not subject to the law of God, neither indeed can be.
8 So then they that are in the flesh cannot please God.
9 But ye are not in the flesh, but in the Spirit, if so be that the Spirit of God dwell in you. Now if any man have not the Spirit of Christ, he is none of his.

When is God pleased according to these verses?
When we serve God, we are worshipping Him, being spiritually minded, trusting Him (8:6; Exodus 5)! We know we belong to God, our Father in heaven. We belong!
How can we know we are in the Spirit? When the Spirit of God dwells in us, we are in the Spirit (8:9). That was when we began to care about the things of God. That was the hour we became His.
Before we were saved, why didn't we want to obey and go God's way?

_____

_____

_____

_____

_____

THE SPIRIT IS LIFE BECAUSE OF RIGHTEOUSNESS :10

Romans 8:7 – 10 (KJV)

⁷ Because the carnal mind *is* enmity against God: for it is not subject to the law of God, neither indeed can be.
⁸ So then they that are in the flesh cannot please God.
⁹ But ye are not in the flesh, but in the Spirit, if so be that the Spirit of God dwell in you. Now if any man have not the Spirit of Christ, he is none of his.
¹⁰ And if Christ *be* in you, the body *is* dead because of sin; but the Spirit *is* life because of righteousness.

This righteousness is in us but not of us (7:6). The Spirit of life abides in us and He is one with our spirit. We are made righteous through the blood of Christ Jesus in our **spiritual veins.** What does God want you to do with His Spirit in you? (see Galatians 5:22 – 23) The Spirit who guides and teaches you is the same Holy Spirit who raised Jesus from the dead (Ephesians 1; John 14:17; 16:13).

THE SPIRIT...THAT RAISED UP JESUS...IN YOU :11

Romans 8:8 – 11 (KJV)

⁸ So then they that are in the flesh cannot please God.
⁹ But ye are not in the flesh, but in the Spirit, if so be that the Spirit of God dwell in you. Now if any man have not the Spirit of Christ, he is none of his.
¹⁰ And if Christ *be* in you, the body *is* dead because of sin; but the Spirit *is* life because of righteousness.
¹¹ But if the Spirit of him that raised up Jesus from the dead dwell in you, he that raised up Christ from the dead shall also quicken your mortal bodies by his Spirit that dwelleth in you.

When the Spirit of God raised Jesus from the dead, He was **raised up in you.**
As we sow a seed for Jesus and the least of these, **we will reap the hand of God** for us and upon our children (1 Corinthians 9:7 – 11).
Your enemy cannot destroy your dream!

_____
_____
_____
_____
_____
_____
_____

_____
_____
_____
_____
_____
_____
_____

IF YE THROUGH THE SPIRIT :13

Romans 8:10 – 13 (KJV)

[10] And if Christ *be* in you, the body *is* dead because of sin; but the Spirit *is* life because of righteousness.

[11] But if the Spirit of him that raised up Jesus from the dead dwell in you, he that raised up Christ from the dead shall also quicken your mortal bodies by his Spirit that dwelleth in you.

[12] Therefore, brethren, we are debtors, not to the flesh, to live after the flesh.

[13] For if ye live after the flesh, ye shall die: but if ye through the Spirit do mortify the deeds of the body, ye shall live.

The word "live" in Scripture is far beyond mere existence. When we continue to kill our past and forget what is behind us and lay aside the sin that entangles us, we will daily practice the teachings of Jesus Christ and **go forward** in the authority of His name.

What kind of life if he talking about in verse 13 in context of verses 1 – 12?

_____
_____
_____
_____
_____

LED BY THE SPIRIT OF GOD… ARE THE SONS :14

Romans 8:11 – 14 (KJV)

[11] But if the Spirit of him that raised up Jesus from the dead dwell in you, he that raised up Christ from the dead shall also quicken your mortal bodies by his Spirit that dwelleth in you.

[12] Therefore, brethren, we are debtors, not to the flesh, to live after the flesh.

[13] For if ye live after the flesh, ye shall die: but if ye through the Spirit do mortify the deeds of the body, ye shall live.

[14] For as many as are led by the Spirit of God, they are the sons of God.

When we have the Spirit of Christ, we are His. Then God has become our Daddy.

As we invest our lives in the things of God, we show Jesus is alive in us and witness for Jesus to others. (see Colossians 1:27; Jeremiah 32:17, 26, 27) God put the internet in the universe but it was thousands of years before mankind discovered it. What can you believe? Nothing shall be impossible to the one who believes. Who leads us?

_____
_____
_____
_____

SPIRIT OF ADOPTION :15

Romans 8:14 – 17 (KJV)
[14] For as many as are led by the Spirit of God, they are the sons of God.
[15] For ye have not received the spirit of bondage again to fear; but ye have received the Spirit of adoption, whereby we cry, Abba, Father.
[16] The Spirit itself beareth witness with our spirit, that we are the children of God:
[17] And if children, then heirs; heirs of God, and joint-heirs with Christ; if so be that we suffer with *him*, that we may be also glorified together.

When a little 2 year old girl reaches up for her daddy, and she wants him to pick her up, what is the little one thinking about daddy?
When I was little, I believed my daddy loved me and would give me the moon if he had it and I asked for it. Where does the Spirit of adoption motivate us? What does the Spirit of wisdom want to do for us?

_____
_____
_____
_____
_____
_____
_____

THE SPIRIT ITSELF BEARETH WITNESS :16

Romans 8:14 – 17 (KJV)
[14] For as many as are led by the Spirit of God, they are the sons of God.
[15] For ye have not received the spirit of bondage again to fear; but ye have received the Spirit of adoption, whereby we cry, Abba, Father.
[16] The Spirit itself beareth witness with our spirit, that we are the children of God:
[17] And if children, then heirs; heirs of God, and joint-heirs with Christ; if so be that we suffer with *him*, that we may be also glorified together.

"…we suffer with him…be also glorified together…" What does that mean for you?
The Spirit in love affirms our adoption. We know whose we are! How has he described the children of God? Who witnesses?

_____
_____
_____
_____
_____
_____
_____

HAVE THE FIRSTFRUITS OF THE SPIRIT :23

Romans 8:19 – 23 (KJV)

¹⁹ For the earnest expectation of the creature waiteth for the manifestation of the sons of God.

²⁰ For the creature was made subject to vanity, not willingly, but by reason of him who hath subjected *the same* in hope,

²¹ Because the creature itself also shall be delivered from the bondage of corruption into the glorious liberty of the children of God.

²² For we know that the whole creation groaneth and travaileth in pain together until now.

²³ And not only *they*, but ourselves also, which have the firstfruits of the Spirit, even we ourselves groan within ourselves, waiting for the adoption, *to wit*, the redemption of our body.

We ourselves have the firstfruits of the Spirit. Whose Spirit is in us? Why and how?

_____

_____

_____

_____

_____

_____

_____

_____

SPIRIT ALSO HELPETH… INTERCESSION :26

Romans 8:23 – 26 (KJV)

²³ And not only *they*, but ourselves also, which have the firstfruits of the Spirit, even we ourselves groan within ourselves, waiting for the adoption, *to wit*, the redemption of our body.

²⁴ For we are saved by hope: but hope that is seen is not hope: for what a man seeth, why doth he yet hope for?

²⁵ But if we hope for that we see not, *then* do we with patience wait for *it*.

²⁶ Likewise the Spirit also helpeth our infirmities: for we know not what we should pray for as we ought: but the Spirit itself maketh intercession for us with groanings which cannot be uttered.

The Spirit in the heart of love, who knows every **word about God**, is praying for you right now (1 John 4:7, 9). (see Isaiah 53; Acts 7:34 – 37)

_____

_____

_____

_____

_____

_____

_____

_____

_____

THE MIND OF THE SPIRIT... INTERCESSION :27

Romans 8:25 – 28 (KJV)

²⁵ But if we hope for that we see not, *then* do we with patience wait for *it*.

²⁶ Likewise the Spirit also helpeth our infirmities: for we know not what we should pray for as we ought: but the Spirit itself maketh intercession for us with groanings which cannot be uttered.

²⁷ And he that searcheth the hearts knoweth what *is* the mind of the Spirit, because he maketh intercession for the saints according to *the will of* God.

²⁸ And we know that all things work together for good to them that love God, to them who are the called according to *his* purpose.

The Spirit prays beyond what we could ask or think. (see Ephesians 3:20) He prays **"with groanings" too deep for words; unspeakable words.** (see 1 Corinthians 2:9 – 10) Who knows the will of God every time? How can we know the perfect will of God? The Spirit of God gives the peace of God to show us His perfect will (8:27; Colossians 3:12 – 17).

_____
_____
_____
_____

CONSCIENCE...IN THE HOLY GHOST

Romans 9:1 – 5 (KJV)

¹ I say the truth in Christ, I lie not, my conscience also bearing me witness in the Holy Ghost,

² That I have great heaviness and continual sorrow in my heart.

³ For I could wish that myself were accursed from Christ for my brethren, my kinsmen according to the flesh:

⁴ Who are Israelites; to whom *pertaineth* the adoption, and the glory, and the covenants, and the giving of the law, and the service *of God,* and the promises;

⁵ Whose *are* the fathers, and of whom as concerning the flesh Christ *came,* who is over all, God blessed for ever. Amen.

Even the great Apostle Paul had family members who rejected **the love of** Christ (9:1 – 7). He was in the perfect will of God and yet he was sad and he wrote to them in Rome (10:9 – 10). The Apostle didn't give up. What does that mean for us?

_____
_____
_____
_____
_____

JOY IN THE HOLY GHOST

Romans 14:14 – 17 (KJV)

[14] I know, and am persuaded by the Lord Jesus, that *there is* nothing unclean of itself: but to him that esteemeth any thing to be unclean, to him *it is* unclean.

[15] But if thy brother be grieved with *thy* meat, now walkest thou not charitably. Destroy not him with thy meat, for whom Christ died.

[16] Let not then your good be evil spoken of:

[17] For the kingdom of God is not meat and drink; but righteousness, and peace, and joy in the Holy Ghost.

The DNA of the meat was fine; but if they knew it was offered to idols and they ate it then they knowingly and openly took part in idol worship and that was when eating it was wrong (Genesis 9:3). Paul never said meats and foods were wrong. He was teaching them about **how to keep from hindering another person from walking in the Spirit.**

_____
_____
_____
_____
_____
_____

POWER OF...SANCTIFIED BY THE HOLY GHOST

Romans 15:13 – 16 (KJV)

[13] Now the God of hope fill you with all joy and peace in believing, that ye may abound in hope, through the power of the Holy Ghost.

[14] And I myself also am persuaded of you, my brethren, that ye also are full of goodness, filled with all knowledge, able also to admonish one another.

[15] Nevertheless, brethren, I have written the more boldly unto you in some sort, as putting you in mind, because of the grace that is given to me of God,

[16] That I should be the minister of Jesus Christ to the Gentiles, ministering the gospel of God, that the offering up of the Gentiles might be acceptable, being sanctified by the Holy Ghost.

Who sanctified us? Paul wrote more boldly to these Gentiles because he was called to them and therefore had the grace to do so. What has God given you the grace to do?

_____
_____
_____
_____
_____

date_____

POWER OF THE SPIRIT
OF GOD

Romans 15:17 – 21 (KJV)

17 I have therefore whereof I may glory through Jesus Christ in those things which pertain to God.

18 For I will not dare to speak of any of those things which Christ hath not wrought by me, to make the Gentiles obedient, by word and deed,

19 Through mighty signs and wonders, by the power of the Spirit of God; so that from Jerusalem, and round about unto Illyricum, I have fully preached the gospel of Christ.

20 Yea, so have I strived to preach the gospel, not where Christ was named, lest I should build upon another man's foundation:

21 But as it is written, To whom he was not spoken of, they shall see: and they that have not heard shall understand.

The Apostle Paul was saying he strived to preach to those who haven't heard. Why did he say "fully preached?" What did Paul say he wouldn't build upon? (see Acts 15:37 – 40)

_____
_____
_____
_____
_____
_____

date_____

LOVE OF THE SPIRIT...
PRAYERS TO GOD

Romans 15:30 – 33 (KJV)

30 Now I beseech you, brethren, for the Lord Jesus Christ's sake, and for the love of the Spirit, that ye strive together with me in *your* prayers to God for me;

31 That I may be delivered from them that do not believe in Judaea; and that my service which *I have* for Jerusalem may be accepted of the saints;

32 That I may come unto you with joy by the will of God, and may with you be refreshed.

33 Now the God of peace *be* with you all. Amen.

What things did Paul ask them to pray for? (15:31 – 32) (see 15:27; 1 Corinthians 9:7 – 11; 10:1 – 4; James 1:1 – 5) What did Paul believe about prayer and the will of God?

The love of the Spirit led to prayer. The most powerful list of Scriptures I've ever read to God as a prayer are the following list: 1 John 1:9; Matthew 6:8 – 14; 1 Corinthians 11:23 – 25; Mark 1:21 – 25; 11:22 – 24. What do you see in those verses?

_____
_____
_____
_____

DEMONSTRATION OF THE SPIRIT AND OF POWER :4

1 Corinthians 2:1 – 4 (KJV)
[1] And I, brethren, when I came to you, came not with excellency of speech or of wisdom, declaring unto you the testimony of God.
[2] For I determined not to know any thing among you, save Jesus Christ, and him crucified.
[3] And I was with you in weakness, and in fear, and in much trembling.
[4] And my speech and my preaching *was* not with enticing words of man's wisdom, but in demonstration of the Spirit and of power:

What did he mean by "demonstration of the Spirit"? How can physical man demonstrate the invisible Spirit? Why did he say "Spirit and of power?" (see Acts 1:8; Ephesians 1:15 – 19) According to these verses in First Corinthians 2:1 – 4, was Paul claiming to be a great speaker? What did Paul say he declared to them? (2:1) (see Revelation 19:10)

_____
_____
_____
_____
_____
_____

HIS SPIRIT: FOR THE SPIRIT SEARCHETH :10

1 Corinthians 2:7 – 10 (KJV)
[7] But we speak the wisdom of God in a mystery, *even* the hidden *wisdom*, which God ordained before the world unto our glory:
[8] Which none of the princes of this world knew: for had they known *it*, they would not have crucified the Lord of glory.
[9] But as it is written, Eye hath not seen, nor ear heard, neither have entered into the heart of man, the things which God hath prepared for them that love him.
[10] But God hath revealed *them* unto us by his Spirit: for the Spirit searcheth all things, yea, the deep things of God.

Now we know we have received the Spirit of God so that we can know all God has given us, but how would we know without a Teacher?
The **searching by the Spirit and the revelation by the Spirit are connected**. Then we may **experience what God wants for us. (see Romans 2:9; 8:26 – 28)**

_____
_____
_____
_____

THE SPIRIT OF GOD :11

1 Corinthians 2:8 – 11 (KJV)
[8] Which none of the princes of this world knew: for had they known *it*, they would not have crucified the Lord of glory.
[9] But as it is written, Eye hath not seen, nor ear heard, neither have entered into the heart of man, the things which God hath prepared for them that love him.
[10] But God hath revealed *them* unto us by his Spirit: for the Spirit searcheth all things, yea, the deep things of God.
[11] For what man knoweth the things of a man, save the spirit of man which is in him? even so the things of God knoweth no man, but the Spirit of God.

Without the Spirit connection we'd miss a lot. Only the Spirit of God can **explain** our life and future in the Spirit, from His Spirit to our spirit; then we may **understand** the things of God. When we are on the edge, **we are on faith. Faith goes forward by love.**
Our faith will stand firm and continue as we fully trust in God's Wisdom.

_____
_____
_____
_____

BUT THE SPIRIT OF GOD :12

1 Corinthians 2:9 – 12 (KJV)
[9] But as it is written, Eye hath not seen, nor ear heard, neither have entered into the heart of man, the things which God hath prepared for them that love him.
[10] But God hath revealed *them* unto us by his Spirit: for the Spirit searcheth all things, yea, the deep things of God.
[11] For what man knoweth the things of a man, save the spirit of man which is in him? even so the things of God knoweth no man, but the Spirit of God.
[12] Now we have received, not the spirit of the world, but the spirit which is of God; that we might know the things that are freely given to us of God.

We don't know what to pray for the right way so the Spirit of Jesus prays for us in a way we couldn't. We may come to His throne of grace any time. We may ask for wisdom any time. What things have freely been given to us? (Romans 8:25 – 27; 1 Corinthians 12:8; Hebrews 4:16; James 1:5) (see John 14:26)

_____
_____
_____
_____

THE HOLY GHOST
TEACHETH :13

1 Corinthians 2:10 – 13

[10] But God hath revealed *them* unto us by his Spirit: for the Spirit searcheth all things, yea, the deep things of God.
[11] For what man knoweth the things of a man, save the spirit of man which is in him? even so the things of God knoweth no man, but the Spirit of God.
[12] Now we have received, not the spirit of the world, but the spirit which is of God; that we might know the things that are freely given to us of God.
[13] Which things also we speak, not in the words which man's wisdom teacheth, but which the Holy Ghost teacheth; comparing spiritual things with spiritual.

The **wisdom teaching** of the Holy Ghost is available. We can grasp the **Writings of the Spirit** only by the Spirit. (see 2 Corinthians 4:6)
Can we imagine sitting in a classroom and hearing a voice say, "Your **Teacher today** will be the Spirit of God." Our **time in His presence is priceless.**

_____
_____
_____
_____
_____

SPIRIT OF GOD...SPIRITUALLY
DISCERNED :14

1 Corinthians 2:11 – 14 (KJV)

[11] For what man knoweth the things of a man, save the spirit of man which is in him? even so the things of God knoweth no man, but the Spirit of God.
[12] Now we have received, not the spirit of the world, but the spirit which is of God; that we might know the things that are freely given to us of God.
[13] Which things also we speak, not in the words which man's wisdom teacheth, but which the Holy Ghost teacheth; comparing spiritual things with spiritual.
[14] But the natural man receiveth not the things of the Spirit of God: for they are foolishness unto him: neither can he know *them*, because they are spiritually discerned.

We can understand the Bible through the Spirit of God who abides in us; for He wrote the Bible through holy men of God who held the pen as He spoke and they wrote His words. We need the Teacher to ask questions. God asked Adam, "Where are you?" (Genesis 3:9) The Spirit can only be discerned spiritually, discerned by the one with the Spirit.

_____
_____

THE SPIRIT OF GOD DWELLETH IN YOU

1 Corinthians 3:5 – 7, 9, 16, 23 (KJV)
[5] Who then is Paul, and who *is* Apollos, but ministers by whom ye believed, even as the Lord gave to every man?
[6] I have planted, Apollos watered; but God gave the increase.
[7] So then neither is he that planteth any thing, neither he that watereth; but God that giveth the increase.
[9] For we are labourers together with God: ye are God's husbandry, *ye are* God's building.
[16] Know ye not that ye are the temple of God, and *that* the Spirit of God dwelleth in you?
[23] And ye are Christ's; and Christ *is* God's.

Our labor is with God. We are His building, **His temple, the house of the Holy Ghost.** (see 2 Samuel 7) God makes the Holy Spirit known in us and visible through us in this life. (see John 10:10) We are each His house therefore we are each His.

_____

_____

_____

_____

_____

_____

THE SPIRIT OF OUR GOD

1 Corinthians 6:9 – 12 (KJV)
[9] Know ye not that the unrighteous shall not inherit the kingdom of God? Be not deceived: neither fornicators, nor idolaters, nor adulterers, nor effeminate, nor abusers of themselves with mankind,
[10] Nor thieves, nor covetous, nor drunkards, nor revilers, nor extortioners, shall inherit the kingdom of God.
[11] And such were some of you: but ye are washed, but ye are sanctified, but ye are justified in the name of the Lord Jesus, and by the Spirit of our God.
[12] All things are lawful unto me, but all things are not expedient: all things are lawful for me, but I will not be brought under the power of any.

God is not mocked. We have sown our life into the kingdom of God and so we shall reap. (see John 3:1 – 8; Mark 10:29 – 30) How and by who are we justified?

_____

_____

_____

_____

_____

_____

TEMPLE OF THE HOLY GHOST

1 Corinthians 6:17 – 20 (KJV)

[17] But he that is joined unto the Lord is one spirit.

[18] Flee fornication. Every sin that a man doeth is without the body; but he that committeth fornication sinneth against his own body.

[19] What? know ye not that your body is the temple of the Holy Ghost *which is* in you, which ye have of God, and ye are not your own?

[20] For ye are bought with a price: therefore glorify God in your body, and in your spirit, which are God's.

Each of us is one in the Spirit and when we submit to God and resist the devils' schemes, the unclean spirits will submit to us (James 4:7). (see Luke 10:19; Galatians 3:29) We are God-adopted. Our body is **the temple, the house of the Holy Ghost** (2 Samuel 7:27).

_____
_____
_____
_____
_____
_____
_____
_____
_____
_____

IN THE LORD...THE SPIRIT OF GOD

1 Corinthians 7:39 – 40 (KJV)

[39] The wife is bound by the law as long as her husband liveth; but if her husband be dead, she is at liberty to be married to whom she will; only in the Lord.

[40] But she is happier if she so abide, after my judgment: and I think also that I have the Spirit of God.

No man should make his daughter feel obligated to get married (7:35 – 38). **Some of the widows thought they had to remarry to please the Lord.** The Apostle Paul didn't want the widows to feel obligated to remarry **to please God** but to remarry in **the Lord's liberty**. Such a marriage has favor with God (Proverbs 18:22). We will all be equally glorified and blessed at the marriage supper of the Lamb, Jesus in heaven.

What does the phrase "only in the Lord" mean? (see Ephesians 5)

_____
_____
_____
_____
_____
_____
_____
_____

CONCERNING SPIRITUAL GIFTS :1 – 2

1 Corinthians 12:1 – 2 (KJV)
¹ Now concerning spiritual *gifts*, brethren, I would not have you ignorant.
² Ye know that ye were Gentiles, carried away unto these dumb idols, even as ye were led.

The oil in the Old Testament represents the gifts given **of the Holy Spirit**. The oil was her gift, not the same as and not to be used the same as other people's gifts (2 Kings 4:1 – 7). The Spirit has given many gifts to lead us the right way. The wrong choices are still there too because we are still in the world. But now we are not of this world so our Teacher and Guide is the Holy Ghost inside. When we ask the Spirit in us first, we can follow and be led by His peace (John 17:11, 14; Colossians 3:15; John 14:27). Spiritual gifts are listed but the facets are innumerable (Romans 12:1 – 18).

_____
_____
_____
_____
_____
_____
_____

THE SPIRIT OF GOD...THE HOLY GHOST :3

1 Corinthians 12:1 – 3 (KJV)
¹ Now concerning spiritual *gifts*, brethren, I would not have you ignorant.
² Ye know that ye were Gentiles, carried away unto these dumb idols, even as ye were led.
³ Wherefore I give you to understand, that no man speaking by the Spirit of God calleth Jesus accursed: and *that* no man can say that Jesus is the Lord, but by the Holy Ghost.

As we exhibit any of the spiritual gifts with giving Jesus the glory, we show evidence of the Spirit. During a Bible Study, I got a word of knowledge a dad would get in touch with his son whom he hadn't seen in over 15 years and it happened a few months later. Could there be a word of knowledge in the Old Testament? (12:8; 2 Kings 6:12)
When someone calls Jesus "Lord" or makes Him the Lord of their life, how do they make Him Lord according to verse 3? (see Romans 10:9 – 10)

_____
_____
_____
_____
_____

DIVERSITIES OF GIFTS, BUT THE SAME SPIRIT :4

1 Corinthians 12:1 – 4 (KJV)
¹ Now concerning spiritual *gifts*, brethren, I would not have you ignorant.
² Ye know that ye were Gentiles, carried away unto these dumb idols, even as ye were led.
³ Wherefore I give you to understand, that no man speaking by the Spirit of God calleth Jesus accursed: and *that* no man can say that Jesus is the Lord, but by the Holy Ghost.
⁴ Now there are diversities of gifts, but the same Spirit.

Why did the Apostle Paul list these spiritual gifts together in one letter?
Every spiritual gift is a spectrum of light from the Light!
Is it necessary to exhibit all the spiritual gifts or manifestations of the Spirit at the same time? (1 Corinthians 12) (see John 3:1 – 8)
Did all these gifts come from the authority of the Holy Spirit?

_____
_____
_____
_____
_____
_____
_____

MANIFESTATION OF THE SPIRIT :7

1 Corinthians 12:5 – 7 (KJV)
⁵ And there are differences of administrations, but the same Lord.
⁶ And there are diversities of operations, but it is the same God which worketh all in all.
⁷ But the manifestation of the Spirit is given to every man to profit withal.

God is the **Admin of administrators** (12:5). When we're operating in the light of God's heart, **voting His Holy Word according to His will written on our hearts**, we will bring His business into ours, and ours **will be His blessed by heaven** (12:6)! But when the spiritual gifts are unveiled, those gifts aren't exactly the same facet for anyone. The same **Spirit who designed the universe** also designed all the **gifts** the Spirit has given unto us (12:7). Did you ever know and tell someone by the Spirit, they were called to preach? Did they believe you right then or did they have to wait and see? (12:8)

_____
_____
_____
_____
_____
_____

date_____

BY THE SPIRIT THE WORD OF WISDOM :8

1 Corinthians 12:7 – 8 (KJV)
[7] But the manifestation of the Spirit is given to every man to profit withal. [8] For to one is given by the Spirit the word of wisdom; to another the word of knowledge by the same Spirit;

Please pray for some ladies who are arguing in the church and refusing to pray. We need wisdom, she asked. After prayer, God impressed me with a message for her like this: 'Get the church on board: Pray for the enemies in the flesh and God will lead them away by His power. Be so nice and forgiving they become sick of you. Overcome their evil with your good.' Then we remembered these words: "If your enemy is hungry, give him bread to eat; And if he is thirsty, give him water to drink; For *so* you will heap coals of fire on his head, And the LORD will reward you" **Proverbs 25:21 – 22 (NKJV).**
Do you want the LORD Himself to reward you? (see Matthew 5:44; 6:1 – 14)

date_____

FAITH...GIFTS OF HEALING BY THE SAME SPIRIT :9

1 Corinthians 12:5 – 9 (KJV)
[5] And there are differences of administrations, but the same Lord. [6] And there are diversities of operations, but it is the same God which worketh all in all. [7] But the manifestation of the Spirit is given to every man to profit withal. [8] For to one is given by the Spirit the word of wisdom; to another the word of knowledge by the same Spirit; [9] To another faith by the same Spirit; to another the gifts of healing by the same Spirit;

The word "gifts" is plural to remind us all these gifts have many **workings or facets.** Healing can be relational! When a woman touched the hem of Jesus' garment, she said, "I will be made well when I touch the hem of His garment."
Then Jesus told her, "Your faith has made you whole." She was healed spiritually, physically and emotionally (Matthew 9:21 – 22).
Jesus had all the facets of all the gifts and He used them for others.

AND THE SELFSAME SPIRIT :11

BY ONE SPIRIT ARE WE ALL BAPTIZED...ONE SPIRIT

1 Corinthians 12:8 – 11 (KJV)
[8] For to one is given by the Spirit the word of wisdom; to another the word of knowledge by the same Spirit;
[9] To another faith by the same Spirit; to another the gifts of healing by the same Spirit;
[10] To another the working of miracles; to another prophecy; to another discerning of spirits; to another *divers* kinds of tongues; to another the interpretation of tongues:
[11] But all these worketh that one and the selfsame Spirit, dividing to every man severally as he will.

All gifts are the workings of the Spirit and all gifts manifest Christ. God works the gifts by love! We work out our own gifts through compassion! (see 11:19 Genesis 1:1 – 2) All gifts manifested through us are the Holy Ghost proving He is available to us and through us (12:10 – 11). Why does He give gifts to each of us?

_____
_____
_____
_____
_____
_____

1 Corinthians 12:10 – 13, 31 (KJV)
[10] To another the working of miracles; to another prophecy; to another discerning of spirits; to another *divers* kinds of tongues; to another the interpretation of tongues:
[11] But all these worketh that one and the selfsame Spirit, dividing to every man severally as he will.
[12] For as the body is one, and hath many members, and all the members of that one body, being many, are one body: so also *is* Christ.
[13] For by one Spirit are we all baptized into one body, whether *we be* Jews or Gentiles, whether *we be* bond or free; and have been all made to drink into one Spirit.
[31] But covet earnestly the best gifts: and yet shew I unto you a more excellent way.

We are connected to God through the one Holy Spirit. (see 11:23 – 24) We get along with the Spirit-filled because we are in one accord with Him! Does God want each Christian to have identical spiritual gifts?

_____
_____
_____
_____
_____

CHARITY...BELIEVETH... HOPETH...ENDURETH

1 Corinthians 13:4 – 7 (KJV)

[4] Charity suffereth long, *and* is kind; charity envieth not; charity vaunteth not itself, is not puffed up,

[5] Doth not behave itself unseemly, seeketh not her own, is not easily provoked, thinketh no evil;

[6] Rejoiceth not in iniquity, but rejoiceth in the truth;

[7] Beareth all things, believeth all things, hopeth all things, endureth all things.

We never give up. God loves us. Jesus is coming soon (13:4 – 5). To **love like Jesus,** making **His kingdom your charity,** is to know **you can't lose** (2 Peter 1:4 – 8). God is Love and love is our power over the enemy. Our love for our enemies will shrink our enemies and destroy their power! Charity shall continue through those who believe through their word and through ours (3:17; John 17:20). (see Romans 5:1 – 8)
Love is the fuel for the kingdom! We have nothing without the Spirit of Love!

IN THE SPIRIT HE SPEAKETH MYSTERIES :2

1 Corinthians 14:2 – 5, 12 (KJV)

[2] For he that speaketh in an *unknown* tongue speaketh not unto men, but unto God: for no man understandeth *him*; howbeit in the spirit he speaketh mysteries.

[3] But he that prophesieth speaketh unto men *to* edification, and exhortation, and comfort.

[4] He that speaketh in an *unknown* tongue edifieth himself; but he that prophesieth edifieth the church.

[5] I would that ye all spake with tongues, but rather that ye prophesied: for greater *is* he that prophesieth than he that speaketh with tongues, except he interpret, that the church may receive edifying.

[12] Even so ye, forasmuch as ye are zealous of spiritual *gifts,* seek that ye may excel to the edifying of the church.

The thing we think everybody else should do (or help us do) is a clue to one of the gifts or the calling the Spirit of God has chosen for us to cause or make happen.

PRAY WITH THE SPIRIT :15

1 Corinthians 14:12 – 15 (KJV)
[12] Even so ye, forasmuch as ye are zealous of spiritual *gifts*, seek that ye may excel to the edifying of the church.
[13] Wherefore let him that speaketh in an *unknown* tongue pray that he may interpret.
[14] For if I pray in an *unknown* tongue, my spirit prayeth, but my understanding is unfruitful.
[15] What is it then? I will pray with the spirit, and I will pray with the understanding also: I will sing with the spirit, and I will sing with the understanding also.

In the Spirit is a created realm that cannot be comprehended by the flesh! Is praying with **the** spirit and praying with **the** understanding the same? Why or why not? Did Paul say he prayed with the Spirit and interpreted and why or why not? How did he say he was singing? On the Day of Pentecost, who interpreted and how were the words understood? (Acts 2:1 – 18) What's the key? (14:12)

_____
_____
_____
_____
_____

BLESS WITH THE SPIRIT :16

1 Corinthians 14:15 – 19 (KJV)
[15] What is it then? I will pray with the spirit, and I will pray with the understanding also: I will sing with the spirit, and I will sing with the understanding also.
[16] Else when thou shalt bless with the spirit, how shall he that occupieth the room of the unlearned say Amen at thy giving of thanks, seeing he understandeth not what thou sayest?
[17] For thou verily givest thanks well, but the other is not edified.

If a minister is giving thanks or saying a blessing in an unknown language to you, would you say 'Amen' if you didn't know what he said? In this context of these 3 verses, who are they who "occupieth the room of the unlearned" and why? Why did he say "the other is not edified"?

_____
_____
_____
_____
_____
_____
_____
_____
_____

date_____
EARNEST OF THE SPIRIT IN OUR HEARTS

2 Corinthians 1:20 – 24 (KJV)

20 For all the promises of God in him *are* yea, and in him Amen, unto the glory of God by us.

21 Now he which stablisheth us with you in Christ, and hath anointed us, *is* God;

22 Who hath also sealed us, and given the earnest of the Spirit in our hearts.

23 Moreover I call God for a record upon my soul, that to spare you I came not as yet unto Corinth.

24 Not for that we have dominion over your faith, but are helpers of your joy: for by faith ye stand.

Anointed. Sealed. Given the Holy Spirit of promise to come! What promise do you need that's all to the praise of His glory! You have the power to ask and receive; to give and receive; to speak and to command – by faith in the mighty name of Jesus. (see 1 Samuel 10:5 – 7; 1 John 2:12 – 14)

_____
_____
_____
_____
_____
_____
_____

date_____
SPIRIT OF THE LIVING GOD

2 Corinthians 3:2 – 5 (KJV)

2 Ye are our epistle written in our hearts, known and read of all men:

3 *Forasmuch as ye are* manifestly declared to be the epistle of Christ ministered by us, written not with ink, but with the Spirit of the living God; not in tables of stone, but in fleshy tables of the heart.

4 And such trust have we through Christ to God-ward:

5 Not that we are sufficient of ourselves to think any thing as of ourselves; but our sufficiency *is* of God;

Through Christ, you are the letters read by others as written with the Spirit of the living God. We say what we say in Christ (2:17). An epistle is a letter, so who does this say is this letter? Who was writing this letter and where was the letter written?

_____
_____
_____
_____
_____
_____
_____
_____
_____

THE SPIRIT GIVETH LIFE

2 Corinthians 3:5 – 8 (KJV)

5 Not that we are sufficient of ourselves to think any thing as of ourselves; but our sufficiency *is* of God;

6 Who also hath made us able ministers of the new testament; not of the letter, but of the spirit: for the letter killeth, but the spirit giveth life.

7 But if the ministration of death, written *and* engraven in stones, was glorious, so that the children of Israel could not stedfastly behold the face of Moses for the glory of his countenance; which *glory* was to be done away:

8 How shall not the ministration of the spirit be rather glorious?

We are ministers of and for the Spirit and thereby ministers of and for life. Our level we minister is equal to all ministers because every one of us ministers by the cross. How does he write we are a different kind of letter? How does he say the results will be different?

———————————————
———————————————
———————————————
———————————————
———————————————
———————————————

MINISTRATION OF THE SPIRIT

2 Corinthians 3:7 – 11 (KJV).

7 But if the ministration of death, written *and* engraven in stones, was glorious, so that the children of Israel could not stedfastly behold the face of Moses for the glory of his countenance; which *glory* was to be done away:

8 How shall not the ministration of the spirit be rather glorious?

9 For if the ministration of condemnation *be* glory, much more doth the ministration of righteousness exceed in glory.

10 For even that which was made glorious had no glory in this respect, by reason of the glory that excelleth.

11 For if that which is done away *was* glorious, much more that which remaineth *is* glorious

As the Spirit is the Minister through each of us, the glory of the Lord's righteousness is revealed and therefore (being uncovered) exceeds the previous glory! Glory to glory.

———————————————
———————————————
———————————————
———————————————
———————————————

SPIRIT OF THE LORD IS, THERE IS LIBERTY

2 Corinthians 3:12 – 17 (KJV).

¹² Seeing then that we have such hope, we use great plainness of speech:

¹³ And not as Moses, *which* put a vail over his face, that the children of Israel could not stedfastly look to the end of that which is abolished:

¹⁴ But their minds were blinded: for until this day remaineth the same vail untaken away in the reading of the old testament; which *vail* is done away in Christ.

¹⁵ But even unto this day, when Moses is read, the vail is upon their heart.

¹⁶ Nevertheless when it shall turn to the Lord, the vail shall be taken away.

¹⁷ Now the Lord is that Spirit: and where the Spirit of the Lord *is*, there *is* liberty.

He removes the veil in Christ (3:14, 17). The veil prevented the people from seeing what was to come! If they saw, they would be converted and then the Gentiles would be lost without hope.

_____
_____
_____
_____
_____

GLORY TO GLORY...BY THE SPIRIT OF THE LORD

2 Corinthians 3:12, 17, 18 (KJV)

¹² Seeing then that we have such hope, we use great plainness of speech:

¹⁷ Now the Lord is that Spirit: and where the Spirit of the Lord *is*, there *is* liberty.

¹⁸ But we all, with open face beholding as in a glass the glory of the Lord, are changed into the same image from glory to glory, *even* as by the Spirit of the Lord.

In conclusion, **in Christ we were changed by the Spirit of the Lord unto liberty** – His liberty of grace. A veil was for them so that the revelation of Jesus Christ could be for us.

_____
_____
_____
_____
_____
_____
_____
_____
_____
_____
_____
_____
_____

THE SPIRIT OF FAITH

2 Corinthians 4:10 – 14 (KJV)

[10] Always bearing about in the body the dying of the Lord Jesus, that the life also of Jesus might be made manifest in our body.

[11] For we which live are alway delivered unto death for Jesus' sake, that the life also of Jesus might be made manifest in our mortal flesh.

[12] So then death worketh in us, but life in you.

[13] We having the same spirit of faith, according as it is written, I believed, and therefore have I spoken; we also believe, and therefore speak;

[14] Knowing that he which raised up the Lord Jesus shall raise up us also by Jesus, and shall present *us* with you.

We suffer for His sake so His life is seen through ours. We will be presented to God the same way. (see Ephesians 2:20) We are in unity from **earth to eternity** (4:8 – 14). Does God want to build our faith? (Matthew 14:13; Mark 6:38; Luke 9:13; John 6:9 – 13)

_____
_____
_____
_____
_____
_____

EARNEST OF THE SPIRIT

2 Corinthians 5:1, 5, 14, 15, 19 (KJV)

[1] For we know that if our earthly house of *this* tabernacle were dissolved, we have a building of God, an house not made with hands, eternal in the heavens.

[5] Now he that hath wrought us for the selfsame thing *is* God, who also hath given unto us the earnest of the Spirit.

[14] For the love of Christ constraineth us; because we thus judge, that if one died for all, then were all dead:

[15] And *that* he died for all, that they which live should not henceforth live unto themselves, but unto him which died for them, and rose again.

[19] To wit, that God was in Christ, reconciling the world unto himself, not imputing their trespasses unto them; and hath committed unto us the word of reconciliation.

We are each the **house of the Holy Ghost** waiting for our eternal house (5:1). What is the message given to us? (5:19)

_____
_____
_____
_____
_____

date_____

BY THE HOLY GHOST, BY LOVE UNFEIGNED

2 Corinthians 6:3 – 7 (KJV)
³ Giving no offence in any thing, that the ministry be not blamed:
⁴ But in all *things* approving ourselves as the ministers of God, in much patience, in afflictions, in necessities, in distresses,
⁵ In stripes, in imprisonments, in tumults, in labours, in watchings, in fastings;
⁶ By pureness, by knowledge, by longsuffering, by kindness, by the Holy Ghost, by love unfeigned,
⁷ By the word of truth, by the power of God, by the armour of righteousness on the right hand and on the left,

We protected the ministry. We are approved by God, the Almighty Father (6:18). If we judge ourselves, we aren't judged with the world (1 Corinthians 11:31 – 32).

_____
_____
_____
_____
_____
_____
_____
_____

date_____

YE (YOU) ARE THE TEMPLE OF THE LIVING GOD

2 Corinthians 6:14 – 17 (KJV)
¹⁴ Be ye not unequally yoked together with unbelievers: for what fellowship hath righteousness with unrighteousness? and what communion hath light with darkness?
¹⁵ And what concord hath Christ with Belial? or what part hath he that believeth with an infidel?
¹⁶ And what agreement hath the temple of God with idols? for ye are the temple of the living God; as God hath said, I will dwell in them, and walk in *them*; and I will be their God, and they shall be my people.
¹⁷ Wherefore come out from among them, and be ye separate, saith the Lord, and touch not the unclean *thing*; and I will receive you,

By the same Spirit, we are each the temple of the living God. We are therefore sons and daughters of the Almighty. (see 1 Corinthians 3:9; 1 Peter 2:5) Who does God walk in? (see Jeremiah 7:23; Ezekiel 11:17 – 20) What does He want us to do with idols?

_____
_____
_____
_____

WALKED WE NOT IN THE SAME SPIRIT?

2 Corinthians 12:15 – 18 (KJV)

[15] And I will very gladly spend and be spent for you; though the more abundantly I love you, the less I be loved.

[16] But be it so, I did not burden you: nevertheless, being crafty, I caught you with guile.

[17] Did I make a gain of you by any of them whom I sent unto you?

[18] I desired Titus, and with *him* I sent a brother. Did Titus make a gain of you? walked we not in the same spirit? *walked we* not in the same steps?

The power of Christ rested on Paul as he ran after the loss for himself but gain for others. Who are those others? You. Paul was used up for the glory of God. We reap the benefit because he was one of those apostles on the foundation, the platform where we now stand firm with **our spirit sealed by the Spirit of Christ** (Ephesians 2:19 – 22). (see 2 Corinthians 1:20 – 24)

COMMUNION OF THE HOLY GHOST

2 Corinthians 13:3, 8, 10, 11, 14 (KJV)

[3] Since ye seek a proof of Christ speaking in me, which to you-ward is not weak, but is mighty in you.

[8] For we can do nothing against the truth, but for the truth.

[10] Therefore I write these things being absent, lest being present I should use sharpness, according to the power which the Lord hath given me to edification, and not to destruction.

[11] Finally, brethren, farewell. Be perfect, be of good comfort, be of one mind, live in peace; and the God of love and peace shall be with you.

[14] The grace of the Lord Jesus Christ, and the love of God, and the communion of the Holy Ghost, *be* with you all. Amen.

Paul called on the **Holy Trinity** as the One and only **presiding Judge** over his case. Do you remember who your Advocate is? (1 John 2:1 – 2)

REVELATION OF JESUS CHRIST

Galatians 1:10 – 12, 15 – 17 (KJV)

[10] For do I now persuade men, or God? or do I seek to please men? for if I yet pleased men, I should not be the servant of Christ.

[11] But I certify you, brethren, that the gospel which was preached of me is not after man.

[12] For I neither received it of man, neither was I taught *it*, but by the revelation of Jesus Christ.

[15] But when it pleased God, who separated me from my mother's womb, and called *me* by his grace,

[16] To reveal his Son in me, that I might preach him among the heathen; immediately I conferred not with flesh and blood:

[17] Neither went I up to Jerusalem to them which were apostles before me; but I went into Arabia, and returned again unto Damascus.

Time alone was more important to him than man (1:11, 17). Revelation comes how?

_____
_____
_____
_____
_____
_____

RECEIVED YE THE SPIRIT BY :2

Galatians 3:1 – 4 (KJV)

[1] O foolish Galatians, who hath bewitched you, that ye should not obey the truth, before whose eyes Jesus Christ hath been evidently set forth, crucified among you?

[2] This only would I learn of you, Received ye the Spirit by the works of the law, or by the hearing of faith?

[3] Are ye so foolish? having begun in the Spirit, are ye now made perfect by the flesh?

[4] Have ye suffered so many things in vain? if *it be* yet in vain.

How did you receive the Spirit of God? If by the law, then why didn't you receive the Spirit before now! Faith comes by hearing; so were we baptized in the Spirit or in the law?

_____
_____
_____
_____
_____
_____
_____
_____
_____

HAVING BEGUN IN THE SPIRIT :3

Galatians 3:2 – 7 (KJV)
² This only would I learn of you, Received ye the Spirit by the works of the law, or by the hearing of faith?
³ Are ye so foolish? having begun in the Spirit, are ye now made perfect by the flesh?
⁴ Have ye suffered so many things in vain? if *it be* yet in vain.
⁵ He therefore that ministereth to you the Spirit, and worketh miracles among you, *doeth he it* by the works of the law, or by the hearing of faith?
⁶ Even as Abraham believed God, and it was accounted to him for righteousness.
⁷ Know ye therefore that they which are of faith, the same are the children of Abraham.

If the apostles received the Spirit by the law then why didn't they receive Him **long before the Day of Pentecost?**
As Abraham believed God, so we believe (verse 7). When we want to climb up, we can aim toward the faith of Abraham. The higher we aim, the higher we will land.

_____
_____
_____
_____

MINISTERETH TO YOU THE SPIRIT :5

Galatians 3:2 – 7 (KJV)
² This only would I learn of you, Received ye the Spirit by the works of the law, or by the hearing of faith?
³ Are ye so foolish? having begun in the Spirit, are ye now made perfect by the flesh?
⁴ Have ye suffered so many things in vain? if *it be* yet in vain.
⁵ He therefore that ministereth to you the Spirit, and worketh miracles among you, *doeth he it* by the works of the law, or by the hearing of faith?
⁶ Even as Abraham believed God, and it was accounted to him for righteousness.
⁷ Know ye therefore that they which are of faith, the same are the children of Abraham.

Paul explained no part of the flesh nor man's efforts could cause us to receive the Spirit. The Spirit of God and miracles come only from above! (see Genesis 1:1; Matthew 16:15 – 19; 1 Corinthians 12; John 3:8)

_____
_____
_____
_____

date_____

PROMISE OF THE SPIRIT THROUGH FAITH :14

Galatians 3:8, 11, 13, 14 (KJV)

[8] And the scripture, foreseeing that God would justify the heathen through faith, preached before the gospel unto Abraham, *saying*, In thee shall all nations be blessed.

[11] But that no man is justified by the law in the sight of God, *it is* evident: for, The just shall live by faith.

[13] Christ hath redeemed us from the curse of the law, being made a curse for us: for it is written, Cursed *is* every one that hangeth on a tree:

[14] That the blessing of Abraham might come on the Gentiles through Jesus Christ; that we might receive the promise of the Spirit through faith.

God never changed nor cancelled the promise He gave to Abraham and Sarah, **even after their mistake.**

_____
_____
_____
_____
_____
_____
_____
_____

date_____

SENT FOR THE SPIRIT OF HIS SON

Galatians 4:4 – 7 (KJV)

[4] But when the fulness of the time was come, God sent forth his Son, made of a woman, made under the law,

[5] To redeem them that were under the law, that we might receive the adoption of sons.

[6] And because ye are sons, God hath sent forth the Spirit of his Son into your hearts, crying, Abba, Father.

[7] Wherefore thou art no more a servant, but a son; and if a son, then an heir of God through Christ.

God so loved us that He sent His one Son to earth to die under the law then by the Spirit of His Son, we can say to Him (God), "Daddy! Papa!"

Have you ever seen a loving daddy and husband's face light up when his wife and toddler enter the room? What will the loving daddy give them? What will the loving daddy do when he sees his little toddler hold up her arms and say "Daddy"?

_____
_____
_____
_____
_____

THAT WAS BORN AFTER THE SPIRIT

Galatians 4:22 – 23, 28 – 29 (KJV)

²² For it is written, that Abraham had two sons, the one by a bondmaid, the other by a freewoman.

²³ But he *who was* of the bondwoman was born after the flesh; but he of the freewoman *was* by promise.

²⁸ Now we, brethren, as Isaac was, are the children of promise.

²⁹ But as then he that was born after the flesh persecuted him *that was born* after the Spirit, even so *it is* now.

We are also mistreated by those who aren't **born again.** This is God's teaching. We are treated nice by those who are born again, born into the kingdom of God. (see Romans 1:12) Each year they had to make a new sacrifice, but Jesus was our **only Sacrifice.**

_____
_____
_____
_____
_____
_____
_____
_____
_____
_____

THROUGH THE SPIRIT :5

Galatians 5:1 – 5 (KJV)

¹ Stand fast therefore in the liberty wherewith Christ hath made us free, and be not entangled again with the yoke of bondage.

² Behold, I Paul say unto you, that if ye be circumcised, Christ shall profit you nothing.

³ For I testify again to every man that is circumcised, that he is a debtor to do the whole law.

⁴ Christ is become of no effect unto you, whosoever of you are justified by the law; ye are fallen from grace.

⁵ For we through the Spirit wait for the hope of righteousness by faith.

God's Word will take a stand by grace through the Spirit in us; for if we try to save ourselves by the law, we have fallen from grace; having misunderstood His cross. Did they understand grace if they were trying to be justified by the law? Is there any part of the law that could **save us for eternity** or could **prepare us for heaven**?

_____
_____
_____
_____
_____

WALK IN THE SPIRIT :16

Galatians 5:13 – 17 (KJV).

¹³ For, brethren, ye have been called unto liberty; only *use* not liberty for an occasion to the flesh, but by love serve one another.

¹⁴ For all the law is fulfilled in one word, *even* in this; Thou shalt love thy neighbour as thyself.

¹⁵ But if ye bite and devour one another, take heed that ye be not consumed one of another.

¹⁶ *This* I say then, Walk in the Spirit, and ye shall not fulfil the lust of the flesh.

¹⁷ For the flesh lusteth against the Spirit, and the Spirit against the flesh: and these are contrary the one to the other: so that ye cannot do the things that ye would.

"Walk in the Spirit…" Gossip grieves the Spirit! (5:10) Love is a connection, but negative talk is resisting the Holy Spirit. (see Romans 13:8 – 12; James 2:8 – 9)

_____
_____
_____
_____
_____
_____

THE SPIRIT AGAINST THE FLESH :17

Galatians 5:14 – 17 (KJV)

¹⁴ For all the law is fulfilled in one word, *even* in this; Thou shalt love thy neighbour as thyself.

¹⁵ But if ye bite and devour one another, take heed that ye be not consumed one of another.

¹⁶ *This* I say then, Walk in the Spirit, and ye shall not fulfil the lust of the flesh.

¹⁷ For the flesh lusteth against the Spirit, and the Spirit against the flesh: and these are contrary the one to the other: so that ye cannot do the things that ye would.

"For the flesh lusteth against the Spirit…" When we prepare to pray, our flesh will remind us of carnal (earthly) things! Our flesh opposes Spirit-time. God wants us near Him. What can you do to draw nearer to Him today?

_____
_____
_____
_____
_____
_____
_____

BUT IF YE BE LED OF THE SPIRIT :18

Galatians 5:14 – 18 (KJV)

¹⁴ For all the law is fulfilled in one word, *even* in this; Thou shalt love thy neighbour as thyself.

¹⁵ But if ye bite and devour one another, take heed that ye be not consumed one of another.

¹⁶ *This* I say then, Walk in the Spirit, and ye shall not fulfil the lust of the flesh.

¹⁷ For the flesh lusteth against the Spirit, and the Spirit against the flesh: and these are contrary the one to the other: so that ye cannot do the things that ye would.

¹⁸ But if ye be led of the Spirit, ye are not under the law.

"...led of the Spirit..." Being led is never being forced. The carnal (human) nature seeks to hinder us from the leadership of the Spirit so we cannot be what God plans and where God wants to take us. By faith, can you imagine sitting beside Jesus?

_____

_____

_____

_____

_____

_____

_____

FRUIT OF THE SPIRIT IS LOVE :22

Galatians 5:17, 18, 22 – 25 (KJV)

¹⁷ For the flesh lusteth against the Spirit, and the Spirit against the flesh: and these are contrary the one to the other: so that ye cannot do the things that ye would.

¹⁸ But if ye be led of the Spirit, ye are not under the law.

²² But the fruit of the Spirit is love, joy, peace, longsuffering, gentleness, goodness, faith,

²³ Meekness, temperance: against such there is no law.

²⁴ And they that are Christ's have crucified the flesh with the affections and lusts.

²⁵ If we live in the Spirit, let us also walk in the Spirit.

"...fruit of the Spirit..." The conduct of a Christian will look odd to the world. (see 6:1; 1 Corinthians 4:21) The conduct of a Christian will also anger the unbeliever. So you will be persecuted but those stories will help more people than your success stories. Did you know that persecution comes with the blessing multiplied by God? (2 Timothy 3:12; Matthew 19:29) What can you believe the Almighty Living God for? Will you ask?

_____

_____

LIVE...ALSO WALK IN THE SPIRIT :25

Galatians 5:22 – 26 (KJV)

²² But the fruit of the Spirit is love, joy, peace, longsuffering, gentleness, goodness, faith,

²³ Meekness, temperance: against such there is no law.

²⁴ And they that are Christ's have crucified the flesh with the affections and lusts.

²⁵ If we live in the Spirit, let us also walk in the Spirit.

²⁶ Let us not be desirous of vain glory, provoking one another, envying one another.

"...live in the Spirit, let us also walk in the Spirit." Walking in the Spirit is living Spirit-visible, living by faith! When Jesus talked about doing things in secret He was referring us to 1-not be like Pharisees and 2-doing things without pride. God wants us to show our faith.

Jesus said: "Let your light so shine before men, that they may see your good works and glorify your Father in heaven" **Matthew 5:16 (NKJV)**.

_____

_____

_____

_____

_____

SPIRITUAL, RESTORE...SPIRIT OF MEEKNESS

Galatians 6:1 – 5 (KJV)

¹ Brethren, if a man be overtaken in a fault, ye which are spiritual, restore such an one in the spirit of meekness; considering thyself, lest thou also be tempted.

² Bear ye one another's burdens, and so fulfil the law of Christ.

³ For if a man think himself to be something, when he is nothing, he deceiveth himself.

⁴ But let every man prove his own work, and then shall he have rejoicing in himself alone, and not in another.

⁵ For every man shall bear his own burden.

"...restore..." Backbiters weren't allowed: being spiritual **by God standards** is when we are meek, realizing our power was given to us to rescue and help others and lead them in the Light of His love; as Jesus did. (see 1 Corinthians 4:21) As we restore and forgive, God restores and forgives on the level we gave. You have the seed to put your life on the right road where you really want to be. What does God want you to do?

_____

_____

_____

_____

SOWETH TO THE SPIRIT SHALL OF THE SPIRIT REAP

Galatians 6:7 – 10 (KJV)

⁷ Be not deceived; God is not mocked: for whatsoever a man soweth, that shall he also reap.

⁸ For he that soweth to his flesh shall of the flesh reap corruption; but he that soweth to the Spirit shall of the Spirit reap life everlasting.

⁹ And let us not be weary in well doing: for in due season we shall reap, if we faint not.

¹⁰ As we have therefore opportunity, let us do good unto all *men*, especially unto them who are of the household of faith.

Every good thing we make or cause to happen for someone else; without pride and not for recognition; the Lord God will make that good thing **multiply and overflow in our life**. When we sow for God's kingdom, we will get it back from God. What would you ask if you knew your Father was listening to make it happen this week?

_____
_____
_____
_____
_____
_____

ALL SPIRITUAL BLESSINGS... LOVE

Ephesians 1:3, 4, 5, 9 (KJV)

³ Blessed *be* the God and Father of our Lord Jesus Christ, who hath blessed us with all spiritual blessings in heavenly *places* in Christ:

⁴ According as he hath chosen us in him before the foundation of the world, that we should be holy and without blame before him in love:

⁵ Having predestinated us unto the adoption of children by Jesus Christ to himself, according to the good pleasure of his will,

⁹ Having made known unto us the mystery of his will, according to his good pleasure which he hath purposed in himself:

Daddy always gives favor (preference, privilege) to His children because of who He is!
(see 1:3; Revelation 3:21) What would He do if He looks at you and you raised your hands toward Him?

_____
_____
_____
_____
_____
_____
_____

date_____

SEALED WITH THAT HOLY SPIRIT OF PROMISE

Ephesians 1:10 – 14 (KJV)

[10] That in the dispensation of the fulness of times he might gather together in one all things in Christ, both which are in heaven, and which are on earth; *even* in him:

[11] In whom also we have obtained an inheritance, being predestinated according to the purpose of him who worketh all things after the counsel of his own will:

[12] That we should be to the praise of his glory, who first trusted in Christ.

[13] In whom ye also *trusted*, after that ye heard the word of truth, the gospel of your salvation: in whom also after that ye believed, ye were sealed with that holy Spirit of promise,

[14] Which is the earnest of our inheritance until the redemption of the purchased possession, unto the praise of his glory.

Their love toward the church, those who were sealed with the Holy Spirit of promise, caused **the Apostle Paul** to pray for them. How important is the truth in us?

_____
_____
_____
_____
_____

date_____

UNTO YOU THE SPIRIT OF WISDOM AND REVELATION

Ephesians 1:17 – 20, 23 (KJV)

[17] That the God of our Lord Jesus Christ, the Father of glory, may give unto you the spirit of wisdom and revelation in the knowledge of him:

[18] The eyes of your understanding being enlightened; that ye may know what is the hope of his calling, and what the riches of the glory of his inheritance in the saints,

[19] And what *is* the exceeding greatness of his power to us-ward who believe, according to the working of his mighty power,

[20] Which he wrought in Christ, when he raised him from the dead, and set *him* at his own right hand in the heavenly *places*,

[23] Which is his body, the fulness of him that filleth all in all.

Praise causes revelation to your spirit! Every one of you has resurrection power in you!
(see Romans 6:1 – 5; 1 Corinthians 2:1 – 10) God has also given each one a talent. What are you doing with His power and His faith? (see 1:3, 20; Acts 2:34)

_____
_____
_____
_____

ACCESS BY ONE SPIRIT UNTO THE FATHER

Ephesians 2:15 – 19 (KJV)

[15] Having abolished in his flesh the enmity, *even* the law of commandments *contained* in ordinances; for to make in himself of twain one new man, *so* making peace;

[16] And that he might reconcile both unto God in one body by the cross, having slain the enmity thereby:

[17] And came and preached peace to you which were afar off, and to them that were nigh.

[18] For through him we both have access by one Spirit unto the Father.

[19] Now therefore ye are no more strangers and foreigners, but fellowcitizens with the saints, and of the household of God;

Love is level as the Spirit gives us all the same access! (see Acts 2:38 – 29) We are seen by **our Father** right now in heavenly places (1:3; 2:9). What do we have by one Spirit? (see 2:4 – 5; John 14:27; 17:2 – 3) How can we demonstrate this access to little ones with prayer?

_____
_____
_____
_____

HABITATION OF GOD THROUGH THE SPIRIT

Ephesians 2:19 – 22 (KJV)

[19] Now therefore ye are no more strangers and foreigners, but fellowcitizens with the saints, and of the household of God;

[20] And are built upon the foundation of the apostles and prophets, Jesus Christ himself being the chief corner *stone*;

[21] In whom all the building fitly framed together groweth unto an holy temple in the Lord:

[22] In whom ye also are builded together for an habitation of God through the Spirit.

We are a holy temple in the Lord, both individually and cooperatively. Our purpose is that we, being already a single dwelling place or house of God, would take part in **the growing co-operation of God. (**see Psalm 91:9, 14; 1 Corinthians 3:16; 1 Peter 2:9) What happened when you gave your heart and soul to Jesus?

_____
_____
_____
_____
_____
_____

date_____
GRANT...BY HIS SPIRIT...
LOVE

Ephesians 3:9, 14 – 17, 19 (KJV)
⁹ And to make all *men* see what *is* the fellowship of the mystery, which from the beginning of the world hath been hid in God, who created all things by Jesus Christ:
¹⁴ For this cause I bow my knees unto the Father of our Lord Jesus Christ,
¹⁵ Of whom the whole family in heaven and earth is named,
¹⁶ That he would grant you, according to the riches of his glory, to be strengthened with might by his Spirit in the inner man;
¹⁷ That Christ may dwell in your hearts by faith; that ye, being rooted and grounded in love,
¹⁹ And to know the love of Christ, which passeth knowledge, that ye might be filled with all the fulness of God.

The Spirit strengthens us to love! **He will grant strength** from the inside from His Spirit more than we can ask or think. (see 1:15 – 23; 3:17 – 20) The fullness of who? (3:19)

_____
_____
_____
_____
_____

date_____
UNITY OF THE SPIRIT...PEACE

Ephesians 4:1 – 3 (KJV)
¹ I therefore, the prisoner of the Lord, beseech you that ye walk worthy of the vocation wherewith ye are called,
² With all lowliness and meekness, with longsuffering, forbearing one another in love;
³ Endeavouring to keep the unity of the Spirit in the bond of peace.

Jesus disarmed principalities and powers (Colossians 2:15)! The preparation for the unity of the Spirit began! Peace is represented in the unity! God sent Jesus and **unity was born** in the church when Jesus died! What do we do to Him when we tell negative news about someone? What happens to the church body when we ignore our calling, vocation from God at home or in the work place? What do we do to Him when we don't live in the unity as He called us?

_____
_____
_____
_____
_____
_____
_____

ONE BODY, AND ONE SPIRIT...
HOPE

Ephesians 4:3 – 8 (KJV)

3 Endeavouring to keep the unity of the Spirit in the bond of peace.

4 *There is* one body, and one Spirit, even as ye are called in one hope of your calling;

5 One Lord, one faith, one baptism,

6 One God and Father of all, who *is* above all, and through all, and in you all.

7 But unto every one of us is given grace according to the measure of the gift of Christ.

8 Wherefore he saith, When he ascended up on high, he led captivity captive, and gave gifts unto men.

Jesus received gifts *for* us by His death on the cross and gave gifts *to* us through the cross (4:3, 8; Psalm 68:17 – 19). Jesus told us and them, "If I don't go, I cannot send the Holy Spirit" (4:7 – 8; John 16:7) Jesus was the house of the Holy Ghost. While He was here in a flesh suit, He was the **only house** for His Spirit. When He left here, **He made us a house.**

_____
_____
_____
_____
_____

EDIFYING...ALL...UNITY...
LOVE

Ephesians 4:11 – 15 (KJV)

11 And he gave some, apostles; and some, prophets; and some, evangelists; and some, pastors and teachers;

12 For the perfecting of the saints, for the work of the ministry, for the edifying of the body of Christ:

13 Till we all come in the unity of the faith, and of the knowledge of the Son of God, unto a perfect man, unto the measure of the stature of the fulness of Christ:

14 That we *henceforth* be no more children, tossed to and fro, and carried about with every wind of doctrine, by the sleight of men, *and* cunning craftiness, whereby they lie in wait to deceive;

15 But speaking the truth in love, may grow up into him in all things, which is the head, *even* Christ:

Faith, hope and love: the greatest of these is service to God and people (Galatians 5:22).

_____
_____
_____
_____
_____
_____

date_____

THEIR MIND...IN THE SPIRIT OF YOUR MIND

Ephesians 4:17, 19, 20, 21, 22, 23 (KJV)

[17] This I say therefore, and testify in the Lord, that ye henceforth walk not as other Gentiles walk, in the vanity of their mind,

[19] Who being past feeling have given themselves over unto lasciviousness, to work all uncleanness with greediness.

[20] But ye have not so learned Christ;

[21] If so be that ye have heard him, and have been taught by him, as the truth is in Jesus:

[22] That ye put off concerning the former conversation the old man, which is corrupt according to the deceitful lusts;

[23] And be renewed in the spirit of your mind;

Having surrendered to Christ, having the mind of Christ, we are concerned with the things of Christ and the spirit of our mind is being continually renewed in Him!

_____
_____
_____
_____
_____
_____

date_____

GRIEVE NOT THE HOLY SPIRIT OF GOD

Ephesians 4:25 – 30 (KJV)

[25] Wherefore putting away lying, speak every man truth with his neighbour: for we are members one of another.

[26] Be ye angry, and sin not: let not the sun go down upon your wrath:

[27] Neither give place to the devil.

[28] Let him that stole steal no more: but rather let him labour, working with *his* hands the thing which is good, that he may have to give to him that needeth.

[29] Let no corrupt communication proceed out of your mouth, but that which is good to the use of edifying, that it may minister grace unto the hearers.

[30] And grieve not the holy Spirit of God, whereby ye are sealed unto the day of redemption.

He isn't leaving. God searches the earth for the one He may reward; **so we grieve the Almighty Himself when He cannot reward us**. We can make the Holy Spirit of God happy as we spend time with Him (see Psalm 37:23; Mark 3:1 – 5; Psalm 91:15).

_____
_____
_____
_____
_____

FRUIT OF THE SPIRIT IS IN ALL GOODNESS

Ephesians 5:7, 8, 9, 13 (KJV)

[7] Be not ye therefore partakers with them.

[8] For ye were sometimes darkness, but now *are ye* light in the Lord: walk as children of light:

[9] (For the fruit of the Spirit *is* in all goodness and righteousness and truth;)

[13] But all things that are reproved are made manifest by the light: for whatsoever doth make manifest is light.

With the wisdom of the light in us; we can ask, "What should I do? And what will or could bring someone else to the Lord Jesus?"

God's goodness brings man to repentance (Romans 2:4). Knowing that, what would you pray? (see Galatians 5:22 – 23)

What is in all goodness and righteousness and truth? (5:9)

_____
_____
_____
_____
_____
_____
_____
_____

BE FILLED WITH THE SPIRIT

Ephesians 5:17, 18, 19, 20, 21, 30 (KJV)

[17] Wherefore be ye not unwise, but understanding what the will of the Lord *is*.

[18] And be not drunk with wine, wherein is excess; but be filled with the Spirit;

[19] Speaking to yourselves in psalms and hymns and spiritual songs, singing and making melody in your heart to the Lord;

[20] Giving thanks always for all things unto God and the Father in the name of our Lord Jesus Christ;

[21] Submitting yourselves one to another in the fear of God.

[30] For we are members of his body, of his flesh, and of his bones.

The power of gratitude stirs up the power of the Spirit. God is moved with compassion when we draw near to Him. Saying "Thank you" is wisdom! (see 5:20; 1 Corinthians 11:24) David penned many Psalms and the people sang them. (see Zephaniah 3:17)

The mystery of Christ and the church is no longer a mystery (3:9; 5:32)

_____
_____
_____
_____
_____

date_____
SWORD OF THE SPIRIT

Ephesians 6:10 – 11, 15 – 17 (KJV)
¹⁰ Finally, my brethren, be strong in the Lord, and in the power of his might.
¹¹ Put on the whole armour of God, that ye may be able to stand against the wiles of the devil.
¹⁵ And your feet shod with the preparation of the gospel of peace;
¹⁶ Above all, taking the shield of faith, wherewith ye shall be able to quench all the fiery darts of the wicked.
¹⁷ And take the helmet of salvation, and the sword of the Spirit, which is the word of God:

We will witness the enemy **stronger** than us in appearance, but no weapon against us will **win** by using the Sword of the Spirit as our **conversation** (Psalm 91:7; 37:14 – 15; 1 Timothy 4:12; Hebrews 13:5, 7; James 3:13). Jesus fought the devil on behalf of people! Where and how was His fight won and finished? (Matthew 12:20; 4:3 – 11)

_____
_____
_____
_____
_____
_____

date_____
SUPPLICATION IN THE SPIRIT

Ephesians 6:17 – 20 (KJV)
¹⁷ And take the helmet of salvation, and the sword of the Spirit, which is the word of God:
¹⁸ Praying always with all prayer and supplication in the Spirit, and watching thereunto with all perseverance and supplication for all saints;
¹⁹ And for me, that utterance may be given unto me, that I may open my mouth boldly, to make known the mystery of the gospel,
²⁰ For which I am an ambassador in bonds: that therein I may speak boldly, as I ought to speak.

Supplication is the case in the briefcase of a lawyer; but God is your Defense Lawyer. (see Philippians 4:6) With the full armor of God there's no weapon against you that can prosper (Isaiah 54:17). No mountain is too tall (Mark 11:23).

_____
_____
_____
_____
_____
_____
_____
_____

SUPPLY OF THE SPIRIT OF JESUS CHRIST

Philippians 1:14, 15, 18, 19, 20 (KJV)

¹⁴ And many of the brethren in the Lord, waxing confident by my bonds, are much more bold to speak the word without fear.

¹⁵ Some indeed preach Christ even of envy and strife; and some also of good will:

¹⁸ What then? notwithstanding, every way, whether in pretence, or in truth, Christ is preached; and I therein do rejoice, yea, and will rejoice.

¹⁹ For I know that this shall turn to my salvation through your prayer, and the supply of the Spirit of Jesus Christ,

²⁰ According to my earnest expectation and *my* hope, that in nothing I shall be ashamed, but *that* with all boldness, as always, *so* now also Christ shall be magnified in my body, whether *it be* by life, or by death.

The benefit of suffering was the boldness of others in the faith to **live and speak the gospel.** Others are **empowered by problems** we overcame and even those we didn't.

_____
_____
_____
_____
_____

STAND FAST IN ONE SPIRIT

Philippians 1:27 – 29 (KJV)

²⁷ Only let your conversation be as it becometh the gospel of Christ: that whether I come and see you, or else be absent, I may hear of your affairs, that ye stand fast in one spirit, with one mind striving together for the faith of the gospel;

²⁸ And in nothing terrified by your adversaries: which is to them an evident token of perdition, but to you of salvation, and that of God.

²⁹ For unto you it is given in the behalf of Christ, not only to believe on him, but also to suffer for his sake;

Paul preached with confidence in the Spirit of Jesus Christ. (see 1 Corinthians 12:11)

When we are made afraid of them because of our faith in Christ, we have the proof they are not a Christian and further proof we are (2 Corinthians 4:4; Psalm 86:17)! The ones who oppose us are proving they don't believe in the Jesus Christ in us! Arguing with them is ungodly and by such we are against God. (see John 15:17)

_____
_____
_____
_____
_____

FELLOWSHIP OF THE SPIRIT

Philippians 2:1 – 5 (KJV)
¹ If *there be* therefore any consolation in Christ, if any comfort of love, if any fellowship of the Spirit, if any bowels and mercies,
² Fulfil ye my joy, that ye be likeminded, having the same love, *being* of one accord, of one mind.
³ *Let* nothing *be done* through strife or vainglory; but in lowliness of mind let each esteem other better than themselves.
⁴ Look not every man on his own things, but every man also on the things of others.
⁵ Let this mind be in you, which was also in Christ Jesus:

The unstoppable congregation is the fellowship of the Spirit! (see 1 Thessalonians 4:9)
Faith in flesh opposes worship in Spirit. Faith in our strength opposes the purposes of God. (see Matthew 6:1 – 14; Mark 11:22 – 25)

WE...WORSHIP GOD IN THE SPIRIT

Philippians 3:2, 3, 9, 15 (KJV)
² Beware of dogs, beware of evil workers, beware of the concision.
³ For we are the circumcision, which worship God in the spirit, and rejoice in Christ Jesus, and have no confidence in the flesh.
⁹ And be found in him, not having mine own righteousness, which is of the law, but that which is through the faith of Christ, the righteousness which is of God by faith:
¹⁵ Let us therefore, as many as be perfect, be thus minded: and if in any thing ye be otherwise minded, God shall reveal even this unto you.

Paul was of "the circumcision" meant he was Jewish. Paul worshipped God in the Spirit, not with confidence in the human dimension. Our citizenship is in heaven (3:13, 14, 20). (see 3:9, 2 Corinthians 5:21; Romans 2:28 – 30; Ephesians 2:8 – 9)

YOUR LOVE IN THE SPIRIT

Colossians 1:3 – 8 (KJV)
3 We give thanks to God and the Father of our Lord Jesus Christ, praying always for you,
4 Since we heard of your faith in Christ Jesus, and of the love *which ye have* to all the saints,
5 For the hope which is laid up for you in heaven, whereof ye heard before in the word of the truth of the gospel;
6 Which is come unto you, as *it is* in all the world; and bringeth forth fruit, as *it doth* also in you, since the day ye heard *of it*, and knew the grace of God in truth:
7 As ye also learned of Epaphras our dear fellowservant, who is for you a faithful minister of Christ;
8 Who also declared unto us your love in the Spirit.

We've heard your deep concern for the things of God; for love is the unquenchable Witness! (see 3 John 3) The people of Colosse saw and reported God's love to who?

_____
_____
_____
_____
_____
_____

PRAY...SPIRITUAL UNDERSTANDING

Colossians 1:9 – 12 (KJV)
9 For this cause we also, since the day we heard *it*, do not cease to pray for you, and to desire that ye might be filled with the knowledge of his will in all wisdom and spiritual understanding;
10 That ye might walk worthy of the Lord unto all pleasing, being fruitful in every good work, and increasing in the knowledge of God;
11 Strengthened with all might, according to his glorious power, unto all patience and longsuffering with joyfulness;
12 Giving thanks unto the Father, which hath made us meet to be partakers of the inheritance of the saints in light:

We then **walk in His steps.** All wisdom and spiritual understanding comes as we **walk in the Light.** Who prayed the church would be filled with **knowing God's will**? We are the Lord's. We do what we do, so others will want to know the Lord!

_____
_____
_____
_____
_____

AM I WITH YOU IN THE SPIRIT

Colossians 2:1 – 5 (KJV)

¹ For I would that ye knew what great conflict I have for you, and *for* them at Laodicea, and *for* as many as have not seen my face in the flesh;

² That their hearts might be comforted, being knit together in love, and unto all riches of the full assurance of understanding, to the acknowledgement of the mystery of God, and of the Father, and of Christ;

³ In whom are hid all the treasures of wisdom and knowledge.

⁴ And this I say, lest any man should beguile you with enticing words.

⁵ For though I be absent in the flesh, yet am I with you in the spirit, joying and beholding your order, and the stedfastness of your faith in Christ.

Paul was encouraging the Christians to continue believing they had received Jesus as Lord (2:1 – 10). What did Paul mean by "with you in the spirit, joying … your order, and the stedfastness of your faith in Christ"? How important to God is order (Genesis 1)?

_____
_____
_____
_____
_____

SPIRITUAL SONGS

Colossians 3:15 – 17 (KJV)

¹⁵ And let the peace of God rule in your hearts, to the which also ye are called in one body; and be ye thankful.

¹⁶ Let the word of Christ dwell in you richly in all wisdom; teaching and admonishing one another in psalms and hymns and spiritual songs, singing with grace in your hearts to the Lord.

¹⁷ And whatsoever ye do in word or deed, *do* all in the name of the Lord Jesus, giving thanks to God and the Father by him.

The word *rule* is like an umpire, the umpire of our soul. He leads us to the peace of God by the Spirit of God who has led us to spiritual songs, singing with grace (3:1 – 17)! What does the word "spiritual" mean? What is the difference between spiritual songs and hymns? Who did he say for the church to sing to as we sing or worship?

_____
_____
_____
_____
_____
_____
_____

GOSPEL...IN THE HOLY GHOST

1 Thessalonians 1:2 – 5 (KJV)
[2] We give thanks to God always for you all, making mention of you in our prayers;
[3] Remembering without ceasing your work of faith, and labour of love, and patience of hope in our Lord Jesus Christ, in the sight of God and our Father;
[4] Knowing, brethren beloved, your election of God.
[5] For our gospel came not unto you in word only, but also in power, and in the Holy Ghost, and in much assurance; as ye know what manner of men we were among you for your sake.

The reputation of the Holy Spirit working through them was the powerful **love influence** that **spread the gospel** around the region (1:1 – 10). (see 1 Corinthians 1:5 – 7; 2:5; Galatians 5:5 – 8; 1 John 3:11, 23) Why does verse 5 start with the word "For"?

_____
_____
_____
_____
_____
_____

WITH JOY OF THE HOLY GHOST

1 Thessalonians 1:5 – 8 (KJV)
[5] For our gospel came not unto you in word only, but also in power, and in the Holy Ghost, and in much assurance; as ye know what manner of men we were among you for your sake.
[6] And ye became followers of us, and of the Lord, having received the word in much affliction, with joy of the Holy Ghost:
[7] So that ye were ensamples to all that believe in Macedonia and Achaia.
[8] For from you sounded out the word of the Lord not only in Macedonia and Achaia, but also in every place your faith to God-ward is spread abroad; so that we need not to speak any thing.

They gave a strong example. The missionary's life caused others to follow their word; and then to others and more. What would be the difference between joy in the Spirit and joy of the Holy Ghost (John 7:39)?

_____
_____
_____
_____
_____
_____

GOD...GIVEN UNTO US HIS HOLY SPIRIT

1 Thessalonians 4:6 – 10 (KJV)

⁶ That no *man* go beyond and defraud his brother in *any* matter: because that the Lord *is* the avenger of all such, as we also have forewarned you and testified.

⁷ For God hath not called us unto uncleanness, but unto holiness.

⁸ He therefore that despiseth, despiseth not man, but God, who hath also given unto us his holy Spirit.

⁹ But as touching brotherly love ye need not that I write unto you: for ye yourselves are taught of God to love one another.

¹⁰ And indeed ye do it toward all the brethren which are in all Macedonia: but we beseech you, brethren, that ye increase more and more;

God gives the Spirit of love for kingdom increase; and our children are taught of the Lord (Isaiah 49:25; 54:13). However, the man who is being or speaking ill of the brethren or one brother is showing how his heart treats God. (see Zechariah 8:17; Romans 1:4)

_____
_____
_____
_____
_____

QUENCH NOT THE SPIRIT

1 Thessalonians 5:18 – 24 (KJV)

¹⁸ In every thing give thanks: for this is the will of God in Christ Jesus concerning you.

¹⁹ Quench not the Spirit.

²⁰ Despise not prophesyings.

²¹ Prove all things; hold fast that which is good.

²² Abstain from all appearance of evil.

²³ And the very God of peace sanctify you wholly; and *I pray God* your whole spirit and soul and body be preserved blameless unto the coming of our Lord Jesus Christ.

²⁴ Faithful *is* he that calleth you, who also will do *it*.

Negative talk about another person stifles and holds back the Spirit. (see Psalm 78:41; Jeremiah 1:12) Allowing it has the same results for the house. What is the will of God? (5:18) How can a Christian be a vessel for God's Spirit? Does God want His Spirit to flow from you? (John 14:17; 4:14; 7:37 – 38)

_____
_____
_____
_____
_____
_____

date_____

SANCTIFICATION OF THE SPIRIT

2 Thessalonians 2:13 – 17 (KJV)

13 But we are bound to give thanks alway to God for you, brethren beloved of the Lord, because God hath from the beginning chosen you to salvation through sanctification of the Spirit and belief of the truth:

14 Whereunto he called you by our gospel, to the obtaining of the glory of our Lord Jesus Christ.

15 Therefore, brethren, stand fast, and hold the traditions which ye have been taught, whether by word, or our epistle.

16 Now our Lord Jesus Christ himself, and God, even our Father, which hath loved us, and hath given *us* everlasting consolation and good hope through grace,

17 Comfort your hearts, and stablish you in every good word and work.

The Holy Spirit has set us apart for God's purposes **since we believed** the love of the truth when He created the universe (2:10; 2 Timothy 1:9). We are growing for His glory!

_____
_____
_____
_____
_____

date_____

JUSTIFIED IN THE SPIRIT

1 Timothy 3:13 – 16 (KJV)

13 For they that have used the office of a deacon well purchase to themselves a good degree, and great boldness in the faith which is in Christ Jesus.

14 These things write I unto thee, hoping to come unto thee shortly:

15 But if I tarry long, that thou mayest know how thou oughtest to behave thyself in the house of God, which is the church of the living God, the pillar and ground of the truth.

16 And without controversy great is the mystery of godliness: God was manifest in the flesh, justified in the Spirit, seen of angels, preached unto the Gentiles, believed on in the world, received up into glory.

Godly living is from the living God who came to us as Jesus and was **sent to live in each of us** through the Spirit. (see Romans 1:3 – 4) God has made good plans for us since God knew our whole life before He created the universe so **God with us is now Christ in us.**

_____
_____
_____
_____

THE SPIRIT SPEAKETH EXPRESSLY

1 Timothy 4:1 – 5, 7 (KJV)

¹ Now the Spirit speaketh expressly, that in the latter times some shall depart from the faith, giving heed to seducing spirits, and doctrines of devils;

² Speaking lies in hypocrisy; having their conscience seared with a hot iron;

³ Forbidding to marry, *and commanding* to abstain from meats, which God hath created to be received with thanksgiving of them which believe and know the truth.

⁴ For every creature of God *is* good, and nothing to be refused, if it be received with thanksgiving:

⁵ For it is sanctified by the word of God and prayer.

⁷ But refuse profane and old wives' fables, and exercise thyself *rather* unto godliness.

The Spirit of love wants to protect us from evil! God invented marriage in the beginning. God approved marriage and meat. (see Genesis 2:24; 9:3) In these verses, what things oppose the faith? (see Acts 13:8)

_____
_____
_____
_____

NEGLECT NOT THE GIFT THAT IS IN THEE

1 Timothy 4:12 – 16 (KJV)

¹² Let no man despise thy youth; but be thou an example of the believers, in word, in conversation, in charity, in spirit, in faith, in purity.

¹³ Till I come, give attendance to reading, to exhortation, to doctrine.

¹⁴ Neglect not the gift that is in thee, which was given thee by prophecy, with the laying on of the hands of the presbytery.

¹⁵ Meditate upon these things; give thyself wholly to them; that thy profiting may appear to all.

¹⁶ Take heed unto thyself, and unto the doctrine; continue in them: for in doing this thou shalt both save thyself, and them that hear thee.

The Spirit warns us not to be judgmental, and not to join in with those who are, but to keep **our conduct with the charity of the Spirit.** (see Philippians 4:8; Psalms 1:1 – 3; 1 Corinthians 12:3 – 12) Who transfers the gift to them? (1 Corinthians 12:8 – 11)

_____
_____
_____
_____

HOLY GHOST WHICH DWELLETH IN US

2 Timothy 1:9 – 10, 13 – 14 (KJV)
[9] Who hath saved us, and called *us* with an holy calling, not according to our works, but according to his own purpose and grace, which was given us in Christ Jesus before the world began,
[10] But is now made manifest by the appearing of our Saviour Jesus Christ, who hath abolished death, and hath brought life and immortality to light through the gospel:
[13] Hold fast the form of sound words, which thou hast heard of me, in faith and love which is in Christ Jesus.
[14] That good thing which was committed unto thee keep by the Holy Ghost which dwelleth in us.

The **Holy Ghost in us declared us** to be **the house of the Holy Ghost**. The word us tells us the same Holy Ghost in Paul was also in Timothy. What happened before?

_____
_____
_____
_____
_____
_____
_____

SCRIPTURE IS GIVEN BY INSPIRATION OF GOD

2 Timothy 3:14 – 17 (KJV)
[14] But continue thou in the things which thou hast learned and hast been assured of, knowing of whom thou hast learned *them*;
[15] And that from a child thou hast known the holy scriptures, which are able to make thee wise unto salvation through faith which is in Christ Jesus.
[16] All scripture *is* given by inspiration of God, and *is* profitable for doctrine, for reproof, for correction, for instruction in righteousness:
[17] That the man of God may be perfect, throughly furnished unto all good works.

Saul/Paul (evangelist), Apollos (a great speaker) and Timothy (pastor) were taught Old Testament wisdom when they were young. All Scripture is the **Voice of the Spirit of God in written form**. (see John 20:22; Joshua 1:5, 8; Psalm 1:1 – 3) Every word of The Holy Scriptures are the **Spirit-word, God's breath on a page.**

_____
_____
_____
_____
_____

date_____

RENEWING OF THE HOLY GHOST

Titus 3:4 – 7 (KJV)
[4] But after that the kindness and love of God our Saviour toward man appeared,
[5] Not by works of righteousness which we have done, but according to his mercy he saved us, by the washing of regeneration, and renewing of the Holy Ghost;
[6] Which he shed on us abundantly through Jesus Christ our Saviour;
[7] That being justified by his grace, we should be made heirs according to the hope of eternal life.

The Holy Ghost has the power to recreate and to restore; and **He is in you.** (see 1 Peter 2:4 – 5) No natural means could save us. **We are heirs** through the supernatural **measure of the gospel of grace** through Jesus Christ (3:1 – 8). (see Joel 2:28 – 29; Acts 2:16 – 18) What is a hindrance and how will you dismantle it this year? (see Habakkuk 2:2)

_____
_____
_____
_____
_____
_____
_____

date_____

BY HIMSELF (THE MAJESTY) PURGED OUR SINS

Hebrews 1:1, 2, 3, 5 (KJV)
[1] God, who at sundry times and in divers manners spake in time past unto the fathers by the prophets,
[2] Hath in these last days spoken unto us by *his* Son, whom he hath appointed heir of all things, by whom also he made the worlds;
[3] Who being the brightness of *his* glory, and the express image of his person, and upholding all things by the word of his power, when he had by himself purged our sins, sat down on the right hand of the Majesty on high;
[5] For unto which of the angels said he at any time, Thou art my Son, this day have I begotten thee? And again, I will be to him a Father, and he shall be to me a Son?

(Psalm 2:7, 8) From the lineage of David, came the Savior, Jesus. We believed through their word and are thereby **children in the faith** (John 17:20).
Christ (the Son of God) suffered for us so He could **present us to God.**

_____
_____
_____
_____

date_____

CAPTAIN OF THEIR SALVATION

Hebrews 2:10 – 12 (KJV)

[10] For it became him, for whom *are* all things, and by whom *are* all things, in bringing many sons unto glory, to make the captain of their salvation perfect through sufferings.

[11] For both he that sanctifieth and they who are sanctified *are* all of one: for which cause he is not ashamed to call them brethren,

[12] Saying, I will declare thy name unto my brethren, in the midst of the church will I sing praise unto thee.

[17] Wherefore in all things it behoved him to be made like unto *his* brethren, that he might be a merciful and faithful high priest in things *pertaining* to God, to make reconciliation for the sins of the people.

Jesus paid for our salvation. He is sanctifying. We are sanctified and we are both of One. We are the children; the ones who benefit! We are His so we inherit from Him.

_____
_____
_____
_____
_____
_____

date_____

HOLY GHOST SAITH, TO DAY

Hebrews 3:5 – 8 (KJV)

[5] And Moses verily *was* faithful in all his house, as a servant, for a testimony of those things which were to be spoken after;

[6] But Christ as a son over his own house; whose house are we, if we hold fast the confidence and the rejoicing of the hope firm unto the end.

[7] Wherefore (as the Holy Ghost saith, To day if ye will hear his voice,

[8] Harden not your hearts, as in the provocation, in the day of temptation in the wilderness:

Jesus didn't come to earth to condemn mankind, but as our High Priest, to love each of us into His kingdom. How can we follow Him?

_____
_____
_____
_____
_____
_____
_____
_____
_____
_____

date_____
THRONE OF GRACE

Hebrews 4:12, 14, 15, 16 (KJV)

¹² For the word of God *is* quick, and powerful, and sharper than any twoedged sword, piercing even to the dividing asunder of soul and spirit, and of the joints and marrow, and *is* a discerner of the thoughts and intents of the heart.

¹⁴ Seeing then that we have a great high priest, that is passed into the heavens, Jesus the Son of God, let us hold fast *our* profession.

¹⁵ For we have not an high priest which cannot be touched with the feeling of our infirmities; but was in all points tempted like as *we are, yet* without sin.

¹⁶ Let us therefore come boldly unto the throne of grace, that we may obtain mercy, and find grace to help in time of need.

LORD JESUS forgive me as if the curse never happened. In the name of JESUS. Amen. (see Romans 8:32)

_____
_____
_____
_____
_____
_____
_____

date_____
CHRIST GLORIFIED NOT HIMSELF

Hebrews 5:1, 2, 4, 5, 7 (KJV)

¹ For every high priest taken from among men is ordained for men in things *pertaining* to God, that he may offer both gifts and sacrifices for sins:

² Who can have compassion on the ignorant, and on them that are out of the way; for that he himself also is compassed with infirmity.

⁴ And no man taketh this honour unto himself, but he that is called of God, as *was* Aaron.

⁵ So also Christ glorified not himself to be made an high priest; but he that said unto him, Thou art my Son, to day have I begotten thee.

⁷ Who in the days of his flesh, when he had offered up prayers and supplications with strong crying and tears unto him that was able to save him from death, and was heard in that he feared;

Jesus is our High Priest; and our Sacrifice; who asked the Father if there was any other way but God let Him know there was only one way, so Jesus said "Your will be done."

_____
_____
_____
_____

PARTAKERS OF THE HOLY GHOST

Hebrews 6:4 – 7, 10 (KJV)
[4] For *it is* impossible for those who were once enlightened, and have tasted of the heavenly gift, and were made partakers of the Holy Ghost,
[5] And have tasted the good word of God, and the powers of the world to come,
[6] If they shall fall away, to renew them again unto repentance; seeing they crucify to themselves the Son of God afresh, and put *him* to an open shame.
[7] For the earth which drinketh in the rain that cometh oft upon it, and bringeth forth herbs meet for them by whom it is dressed, receiveth blessing from God:
[10] For God *is* not unrighteous to forget your work and labour of love, which ye have shewed toward his name, in that ye have ministered to the saints, and do minister.

The sermon that isn't preached, but lived openly, is the **hardest sermon to ignore**.

_____
_____
_____
_____
_____
_____

BETTER HOPE...OFFERED UP HIMSELF

Hebrews 7:19, 24, 27, 28 (KJV)
[19] For the law made nothing perfect, but the bringing in of a better hope *did*; by the which we draw nigh unto God.
[24] But this *man*, because he continueth ever, hath an unchangeable priesthood.
[27] Who needeth not daily, as those high priests, to offer up sacrifice, first for his own sins, and then for the people's: for this he did once, when he offered up himself.
[28] For the law maketh men high priests which have infirmity; but the word of the oath, which was since the law, *maketh* the Son, who is consecrated for evermore.

Jesus did for us what we couldn't do for ourselves, being that we are only human; but He is the Lamb of God: He offered Himself. (see 5:1 – 8) When we 'draw nigh' to God, He comes nearer to us too. What happens when the Creator gets nearer to us?

_____
_____
_____
_____
_____
_____

date_____

THE MAJESTY IN THE HEAVENS

Hebrews 8:1, 2, 3, 4, 12 (KJV)

¹ Now of the things which we have spoken *this is* the sum: We have such an high priest, who is set on the right hand of the throne of the Majesty in the heavens;

² A minister of the sanctuary, and of the true tabernacle, which the Lord pitched, and not man.

³ For every high priest is ordained to offer gifts and sacrifices: wherefore *it is* of necessity that this man have somewhat also to offer.

⁴ For if he were on earth, he should not be a priest, seeing that there are priests that offer gifts according to the law:

¹² For I will be merciful to their unrighteousness, and their sins and their iniquities will I remember no more.

The New Covenant says God will not remember our sin because He remembers Jesus on the cross for us! How can God pass over our sins? Jesus, the Majesty in the heavens, took away our sin when He was dying and died on the cross.

_____

_____

_____

_____

date_____

THE HOLY GHOST THIS SIGNIFYING

Hebrews 9:7, 8, 11, 12 (KJV)

⁷ But into the second *went* the high priest alone once every year, not without blood, which he offered for himself, and *for* the errors of the people:

⁸ The Holy Ghost this signifying, that the way into the holiest of all was not yet made manifest, while as the first tabernacle was yet standing:

¹¹ But Christ being come an high priest of good things to come, by a greater and more perfect tabernacle, not made with hands, that is to say, not of this building;

¹² Neither by the blood of goats and calves, but by his own blood he entered in once into the holy place, having obtained eternal redemption *for us.*

Jesus paid for everything for us to have His eternal redemption, His redemption (9:17)! The Holy Ghost is our Teacher and Guide to show us the way. So now we are both here and seated with Jesus in heavenly places with a whole new view of mankind and view of life on earth.

_____

_____

_____

_____

date_____

ETERNAL SPIRIT...ETERNAL INHERITANCE :14

Hebrews 9:13, 14, 15, 17 (KJV)

¹³ For if the blood of bulls and of goats, and the ashes of an heifer sprinkling the unclean, sanctifieth to the purifying of the flesh:

¹⁴ How much more shall the blood of Christ, who through the eternal Spirit offered himself without spot to God, purge your conscience from dead works to serve the living God?

¹⁵ And for this cause he is the mediator of the new testament, that by means of death, for the redemption of the transgressions *that were* under the first testament, they which are called might receive the promise of eternal inheritance.

¹⁷ For a testament *is* of force after men are dead: otherwise it is of no strength at all while the testator liveth.

Jesus had to die! Why? So God could raise Jesus from the dead. **We are accepted** in The Beloved Christ Jesus forever because His Spirit is the Eternal Spirit in us – by faith.

_____
_____
_____
_____
_____
_____

date_____

THE HOLY GHOST ALSO IS A WITNESS TO US

Hebrews 10:10, 14, 15, 17 (KJV)

¹⁰ By the which will we are sanctified through the offering of the body of Jesus Christ once *for all*.

¹⁴ For by one offering he hath perfected for ever them that are sanctified.

¹⁵ *Whereof* the Holy Ghost also is a witness to us: for after that he had said before,

¹⁷ And their sins and iniquities will I remember no more.

No offering for sin can top the offering of the body of Jesus for our sin at the cross, seeing we are already entering the Holiest of all through the veil (10:19, 20)! God isn't punishing us. God sent His only Son to pay for our sins so we could enter His mercy.

_____
_____
_____
_____
_____
_____
_____
_____
_____
_____
_____
_____

date_____
SPIRIT OF GRACE

Hebrews 10:25, 28, 29, 35 (KJV)
²⁵ Not forsaking the assembling of ourselves together, as the manner of some *is*; but exhorting *one another*: and so much the more, as ye see the day approaching.
²⁸ He that despised Moses' law died without mercy under two or three witnesses:
²⁹ Of how much sorer punishment, suppose ye, shall he be thought worthy, who hath trodden under foot the Son of God, and hath counted the blood of the covenant, wherewith he was sanctified, an unholy thing, and hath done despite unto the Spirit of grace?
³⁵ Cast not away therefore your confidence, which hath great recompence of reward.

If we have asked for forgiveness again and again for the same sin, then we are under condemnation and this is not of God! We can trust the Covenant of God!

_____
_____
_____
_____
_____
_____
_____

date_____
WHO IS INVISIBLE

Hebrews 11:24 – 27 (KJV)
²⁴ By faith Moses, when he was come to years, refused to be called the son of Pharaoh's daughter;
²⁵ Choosing rather to suffer affliction with the people of God, than to enjoy the pleasures of sin for a season;
²⁶ Esteeming the reproach of Christ greater riches than the treasures in Egypt: for he had respect unto the recompence of the reward.
²⁷ By faith he forsook Egypt, not fearing the wrath of the king: for he endured, as seeing him who is invisible.

Moses worshipped in Spirit and knew the Christ would come, for he said, "God will raise up a Prophet" (Deuteronomy 18:1). (see 11:11; Matthew 5:8)

_____
_____
_____
_____
_____
_____
_____
_____
_____

FATHER OF SPIRITS

Hebrews 12:2, 3, 9, 10 (KJV)

2 Looking unto Jesus the author and finisher of *our* faith; who for the joy that was set before him endured the cross, despising the shame, and is set down at the right hand of the throne of God.

3 For consider him that endured such contradiction of sinners against himself, lest ye be wearied and faint in your minds.

9 Furthermore we have had fathers of our flesh which corrected *us*, and we gave *them* reverence: shall we not much rather be in subjection unto the Father of spirits, and live?

10 For they verily for a few days chastened *us* after their own pleasure; but he for *our* profit, that *we* might be partakers of his holiness.

We see holiness only through our relationship with Jesus! (see James 1:18; 2 Corinthians 6:17 – 7:2; Romans 1:4; 1 Thessalonians 3:11 – 13) Grace is the right road to be on!

SPIRITS OF JUST MEN MADE PERFECT

Hebrews 12:22, 23, 24, 28 (KJV)

22 But ye are come unto mount Sion, and unto the city of the living God, the heavenly Jerusalem, and to an innumerable company of angels,

23 To the general assembly and church of the firstborn, which are written in heaven, and to God the Judge of all, and to the spirits of just men made perfect,

24 And to Jesus the mediator of the new covenant, and to the blood of sprinkling, that speaketh better things than *that of* Abel.

28 Wherefore we receiving a kingdom which cannot be moved, let us have grace, whereby we may serve God acceptably with reverence and godly fear:

The blood of Jesus speaks the covenant of God over us. So we take part in the kingdom of grace, the kingdom that's forever (12:22 – 28). (see 1 Corinthians 11:24; Genesis 17:1)

OUR LORD JESUS, THAT GREAT SHEPHERD

Hebrews 13:18 – 21 (KJV)

[18] Pray for us: for we trust we have a good conscience, in all things willing to live honestly.

[19] But I beseech *you* the rather to do this, that I may be restored to you the sooner.

[20] Now the God of peace, that brought again from the dead our Lord Jesus, that great shepherd of the sheep, through the blood of the everlasting covenant,

[21] Make you perfect in every good work to do his will, working in you that which is wellpleasing in his sight, through Jesus Christ; to whom *be* glory for ever and ever. Amen.

God is working out His will through us to bring about the purpose of His goodness. As we live our life as if **Jesus were coming this evening**, others will see Jesus in us. (see Philippians 2:10 – 13; Romans 2:4)

_____
_____
_____
_____
_____
_____
_____

SANCTIFICATION OF THE SPIRIT

1 Peter 1:2 – 5 (KJV)

[2] Elect according to the foreknowledge of God the Father, through sanctification of the Spirit, unto obedience and sprinkling of the blood of Jesus Christ: Grace unto you, and peace, be multiplied.

[3] Blessed *be* the God and Father of our Lord Jesus Christ, which according to his abundant mercy hath begotten us again unto a lively hope by the resurrection of Jesus Christ from the dead,

[4] To an inheritance incorruptible, and undefiled, and that fadeth not away, reserved in heaven for you,

[5] Who are kept by the power of God through faith unto salvation ready to be revealed in the last time.

Sanctification is the ongoing process of cleansing us and forgiving us through the sacrifice of our Lord Jesus, by the Spirit of Christ in us. (Ephesians 1:15 – 20)

_____
_____
_____
_____
_____
_____
_____

BY THE SPIRIT OF CHRIST

WITH THE HOLY GHOST

1 Peter 1:8 – 11 (KJV)
[8] Whom having not seen, ye love; in whom, though now ye see *him* not, yet believing, ye rejoice with joy unspeakable and full of glory:
[9] Receiving the end of your faith, *even* the salvation of *your* souls.
[10] Of which salvation the prophets have enquired and searched diligently, who prophesied of the grace *that should come* unto you:
[11] Searching what, or what manner of time the Spirit of Christ which was in them did signify, when it testified beforehand the sufferings of Christ, and the glory that should follow.

The determination of the Spirit testified! The Spirit signified. By the prophecy in them, the prophets searched for the time of Christ.

_____
_____
_____
_____
_____
_____
_____
_____
_____

1 Peter 1:10 – 12 (KJV)
[10] Of which salvation the prophets have enquired and searched diligently, who prophesied of the grace *that should come* unto you:
[11] Searching what, or what manner of time the Spirit of Christ which was in them did signify, when it testified beforehand the sufferings of Christ, and the glory that should follow.
[12] Unto whom it was revealed, that not unto themselves, but unto us they did minister the things, which are now reported unto you by them that have preached the gospel unto you with the Holy Ghost sent down from heaven; which things the angels desire to look into.

Jesus suffered so we could receive the gospel by the grace that witnessed in the prophets.
(see Nehemiah 9:30)

_____
_____
_____
_____
_____
_____
_____

TRUTH THROUGH THE SPIRIT

1 Peter 1:18 – 23 (KJV)

[18] Forasmuch as ye know that ye were not redeemed with corruptible things, *as* silver and gold, from your vain conversation *received* by tradition from your fathers;

[19] But with the precious blood of Christ, as of a lamb without blemish and without spot:

[20] Who verily was foreordained before the foundation of the world, but was manifest in these last times for you,

[21] Who by him do believe in God, that raised him up from the dead, and gave him glory; that your faith and hope might be in God.

[22] Seeing ye have purified your souls in obeying the truth through the Spirit unto unfeigned love of the brethren, *see that ye* love one another with a pure heart fervently:

[23] Being born again, not of corruptible seed, but of incorruptible, by the word of God, which liveth and abideth for ever.

The Incorruptible Spirit of Christ came to live inside us and He changed our want-tos.

_____
_____
_____
_____

YE...ARE BUILT UP A SPIRITUAL HOUSE

1 Peter 2:1 – 5 (KJV)

[1] Wherefore laying aside all malice, and all guile, and hypocrisies, and envies, and all evil speakings,

[2] As newborn babes, desire the sincere milk of the word, that ye may grow thereby:

[3] If so be ye have tasted that the Lord *is* gracious.

[4] To whom coming, *as unto* a living stone, disallowed indeed of men, but chosen of God, *and* precious,

[5] Ye also, as lively stones, are built up a spiritual house, an holy priesthood, to offer up spiritual sacrifices, acceptable to God by Jesus Christ.

We are a spiritual house, the house of the Holy Ghost! We go about teaching the Holy Word and living the gospel of Jesus Christ (2:1 – 9). (see 1 Corinthians 3:9; 9:7 – 14; 2 Corinthians 6:14 – 18; Romans 12 1 – 2; 2 Samuel 7:11)

_____
_____
_____
_____
_____
_____
_____
_____

QUICKENED BY THE SPIRIT

1 Peter 3:14 – 18 (KJV)
[14] But and if ye suffer for righteousness' sake, happy *are ye*: and be not afraid of their terror, neither be troubled;
[15] But sanctify the Lord God in your hearts: and *be* ready always to *give* an answer to every man that asketh you a reason of the hope that is in you with meekness and fear:
[16] Having a good conscience; that, whereas they speak evil of you, as of evildoers, they may be ashamed that falsely accuse your good conversation in Christ.
[17] For *it is* better, if the will of God be so, that ye suffer for well doing, than for evil doing.
[18] For Christ also hath once suffered for sins, the just for the unjust, that he might bring us to God, being put to death in the flesh, but quickened by the Spirit:

Through Christ we are all called to suffer for His name. As we do, He empowers us. (see 1:15; 2:9; 5:10; 2 Peter 1:3; 2 Timothy 1:8 – 9; 6:12; Colossians 3:15; Romans 8:28)

_____
_____
_____
_____

ACCORDING TO GOD IN THE SPIRIT

1 Peter 4:4 – 7, 10 (KJV)
[4] Wherein they think it strange that ye run not with *them* to the same excess of riot, speaking evil of *you*:
[5] Who shall give account to him that is ready to judge the quick and the dead.
[6] For for this cause was the gospel preached also to them that are dead, that they might be judged according to men in the flesh, but live according to God in the spirit.
[7] But the end of all things is at hand: be ye therefore sober, and watch unto prayer.
[10] As every man hath received the gift, *even so* minister the same one to another, as good stewards of the manifold grace of God.

The gospel *was preached* (past tense) to them while they were alive and believed but they *are dead* (present tense) here, so they **now live in the presence of Almighty God and in the Spirit-dimension.** We are the managers here of His infinite grace.
As we use our **gifts of grace** here and now, may we be used up for His glory.

_____
_____
_____
_____

THE SPIRIT OF GLORY AND OF GOD

1 Peter 4:11 – 14 (KJV)

[11] If any man speak, *let him speak* as the oracles of God; if any man minister, *let him do it* as of the ability which God giveth: that God in all things may be glorified through Jesus Christ, to whom be praise and dominion for ever and ever. Amen.

[12] Beloved, think it not strange concerning the fiery trial which is to try you, as though some strange thing happened unto you:

[13] But rejoice, inasmuch as ye are partakers of Christ's sufferings; that, when his glory shall be revealed, ye may be glad also with exceeding joy.

[14] If ye be reproached for the name of Christ, happy *are ye*; for the spirit of glory and of God resteth upon you: on their part he is evil spoken of, but on your part he is glorified.

When we know and believe our destination and position in Christ, we will become unstoppable by the Spirit of God because of His provision (Genesis 22:14)! (see John 17:10)

_____
_____
_____
_____
_____

MOVED BY THE HOLY GHOST

2 Peter 1:19 – 21 (KJV)

[19] We have also a more sure word of prophecy; whereunto ye do well that ye take heed, as unto a light that shineth in a dark place, until the day dawn, and the day star arise in your hearts:

[20] Knowing this first, that no prophecy of the scripture is of any private interpretation.

[21] For the prophecy came not in old time by the will of man: but holy men of God spake *as they were* moved by the Holy Ghost.

God knows how to deliver the righteous (1:18; 2:4 – 9)!

The Bible is God-breathed and Holy Spirit-interpreted as He spoke to holy men who put **God's breath on paper** – for you. What happens when **your vision, God's plan in you**, comes from His Word?

_____
_____
_____
_____
_____
_____
_____
_____
_____
_____

BORN OF GOD...CHILDREN OF GOD

1 John 3:2, 3, 10, 11 (KJV)

[2] Beloved, now are we the sons of God, and it doth not yet appear what we shall be: but we know that, when he shall appear, we shall be like him; for we shall see him as he is.

[3] And every man that hath this hope in him purifieth himself, even as he is pure.

[10] In this the children of God are manifest, and the children of the devil: whosoever doeth not righteousness is not of God, neither he that loveth not his brother.

[11] For this is the message that ye heard from the beginning, that we should love one another.

How do we speak of ourselves? How do we speak of others?

"Born of God" is born of Spirit; of the Spirit of our Father; born again (John 3:1 – 3). (see 1 John 5:4 – 5) We have the Spirit of God in us and we therefore want to please our heavenly Father. We desire nearness with our Father. Fellowship is of the Spirit of unity (1 John 1). We are His kids and we know He loves us because His love is in us!

BY THE SPIRIT HE HATH GIVEN US

1 John 3:20 – 24 (KJV)

[20] For if our heart condemn us, God is greater than our heart, and knoweth all things.

[21] Beloved, if our heart condemn us not, *then* have we confidence toward God.

[22] And whatsoever we ask, we receive of him, because we keep his commandments, and do those things that are pleasing in his sight.

[23] And this is his commandment, That we should believe on the name of his Son Jesus Christ, and love one another, as he gave us commandment.

[24] And he that keepeth his commandments dwelleth in him, and he in him. And hereby we know that he abideth in us, by the Spirit which he hath given us.

When we have surrendered to the living God, He gave us the prayer at that moment. He also gives us the prayers **He has already answered** (Psalm 37:4). We've been **tracing the steps of the Spirit.** His steps have led to you! Who is the Seed who remains in us? (3:9, 24) (see 3:24; Acts 17:31; Psalm 37:23)

HEREBY KNOW YE THE SPIRIT OF GOD

1 John 4:1 – 3 (KJV)
[1] Beloved, believe not every spirit, but try the spirits whether they are of God: because many false prophets are gone out into the world.
[2] Hereby know ye the Spirit of God: Every spirit that confesseth that Jesus Christ is come in the flesh is of God:
[3] And every spirit that confesseth not that Jesus Christ is come in the flesh is not of God: and this is that *spirit* of antichrist, whereof ye have heard that it should come; and even now already is it in the world.

If we are for Him, we aren't against Him! He has chosen us and we have chosen to live for Him because we are Christ's **so we come together** (1 John 3:3; Galatians 3:29, 5:24).
We love the brethren and thereby we confess Jesus Christ to the world and one another (4:2; 3:10 – 11). Who are they who are against the Spirit of God?

_____
_____
_____
_____
_____
_____
_____

THE SPIRIT OF TRUTH

1 John 4:5 – 7 (KJV)
[5] They are of the world: therefore speak they of the world, and the world heareth them.
[6] We are of God: he that knoweth God heareth us; he that is not of God heareth not us. Hereby know we the spirit of truth, and the spirit of error.
[7] Beloved, let us love one another: for love is of God; and every one that loveth is born of God, and knoweth God.

Did you ever want to know for sure? He just told us infallible discernment. The Spirit of truth will listen to and love the truth and those of the Truth! (1 John 4) (see John 15:26)
God is Love. God is Spirit. The love of God (in our hearts) made visible to others will assure us (in our hearts) and this truth will make us free. We perceive God in us by and through **His love working in and through us** (3:16; 4:7 – 8; John 4:24). (see 5:7 – 10; John 19:35) When we are born of God, who does that make God to us? (Matthew 6:9)

_____
_____
_____
_____
_____

date_____

GIVEN US OF HIS (GOD'S) SPIRIT

1 John 4:9, 10, 13, 14, 15 (KJV)

⁹ In this was manifested the love of God toward us, because that God sent his only begotten Son into the world, that we might live through him.

¹⁰ Herein is love, not that we loved God, but that he loved us, and sent his Son *to be* the propitiation for our sins.

¹³ Hereby know we that we dwell in him, and he in us, because he hath given us of his Spirit.

¹⁴ And we have seen and do testify that the Father sent the Son *to be* the Saviour of the world.

¹⁵ Whosoever shall confess that Jesus is the Son of God, God dwelleth in him, and he in God.

Being born of God, we are His children. He will not hold back any good thing from us. He cares for us more than we could understand (Psalm 84:11; 1 Peter 5:7). (see 4:19)

_____
_____
_____
_____
_____
_____
_____
_____

date_____

SPIRIT...BECAUSE THE SPIRIT IS TRUTH

1 John 5:2 – 6 (KJV)

² By this we know that we love the children of God, when we love God, and keep his commandments.

³ For this is the love of God, that we keep his commandments: and his commandments are not grievous.

⁴ For whatsoever is born of God overcometh the world: and this is the victory that overcometh the world, *even* our faith.

⁵ Who is he that overcometh the world, but he that believeth that Jesus is the Son of God?

⁶ This is he that came by water and blood, *even* Jesus Christ; not by water only, but by water and blood. And it is the Spirit that beareth witness, because the Spirit is truth.

The Witness is the Holy Spirit living in us, causing us to want to live closer to Him! We make a difference for one, with the Spirit of Jesus in us. (see Hebrews 10:15)

_____
_____
_____
_____
_____
_____

FATHER, THE WORD, AND THE HOLY GHOST

1 John 5:4 – 7 (KJV)

[4] For whatsoever is born of God overcometh the world: and this is the victory that overcometh the world, *even* our faith.

[5] Who is he that overcometh the world, but he that believeth that Jesus is the Son of God?

[6] This is he that came by water and blood, *even* Jesus Christ; not by water only, but by water and blood. And it is the Spirit that beareth witness, because the Spirit is truth.

[7] For there are three that bear record in heaven, the Father, the Word, and the Holy Ghost: and these three are one.

We are born of God and focused on His kingdom as one, to help one more life. We are coming out by the Father's love! We overcome by believing Jesus is the one and only Son of God. When **we focus on His kingdom, He will focus on our dream**; and He will make it bigger than we could have thought (Isaiah 55:8 – 9; Jeremiah 29:11).

_____
_____
_____
_____
_____

THE SPIRIT...WATER...BLOOD

1 John 5:8, 9, 13 (KJV)

[8] And there are three that bear witness in earth, the Spirit, and the water, and the blood: and these three agree in one.

[9] If we receive the witness of men, the witness of God is greater: for this is the witness of God which he hath testified of his Son.

[13] These things have I written unto you that believe on the name of the Son of God; that ye may know that ye have eternal life, and that ye may believe on the name of the Son of God.

When the Roman speared Jesus after He died on the cross, water and blood came from the side of Jesus. It was the **inauguration of the church**, the body of Jesus, whom God raised from the dead and He is alive forever more. We are without limits in His name!

As we read God's words to Him as our prayer of faith, He hears and we have the Petition of Truth. We are **expecting heaven's answer** (5:14 – 15).

_____
_____
_____
_____
_____
_____

SENSUAL, HAVING NOT THE SPIRIT

Jude 1:17 – 20 (KJV)
17 But, beloved, remember ye the words which were spoken before of the apostles of our Lord Jesus Christ;
18 How that they told you there should be mockers in the last time, who should walk after their own ungodly lusts.
19 These be they who separate themselves, sensual, having not the Spirit.
20 But ye, beloved, building up yourselves on your most holy faith, praying in the Holy Ghost,

As we pray in the Spirit, we are covered in grace! When is God praying on our behalf? What is the difference between having not the Spirit and praying in the Holy Ghost? Why did translators of the KJV use "Spirit" and "Holy Ghost" in the same 2 verses? In reverence, the first translators made a distinction between Spirit and Holy Ghost.
Lord, to be with You is everything!

_____
_____
_____
_____
_____
_____

PRAYING IN THE HOLY GHOST

Jude 1:20, 21, 22, 24 (KJV)
20 But ye, beloved, building up yourselves on your most holy faith, praying in the Holy Ghost,
21 Keep yourselves in the love of God, looking for the mercy of our Lord Jesus Christ unto eternal life.
22 And of some have compassion, making a difference:
24 Now unto him that is able to keep you from falling, and to present *you* faultless before the presence of his glory with exceeding joy,

We rescue others and we are **defended by mercy** (Jude 1:23). (see 1 John 2:1; Matthew 5:7; James 2:13) Compassion defends the faith! Our compassion for others is making a difference one life at a time! (see Luke 10:33; Matthew 6:13) Jesus works that way too. In verse 24, who can present us "faultless" before the presence of His Glory? How does verse 22 describe making a difference?

_____
_____
_____
_____
_____
_____

THE REVELATION OF JESUS CHRIST
WORD OF GOD

Revelation 1:1 – 3, 5 (KJV)

[1] The Revelation of Jesus Christ, which God gave unto him, to shew unto his servants things which must shortly come to pass; and he sent and signified *it* by his angel unto his servant John:

[2] Who bare record of the word of God, and of the testimony of Jesus Christ, and of all things that he saw.

[3] Blessed *is* he that readeth, and they that hear the words of this prophecy, and keep those things which are written therein: for the time *is* at hand.

[5] And from Jesus Christ, *who is* the faithful witness, *and* the first begotten of the dead, and the prince of the kings of the earth. Unto him that loved us, and washed us from our sins in his own blood,

Jesus was made the curse for us (Galatians 3:13). He is the Faithful Witness. **In His agony, He cleansed us** (Romans 8:32). What is His testimony?

_____
_____
_____
_____
_____

TESTIMONY OF JESUS CHRIST IN THE SPIRIT ON THE LORD'S DAY

Revelation 1:9 – 12 (KJV)

[9] I John, who also am your brother, and companion in tribulation, and in the kingdom and patience of Jesus Christ, was in the isle that is called Patmos, for the word of God, and for the testimony of Jesus Christ.

[10] I was in the Spirit on the Lord's day, and heard behind me a great voice, as of a trumpet,

[11] Saying, I am Alpha and Omega, the first and the last: and, What thou seest, write in a book, and send *it* unto the seven churches which are in Asia; unto Ephesus, and unto Smyrna, and unto Pergamos, and unto Thyatira, and unto Sardis, and unto Philadelphia, and unto Laodicea.

[12] And I turned to see the voice that spake with me. And being turned, I saw seven golden candlesticks;

John would live by himself on an island. Where would he visit and was he alone?

_____
_____
_____
_____
_____

THE CHURCH OF EPHESUS HEAR WHAT THE SPIRIT SAITH

Revelation 2:1, 2, 4, 7 (KJV)

[1] Unto the angel of the church of Ephesus write; These things saith he that holdeth the seven stars in his right hand, who walketh in the midst of the seven golden candlesticks;

[2] I know thy works, and thy labour, and thy patience, and how thou canst not bear them which are evil: and thou hast tried them which say they are apostles, and are not, and hast found them liars:

[4] Nevertheless I have *somewhat* against thee, because thou hast left thy first love.

[7] He that hath an ear, let him hear what the Spirit saith unto the churches; To him that overcometh will I give to eat of the tree of life, which is in the midst of the paradise of God.

God adorns His kingdom with His ministries! Evils fade and lives are transformed when there's more **Jesus kingdom on the calendar.** (see Luke 8:8; 23:43; 1 John 5:1 – 4) Jesus is speaking. Who are the overcomers He speaks about?

_____
_____
_____
_____

CHURCH IN SMYRNA …PERGAMOS HEAR WHAT THE SPIRIT SAITH

Revelation 2:8, 11, 12, 17 (KJV)

[8] And unto the angel of the church in Smyrna write; These things saith the first and the last, which was dead, and is alive;

[11] He that hath an ear, let him hear what the Spirit saith unto the churches; He that overcometh shall not be hurt of the second death.

[12] And to the angel of the church in Pergamos write; These things saith he which hath the sharp sword with two edges;

[17] He that hath an ear, let him hear what the Spirit saith unto the churches; To him that overcometh will I give to eat of the hidden manna, and will give him a white stone, and in the stone a new name written, which no man knoweth saving he that receiveth *it*.

As they **vote in Jesus name,** they would receive **the pardon vote from God.** Josiah earned a pardon for himself and even for his whole nation when he humbled himself through pure obedience to the Holy Word of God (2 Kings 22). What's your gift?

_____
_____
_____

date_____

I (JESUS) GIVE POWER OVER THE NATIONS
HERE WHAT THE SPIRIT SAITH

Revelation 2:18, 25 – 29 (KJV)

[18] And unto the angel of the church in Thyatira write; These things saith the Son of God, who hath his eyes like unto a flame of fire, and his feet *are* like fine brass;

[25] But that which ye have *already* hold fast till I come.

[26] And he that overcometh, and keepeth my works unto the end, to him will I give power over the nations:

[27] And he shall rule them with a rod of iron; as the vessels of a potter shall they be broken to shivers: even as I received of my Father.

[28] And I will give him the morning star.

[29] He that hath an ear, let him hear what the Spirit saith unto the churches.

Jesus promises power to the faithful **in the same church. He distributes power** over the enemies to the overcomers (2:24, 26). (see Psalm 2:8) Jesus received the power to rule and who else received the power? (see 2:17, 27; 3:21; John 17:22; Acts 20:24)

date_____

CHURCH IN PHILADELPHIA
WHAT THE SPIRIT SAITH

Revelation 3:6 – 8, 10, 13 (KJV)

[6] He that hath an ear, let him hear what the Spirit saith unto the churches.

[7] And to the angel of the church in Philadelphia write; These things saith he that is holy, he that is true, he that hath the key of David, he that openeth, and no man shutteth; and shutteth, and no man openeth;

[8] I know thy works: behold, I have set before thee an open door, and no man can shut it: for thou hast a little strength, and hast kept my word, and hast not denied my name.

[10] Because thou hast kept the word of my patience, I also will keep thee from the hour of temptation, which shall come upon all the world, to try them that dwell upon the earth.

[13] He that hath an ear, let him hear what the Spirit saith unto the churches.

Protection granted! The church congregation may look small, but Jesus is on the other side of the door and God's Word remains strong forever for you. (see 2 Timothy 4:2) Jesus will shut the door of temptation for you. (see Luke 11:4)

I (JESUS) WILL...SUP WITH HIM
SPIRIT SAITH UNTO THE CHURCHES

Revelation 3:14, 16, 19 – 22 (KJV)

¹⁴ And unto the angel of the church of the Laodiceans write; These things saith the Amen, the faithful and true witness, the beginning of the creation of God;

¹⁶ So then because thou art lukewarm, and neither cold nor hot, I will spue thee out of my mouth.

¹⁹ As many as I love, I rebuke and chasten: be zealous therefore, and repent.

²⁰ Behold, I stand at the door, and knock: if any man hear my voice, and open the door, I will come in to him, and will sup with him, and he with me.

²¹ To him that overcometh will I grant to sit with me in my throne, even as I also overcame, and am set down with my Father in his throne.

²² He that hath an ear, let him hear what the Spirit saith unto the churches.

The grant! We became an overcomer through repentance. Jesus **granted us a seat with Him.** (see John 10:27; 21:12; Ephesians 1:3). The throne of grace is open wide for us.

_____
_____

COME UP HITHER
I (JOHN) WAS IN THE SPIRIT
Revelation 4:1, 2, 4 (KJV)

¹ After this I looked, and, behold, a door *was* opened in heaven: and the first voice which I heard *was* as it were of a trumpet talking with me; which said, Come up hither, and I will shew thee things which must be hereafter.

² And immediately I was in the spirit: and, behold, a throne was set in heaven, and *one* sat on the throne.

⁴ And round about the throne *were* four and twenty seats: and upon the seats I saw four and twenty elders sitting, clothed in white raiment; and they had on their heads crowns of gold.

John accepted the invitation from **inside heaven**. Then suddenly he was there. (see 3:18) **The Voice from the throne** said He would "shew" him things to come. Who was the Voice? (see John 16:13; 10:27) What did John write was his location? What did he mean when he said "in the spirit"? (see Acts 2:1 – 4, 17 – 18; Joel 2:28)

_____
_____
_____
_____
_____
_____

date_____
COME UP HITHER
SPIRIT OF LIFE FROM GOD
Revelation 11:11 – 12 (KJV)

[11] And after three days and an half the Spirit of life from God entered into them, and they stood upon their feet; and great fear fell upon them which saw them.
[12] And they heard a great voice from heaven saying unto them, Come up hither. And they ascended up to heaven in a cloud; and their enemies beheld them.

No condemnation can overtake us in Christ Jesus (Romans 8:1 – 2, 10). The Spirit of life from God will call His witnesses (who have died) and their enemies will watch powerless as God puts life back into these witnesses of Jesus (17:6). Then the witnesses will hear His voice and ascend into heaven. God breathes life. What did the Voice say to them? Your enemies will also be confounded as they see God is more powerful than their gods (11:11 – 12; Isaiah 41:11). When will He say to us, "Come up hither?"

_____
_____
_____
_____
_____
_____

date_____
FAITH OF JESUS
YEA, SAITH THE SPIRIT...
Revelation 14:12 – 15 (KJV)

[12] Here is the patience of the saints: here *are* they that keep the commandments of God, and the faith of Jesus.
[13] And I heard a voice from heaven saying unto me, Write, Blessed *are* the dead which die in the Lord from henceforth: Yea, saith the Spirit, that they may rest from their labours; and their works do follow them.
[14] And I looked, and behold a white cloud, and upon the cloud *one* sat like unto the Son of man, having on his head a golden crown, and in his hand a sharp sickle.
[15] And another angel came out of the temple, crying with a loud voice to him that sat on the cloud, Thrust in thy sickle, and reap: for the time is come for thee to reap; for the harvest of the earth is ripe.

Our faith has come from Jesus and He will say to us, "Come on up" and we will surely be rewarded with our crowns for service without a face. (see Hebrews 4:11; Matthew 25:40)

_____
_____
_____
_____
_____

TESTIMONY OF JESUS IS THE SPIRIT OF PROPHECY

Revelation 19:4, 5, 9, 10 (KJV)

⁴ And the four and twenty elders and the four beasts fell down and worshipped God that sat on the throne, saying, Amen; Alleluia.

⁵ And a voice came out of the throne, saying, Praise our God, all ye his servants, and ye that fear him, both small and great.

⁹ And he saith unto me, Write, Blessed *are* they which are called unto the marriage supper of the Lamb. And he saith unto me, These are the true sayings of God.

¹⁰ And I fell at his feet to worship him. And he said unto me, See *thou do it not*: I am thy fellowservant, and of thy brethren that have the testimony of Jesus: worship God: for the testimony of Jesus is the spirit of prophecy.

"Alleluia" is a heavenly language. We can **pray and write our testimony** and put it at the feet of Jesus. (see John 17; 1 John 5:14 – 15) If someone says "Come again" what do they mean by it? (see Hebrews 1:14) What did the angel say when John fell at his feet?

_____
_____
_____
_____
_____

THE WORD OF GOD KING OF KINGS, AND LORD OF LORDS

Revelation 19:12 – 16 (KJV)

¹² His eyes *were* as a flame of fire, and on his head *were* many crowns; and he had a name written, that no man knew, but he himself.

¹³ And he *was* clothed with a vesture dipped in blood: and his name is called The Word of God.

¹⁴ And the armies *which were* in heaven followed him upon white horses, clothed in fine linen, white and clean.

¹⁵ And out of his mouth goeth a sharp sword, that with it he should smite the nations: and he shall rule them with a rod of iron: and he treadeth the winepress of the fierceness and wrath of Almighty God.

¹⁶ And he hath on *his* vesture and on his thigh a name written, KING OF KINGS, AND LORD OF LORDS.

THIS IS JESUS. (see Matthew 25:37 – 40; Genesis 37:1 – 31)

_____
_____
_____
_____
_____
_____
_____

ALPHA AND OMEGA
ATHIRST...FOUNTAIN OF THE
WATER OF LIFE

Revelation 21:4 – 7 (KJV)

⁴ And God shall wipe away all tears from their eyes; and there shall be no more death, neither sorrow, nor crying, neither shall there be any more pain: for the former things are passed away.

⁵ And he that sat upon the throne said, Behold, I make all things new. And he said unto me, Write: for these words are true and faithful.

⁶ And he said unto me, It is done. I am Alpha and Omega, the beginning and the end. I will give unto him that is athirst of the fountain of the water of life freely.

⁷ He that overcometh shall inherit all things; and I will be his God, and he shall be my son.

John told us the splendor we will inherit and the words he heard at the throne where our mind will reach up to an unknown degree. (see 21:23; John 1:12; 3:16; 4:10, 14, 23). We are heirs of God through Jesus. What words does He use to describe us? (21:7)

_____
_____
_____
_____

THE LAMB IS THE LIGHT
CARRIED ME AWAY IN THE
SPIRIT

Revelation 21:10, 23, 24, 25 (KJV)

¹⁰ And he carried me away in the spirit to a great and high mountain, and shewed me that great city, the holy Jerusalem, descending out of heaven from God,

²³ And the city had no need of the sun, neither of the moon, to shine in it: for the glory of God did lighten it, and the Lamb *is* the light thereof.

²⁴ And the nations of them which are saved shall walk in the light of it: and the kings of the earth do bring their glory and honour into it.

²⁵ And the gates of it shall not be shut at all by day: for there shall be no night there.

The highest government officials on earth, who believed on Jesus here, will be seen in heaven. (see 21:7; John 1:7; Luke 2:30 – 32; Matthew 17:1) How did John go to the "high mountain"?

_____
_____
_____
_____
_____
_____
_____

THRONE OF GOD AND OF THE LAMB
RIVER OF WATER OF LIFE

Revelation 22:1, 4 – 7 (KJV)

[1] And he shewed me a pure river of water of life, clear as crystal, proceeding out of the throne of God and of the Lamb.

[4] And they shall see his face; and his name *shall be* in their foreheads.

[5] And there shall be no night there; and they need no candle, neither light of the sun; for the Lord God giveth them light: and they shall reign for ever and ever.

[6] And he said unto me, These sayings *are* faithful and true: and the Lord God of the holy prophets sent his angel to shew unto his servants the things which must shortly be done.

[7] Behold, I come quickly: blessed *is* he that keepeth the sayings of the prophecy of this book.

The same Spirit was in or on or with the prophets and He abides in and with us now (Joel 2:28; Numbers 11:29; John 14:17; Acts 1:4 – 5; 2:1 – 4, 17 – 18; Acts 16:7; Ephesians 3:5; 1 Peter 1:11) Who are the blessed according to verse 7?

_____
_____
_____
_____

I JESUS HAVE SENT MINE ANGEL
THE SPIRIT...ATHIRST... WATER OF LIFE FREELY

Revelation 22:12, 13, 14, 16, 17 (KJV)

[12] And, behold, I come quickly; and my reward *is* with me, to give every man according as his work shall be.

[13] I am Alpha and Omega, the beginning and the end, the first and the last.

[14] Blessed *are* they that do his commandments, that they may have right to the tree of life, and may enter in through the gates into the city.

[16] I Jesus have sent mine angel to testify unto you these things in the churches. I am the root and the offspring of David, *and* the bright and morning star.

[17] And the Spirit and the bride say, Come. And let him that heareth say, Come. And let him that is athirst come. And whosoever will, let him take the water of life freely.

Come. (see John 1:12) He is the Lord God of the Breakthrough (1 Chronicles 14:11)! Now He wants everyone to see Him through us. Jesus invited everyone to invite more. Come. **Take the water of life freely.**

_____
_____
_____
_____

You will have so much fun meditating on these Scriptures in the presence of our Father, you will not know where the time went:

Luke 1:41

_____

_____

Luke 1:67

_____

_____

SET ONE:
IN THE WORDS OF JESUS:

John 14:15 – 17, 21 – 24, 25 – 27

John 15:4 – 5, 7 – 8, 15 – 18, 19 – 23, 24 – 27

John 16:4 – 7, 12 – 15, 21 – 24, 25 – 28

SET TWO
FILLED WITH THE HOLY GHOST:

Peter said the Gentiles were filled with the Holy Ghost just as he and others were filled. Did God want the Holy Ghost to keep on filling?

Luke 1:15

_____

_____

Acts 2:4, 44 – 45

_____

_____

Acts 4:8, 34 – 35

_____

_____

Acts 4:31

_____

_____

Acts 9:17

_____

_____

Acts 13:9

_____

_____

Acts 13:52 "...filled with joy, and with the Holy Ghost" (KJV).

_____

_____

SET THREE
ONLY TWICE DOES THE
(KJV) SCRIPTURE SAY
"FILLED WITH THE SPIRIT":
FILLED WITH THE SPIRIT

Exodus 28:3 (KJV)

_____

_____

Ephesians 5:18 (KJV)

_____

_____

Deuteronomy 34:9 (HCSB)

_____

_____

As you've studied, have you decided why Jesus is never described as being "filled with the Spirit" or "filled with the Holy Ghost" but He is described as "full of the Holy Ghost"?

SET FOUR
Whose speaking and whose hearing?

God was talking: Joel 2:28 – 29

_____

_____

Jesus was talking: Luke 24:45 – 49

_____

_____

Jesus was talking: Acts 1:4 – 5

_____

_____

Jesus was talking: Acts 1:8

_____

_____

Peter quotes Jesus: Acts 11:15 – 17

_____

_____

Who was speaking? Acts 9:1 – 4

_____

_____

How many believed? Acts 9:5 – 8

_____

_____

How many and who went to visit Saul? Acts 9:10 – 12

_____

_____

Who is in this conversation? Acts 9:13 – 16

_____

_____

What did he do after he was saved? Acts 9:19 – 20

_____

_____

What is the window of opportunity God has opened for you? What one person does God want you to reach out to? Where is the place of your purpose?

Mark 16:15

_____

_____

Luke 3:16, 21 – 22

_____

_____

SET FIVE
FULFILL

Jesus left heaven so did He have any needs He couldn't fulfill in heaven? Why did Jesus say "thus it becometh us"? Why did Jesus say to John the Baptist "to fulfill all righteousness"?

Luke 10:38 – 42

_____

_____

Luke 24:45 – 49

_____

_____

Matthew 3:1 – 6

_____

_____

John 1:29 – 34

_____

_____

Matthew 3:11

_____

_____

John 13:12 – 15

_____

_____

Matthew 3:13 – 17

_____

_____

John 19:25 – 30

_____

_____

Matthew 28:18 – 20

_____

_____

Acts 14:21 – 22

_____

_____

Mark 1:8 – 11

_____

_____

Hebrews 1:1 – 3

_____

_____

Hebrews 4:15 – 16
_____
_____

When we seek to be near Him, we are doing His will. The things that make us angry give us a glimpse into the gift, purpose, ministry, calling or opportunity God has given to us. The Bible tells us not to stay angry. Could that be a note for us to look into why we are angry to help us see the person and the window God has set in front of us?

SET SIX
THE PROMISE

Joel 2:28 – 29
Who made the promise?
_____
_____

Luke 24:49
Who does Jesus say made the promise?
_____
_____

Acts 1:4
Jesus said to wait for whose promise?
_____
_____

Acts 1:5
How did Jesus speak of being baptized?
_____
_____

Acts 2:1 – 4
What day was the promise seen and heard?
_____
_____

That was the fulfillment of the promise for all those who were waiting and believing. Were they all showered and drenched in the water of the Spirit?
_____
_____

SET SEVEN
THE CASE FOR THE HOLY GHOST: The following list is what sparked the books HOUSE OF THE HOLY GHOST and THE HOLY GHOST BIBLE when I was asking God to let me be nearer to Him:

Joel 2:28 – 29
_____
_____

Luke 24:45 – 49
_____
_____

Acts 1:4 – 5

_____

_____

Acts 1:8

_____

_____

Acts 2:1 – 4

_____

_____

Acts 2:17 – 18

_____

_____

Acts 2:32 – 33
Where is Jesus?

_____

_____

Acts 2:36 – 39

_____

_____

Acts 8:12 – 20
What did he mean by the phrase "in the name of Jesus?"

_____

_____

Acts 9:17

_____

_____

Acts 10:44 – 48

_____

_____

Acts 11:12 – 18

_____

_____

Acts 15:5 – 8

_____

_____

Acts 16:30 – 32

_____

_____

Acts 19:1 – 5

_____

_____

SET EIGHT
WHEN THE SPIRIT GIVES POWER: What words describe what the Spirit does?

Judges 6:34 – 35

_____

_____

Judges 14:6

_____

_____

1 Samuel 10:10

_____

_____

Joel 2:28 – 29
What things will change?

_____

_____

John 1:12

_____

_____

John 14:17

_____

_____

Acts 1:8

_____

_____

Acts 2:37 – 39, 44

_____

_____

2 Corinthians 5:17, 21

_____

_____

Romans 8:14 – 17

_____

_____

SET NINE
In each of these sets of verses, who is saved or who is not?
Luke 1:13 – 15

_____

_____

John 3:1 – 8, 16

_____

_____

John 4:39 – 44

_____

_____

Acts 2:17 – 18

_____

_____

Acts 8:14 – 17

_____

_____

Acts 10:44 – 47

_____

_____

Acts 11:14 – 17

_____

_____

Acts 16:31 – 32

_____

_____

In the Old Testament they could believe in God and go to heaven (like babies) but they aren't described as saved since the Holy Spirit didn't continually live in them. Who did the Holy Spirit first come upon and remain on? Was He our Example?

Acts 9:4 – 5
What happened before?

_____

_____

Joel 2:28 – 29
Before that?

_____

_____

SET TEN
BEFORE
2 Timothy 1:14
He said "us" so what happened before?

_____

_____

Genesis 1:26
Before that?

_____

_____

Genesis 1:1 – 3

2 Timothy 1:5 – 6
He is the same Holy Spirit so what happened before?

_____

_____

Acts 16:1
What happened before?

_____

_____

Acts 9:10, 17, 29
What happened before?

_____

_____

HOUSE OF THE HOLY GHOST

OTHER BOOKS BY MARY KING...

1 – *Series:* **KID POWER – For Mature Boys Only** ...With Connections (The first in a series, originally written to encourage adults to have every answer to prayer. Connections are Bible stories or personal stories or some of both in a devotional.) **BOOK ONE**

2 – **THEY CAN SEE US FROM HEAVEN (**This book was written to comfort grandmother after papa suddenly went to be with the Lord.)

3 – **HOLY GHOST BIBLE** Compiled by Mary King. (HOLY GHOST BIBLE is the story of the Holy Ghost according to only **the words in the Holy Bible. As we walk in the Spirit, we are tapping into the Holy Ghost.)**

....

2 Peter 1:17-21 (NKJV)

¹⁷ For He received from God the Father honor and glory when such a voice came to Him from the Excellent Glory: "This is My beloved Son, in whom I am well pleased."

¹⁸ And we heard this voice which came from heaven when we were with Him on the holy mountain.

¹⁹ And so we have the prophetic word confirmed, which you do well to heed as a light that shines in a dark place, until the day dawns and the morning star rises in your hearts;

²⁰ knowing this first, that no prophecy of Scripture is of any private interpretation,

²¹ for prophecy never came by the will of man, but holy men of God spoke *as they were* moved by the Holy Spirit. Would you like to receive Jesus as your personal Savior and Lord? If so, you can pray this simple prayer in faith in Jesus. He is the only One who died on His cross for you:

Jesus, I am a sinner but I want to turn to You and follow You now. Jesus, please forgive me of all my wrongs whether in words or actions or thought. Jesus save me. Jesus, come into my heart and You are my Lord. By faith, I am Yours now and I want to make my choices with You. Jesus, I'm trusting my salvation to You and to You only. Amen. Jesus, I will be looking for Your return. I am now a new person in Christ Jesus my Lord and I want to live for You.

_____

If you prayed that prayer sincerely to Jesus, then you can confess Jesus by signing above and removing this page and giving it to someone you love.

Printed in the United States
by Baker & Taylor Publisher Services